a bi

MISS BERTHA

Woman of Revival

Lewis Drummond

BROADMAN
& HOLMAN
PUBLISHERS

Nashville, Tennessee

4211-64
0-8054-1164-X

Dewey Decimal Classification: 266.092
Subject Heading: SMITH, BERTHA \ SPIRITUAL LIFE
Library of Congress Card Catalog Number: 95-23591

Unless otherwise noted all Scripture quotations are from the King James Version

Photo credits designated "FMB" are courteous of The Foreign Mission Board of the Southern Baptist Convention; those designated "Melten" are courteous of the Peniel Prayer Center, Cowpens, S.C., Gerald Melten Director.

Interior design by Leslie Joslin
Cover design by Rodgers & Company

Library of Congress Cataloging-in-Publication Data
Drummond, Lewis A.
      Miss Bertha: woman of revival / Lewis A. Drummond.
          p. cm.
      ISBN 0-8054-1164-X (hardbound)
      1.Smith, Bertha. 2.Missionaries—China—Biography. 3. Missionaries—
Taiwan—Biography. 4. Missionaries—United States—Biography. 5. Southern
Baptist Convention—Biography. 6. Baptists—United States—Biography. 7. Evan-
gelists—United States—Biography.
    I. Title.
    BV3427.S6D781996
    266'.6132'092—dc20   95-23591
    [B]   CIP

01 02 03 04 05 06 01 00 99 98 97 96

Contents

Contents

Foreword

William Taylor Thorn and Mary Turner Thorn, Miss
Bertha's maternal grandparents. *Credit: Melten*

To know her was to love her and to be spiritually challenged by her. Bertha Smith influenced the lives of all she touched in a most significant and unmistakable way. It was a rare treat and privilege to have her in our home at "Melody Lane."

Bertha Smith's dedication and love for Christ became a true inspiration, not only to me, but to the thousands she touched in China, Taiwan, America, and around the globe. Rarely has the world seen such a personality. Not only were countless Christians blessed by her life and ministry; she was a most effective evangelist in her own unique manner. Only heaven will record the many she personally won to faith in Jesus Christ. The twentieth century (for she lived through most of it) became a better century because of "Miss Bertha." Those who experienced the prayer fellowship at Peniel in Cowpens, South Carolina, will long remember the experience.

It is fitting that an extensive biography of this intriguing missionary be written. To look into the exciting aspects of her life and Christian service will challenge any reader to a deeper commitment to the work of Christ. If

that happens, she would be well pleased. Therefore, I most heartily recommend a careful, open-hearted reading of Bertha Smith's fascinating life.

—Cliff Barrows
Greenville, South Carolina

Preface

John M. Smith and Francis E. Smith, Miss Bertha's parents. *Credit: Melten*

Revival always stands as the pressing need of the Church of Jesus Christ. At times, God in His infinite grace pours out His Spirit on His people and they are powerfully renewed. Such times become blessed moments for Christians, and for society as well. The Church is reawakened while multitudes enter into the Kingdom of God. Little wonder a revival can be termed a time "of refreshing . . . from the presence of the Lord" (Acts 3:19).

That kind of spiritual awakening burst on the Chinese people in the latter 1920s. Beginning in Shantung Province, the Holy Spirit fell on a small group of Baptist missionaries, and for years the fires of revival burned. Right at the center of this exciting movement stood Miss Bertha Smith. God used this "Woman of Revival" in a most unusual manner. The story of her life and ministry in China, and later in America, portrays a saga of spiritual awakening. Her story needs to be told!

A restrictive, rigid chronological structure of Miss Bertha Smith's life is not sought in this biography. At times a more topical approach is taken in order to put all the events of her fascinating life into a more logical and comprehensive format. Yet, the unfolding of her one hundred years follows a basic sequence of all that took place in her ministry for Jesus Christ.

Words of sincere appreciation are in order to those who contributed to "Miss Bertha's" story. Mrs. Charlotte Baughn toiled for hours over the manuscript. Gerald Melton, director of Miss Bertha's Peniel Prayer Center in Cowpens, South Carolina, helped give birth to this biography and provided invaluable original archives. Also, the *Spartanburg Journal*, the Foreign Mission Board of the Southern Baptist Convention, and Mrs. Rebecca Knight (working in the archives at Samford University) provided much help, as did Mrs. Joan Watterson, who corrected the original manuscript. A further word of appreciation must be expressed to the editor, John Landers, the staff of Broadman & Holman, and also to James T. Draper Jr. president of the Southern Baptist Sunday School Board, who provided helpful assistance in the project.

Additional thanks is extended to Victoria Bleick of the Foreign Mission Board SBC for her generous cooperation and assistance. She went "above and beyond the call of duty" in providing photographs to the publisher on an extremely tight schedule. Thanks, also, to Gerald Melten, Director of the Peniel Prayer Center, for the additional photographs included in this book. These photos add immensely to the book and are gratefully appreciated.

Above all, gratitude goes to Mrs. June Andrews. She worked through Miss Bertha Smith's papers and integrated them into their proper places in the manuscript. She saved this author untold hours of research and all but coauthored this work. As Mrs. Andrew's testimony indicates in the Prologue of this book, her work on this manuscript was a labor of love in thanksgiving for a woman who significantly touched her life.

Quotations from letters are not footnoted in some instances. Those not noted are found in the archives of the Peniel Prayer Center of Cowpens, South Carolina. Furthermore, the letters in some instances are punctuated as Bertha Smith wrote them; otherwise the punctuation was corrected.

This biography goes forth with the prayer that the life story of Bertha Smith, "Woman of Revival," will spawn interest, concern, and above all, intercession for a true revival in our day. If this happens, all the labor to produce this work will be amply repaid.

—Lewis A. Drummond
Birmingham, Alabama

Prologue

Portrait of Bertha and two of her sisters. Left to right: Jennie, Ethel, and Bertha. *Credit: Melten*

I came to know Christ at an early age. Yet, for years my spiritual life was very nominal. Then one day while I was vacuuming the living room, the Spirit of God deeply convicted me. God seemed to say, "June, you have three children, but you aren't telling them about Jesus." The next Sunday the children and I went to church. The following week, I transferred my membership and soon busied myself doing things for the Lord. A change was underway.

Later I became actively involved in the mission church I had joined. The Woman's Missionary Union asked me to serve. I worked and worked and worked. Still, I found no deep peace in much serving. I was a mere activist. Frustration set in. I became depressed and resigned virtually all my positions. Spiritual stagnation seemed my lot. Then, God did a deep work of grace in my life.

While visiting friends in Atlanta, I attended a mission book study. The book was *Go Home and Tell*, written by Miss Bertha Smith. As I read, I looked at my life and became frightened at what I saw. My life revolved around doing, doing, doing—not *being!* Finally, I came to the place that I prayed, "Lord Jesus, I've made such a mess of my life. I have given it to You and taken it back many times. Please forgive me. Will You take my life and the mess it's in and do something with it?" He did.

That fall I began serving in the Woman's Missionary Union at my church. It was in the setting of a Woman's Missionary Union conference that I heard Bertha Smith speak. She was a bold, powerful speaker who pointed her finger at us and said, "Do you know why you aren't living effective, abundant lives for Christ? Unconfessed sin keeps your lives dirty and ineffective." She seemed to be peering right into my heart, revealing what she saw.

While driving back home from the meeting, I confessed my sins aloud to God. When the last sin had been confessed, I asked the Lord to fill me with His Spirit. At that moment something wonderful happened. A profound peace and joy filled my very soul. Love permeated my being and I knew the presence of Jesus in a way I had never known before. Tears of joy trickled down my cheeks. God was there—by my side, within me, loving me in a way words cannot express.

From that moment on, life became radically different. My understanding of the whole Christian experience forever changed. Service to the Savior would never again be the same. The Scriptures came alive. I loved being alone in Bible study and prayer. Worship with fellow believers was a delight. I felt like a dry sponge being saturated with the fullness of Christ and His love.

I praise and thank the Lord for crossing paths with Miss Bertha Smith who so moved me towards the fullness of life only Jesus Christ can give.

—*June Andrews*

What kind of woman was Bertha Smith? You must meet her.

Part I

The Early Years

Smith family portrait. Pictured five of eight children: Bertha is in her mother's lap. *Credit: Melten*

1

Meet Bertha Smith,
Woman of Revival

Bertha Smith *Credit: Melten*

All who knew and loved her, knew her affectionately as "Miss Bertha": missionary, speaker, Bible teacher, "Woman of Revival." Thousands who crossed her path will never be quite the same again. After coming into contact with this crusader, few were left unmoved. Rarely has a more spiritually-minded, powerful witness for the Lord Jesus Christ tread across the pages of China's Christian history—and American Christian history as well. But to say that Bertha Smith stood as a spiritual giant does not mean she was so "other worldly" that she had no concern for the more mundane things of life. In her first ten years of missionary service in China, she lived with Miss Alice Huey, a Southern Baptist missionary from Alabama. Dr. Jeannette Beall, another fellow missionary, would say teasingly, "Huey is of the heavens, heavenly; Bertha is of the earth, earthy."[1] Very true. Although Bertha Smith was deeply and profoundly concerned for the advancement of God's Kingdom, she never lost contact with or interest in the down-to-earth affairs of everyday life.

Miss Bertha beautifully balanced commitment to spiritual matters with earthly things, and "thus the common people heard . . . gladly" (Mark 12:37). For example, one day during the Christmas season half a dozen little Chinese boys were making sport, throwing sticks and rocks into a small religious temple. Miss Bertha, passing by on her way to mid-week prayer service at the church, asked the boys, "What is the fun?" "There is an old Chinese beggar woman inside," the boys gleefully replied. Bertha walked on some distance, then turned around and went back. Climbing up the stone bank and peering into the temple, she saw a poor, pitiful, ancient Chinese woman huddled on the brick floor in a cramped space about three feet long. "Old grandmother," Bertha called. A disheveled gray head raised up. As a lean hand pushed back the gray hair, Miss Bertha recognized the wrinkled face of a beggar whom she had seen on the street a few days before. "Oh, pity me! Pity me!" the old woman cried, "I am hungry and cold and sick. If I were not sick I could walk on my frozen feet to beg. Won't you give me some money?"

Without a reply Bertha turned and went on to church. She knew money was not the woman's most pressing need. But something must be done—she would think it through first. The sun was just setting, and nights get very cold in Shantung at Christmastime. Yet this old soul had no bedding for the night, wore a ragged wadded garment or two, and lay sick on a brick floor—a cramped brick floor not big enough to lie on! She might freeze to death before morning; and if she didn't actually freeze, how she would suffer! Miss Bertha resolved to provide food and bedding.

The food could be easily found, but where would the bedding come from? Bertha could give her straw mattress, but the old woman must have covers. Her own supply of bedding passed through her mind; each piece did not pass quickly, however. One quilt lingered on. It was Bertha's oldest quilt, the one she loved most. She had made it herself as a child. Would she take that quilt and cover the shivering woman? Give up a prized possession?

On her way home from church Bertha wrestled with the question. Perhaps she had some old clothes that would do as well, but when she looked through the box of clothes, she found none that would answer the need. So she went to the room where the favorite quilt lay on a bed and reluctantly picked it up. As she longingly looked at her handiwork, she recalled the happy days she sat in her child's chair, under the blooming pear trees in the backyard of her South Carolina home, slowly sewing the pieces of cloth together in a log-cabin pattern. The quilt was her first piece of work worth saving. She hesitatingly folded it as she glimpsed scraps of the dresses that made up the pattern, scraps her mother and sisters had worn long ago. There was even a piece of the little red dress from her own

2

childhood. She had not realized before how pretty her quilt really was. She almost laid it down.

But what is sentiment when one is in need? I'll be practical and helpful, Bertha resolved. She thought she had conquered her reluctance to part with her prized quilt, but before she reached the door she stopped and hesitated again. Then Jesus' words, "I was hungry and you fed me, naked and you clothed me, sick and you visited me," came to her mind, followed by, "In as much . . ." And Christ conquered.

Bertha walked briskly and joyfully with the quilt on her arm. She went through her kitchen where she gathered as much food as the sick woman could eat, and with a servant and lantern went to the woman in need. The old grandmother raised her head when called to sit up and eat supper. Hungry as she was, she did not eat until she first pushed a brick out in front of her and invited Miss Bertha to have a seat and eat with her.

The seat was accepted and the missionary sat on the brick at the foot of the temple idol with tears streaming down her cheeks, tears she hoped the happy woman did not see. The old beggar ate four bowls of hot millet with a childish laugh between each. As Bertha sat looking at her, she could not help contrasting herself with this poor beggar in the bundle of rags. *Why, oh, why the difference?* thought Miss Bertha. Was not the reason before her very eyes? Three heathen idols still dominated the temple, two tumbled down. This was the spiritual and cultural background of the poor wreck of humanity—a woman once made in the image of God who had long since lost the likeness. All that had gone into the making of the poor beggar, bringing her to such a pitiful condition, was the fruit of idolatry and heathen worship. Bertha had been fashioned into Christ's image by the grace of God. Oh, that people would hear the Good News and come to Christ!

Bertha had left the quilt outside the temple, unseen as the woman ate. While the servant returned home to bring the straw mattress, Bertha made an honest effort to get something of the saving knowledge of Christ into the woman's dull mind and empty heart. The woman knew the "Old Heavenly Grandfather" who sent the rain and sunshine. However, Bertha did not know how much the woman understood of what she told her about the true God who sent His Son into the world to save her and who alone must be worshiped; Bertha only knew that she presented the gospel faithfully and lovingly.

As the servant returned with the mattress, Bertha surveyed the scene. The idol that had fallen down from the wall at the end of the little temple needed to be moved to make room for a comfortable bed. But when the superstitious servant saw the situation, he would not touch it. Bertha was able to move the idol only a few inches.

They finally cleared enough space for the mattress. When the woman laid down on it, she exclaimed how warm she would be. Then Bertha stepped back to the temple door for the quilt, and as she spread it over her and tucked her in, the grateful old beggar said, "A quilt! A quilt! She is going to cover me with a quilt." Another childish laugh followed.

Do you think Bertha remembered the sentiment connected with that quilt when she gave it to the woman? Hardly. Bertha was overjoyed that she had made it to give. She returned to her comfortable home. Red geraniums were in bloom on the window sills and Christmas bells were hanging from the shades. She appreciated as never before the greatest of all gifts, the inexpressible gift of our Lord Jesus Christ.

This was the spirit of our "Woman of Revival." Bertha Smith loved the people of China and joyfully sought to meet all their needs, physical as well as spiritual. Still, she was primarily concerned about the salvation of the Chinese people and their development in the faith. The biblical balance between meeting both temporal and eternal needs, as exemplified in our Lord Jesus Christ, characterized Bertha's entire life and gave her real rapport with the people. Even though she was known among her missionary friends as "earthy Bertha," she exuded a heavenly aura that endued her with tremendous power for ministering the Word of God.

The Beginning of It All

After a normal upbringing in the town of Cowpens, South Carolina, Miss Bertha came to faith in Jesus Christ and soon felt the Spirit's tug to become a missionary. After college, she enrolled at the Woman's Missionary Union Training School at The Southern Baptist Theological Seminary in Louisville, Kentucky. Soon after her appointment by the Foreign Mission Board of the Southern Baptist Convention on July 3, 1917, she was on her way to China.

After spending two years studying the Chinese language, Bertha began to adjust to China. For a Southern lady to fit into the China of 1917 could hardly be easy. But circumstances never daunted her. After all, she had felt the call of the Lord Jesus Christ.

Miss Bertha arrived in China with a good grasp of the evangelical Christian faith. Yet something was lacking. Missionaries were deeply concerned about the limited spiritual development of most Chinese church members. Even the missionaries themselves—Miss Bertha included—confessed to a need for a deep movement of God in their own lives. She discovered that leaders on virtually every mission station were praying for a spiritual awakening for themselves and for the churches. The longing for real revival had subtly settled upon them like the morning dew. In 1919

Bertha attended a missionary conference led by Dr. R. A. Torrey of the Moody Bible Institute. The following summer, she attended another missionary conference and heard Dr. Charles G. Trumbull, editor of the *Sunday School Times*, and Miss Ruth Paxon, the author of *Life on the Highest Plane*. Before the conference, Bertha had felt reasonably satisfied with her Christian life. But through the ministry of these godly leaders, she discovered that Christ Himself was to be her life and victory. She realized that she did not need to strive to be a "good missionary." All she needed as a Christian resided in the indwelling presence of Jesus Christ. He constituted her life, her all. She learned the principle that a believer stands identified with Christ in His death and resurrection, and therefore a Christian is dead to sin and alive to God in Christ (Rom. 6:1–12). Bertha received that glorious fact as the key to victory and it unlocked a treasure of spiritual reality within her. Her life and service could never be the same again, for she received a deepening and awakening touch.

Through conferences like those of Torrey, Trumbull, Paxon, and others, God began to prepare His people for the spiritual awakening that came to China in 1927, largely on the wings of a special speaker, Miss Marie Monsen, a Lutheran evangelical missionary from Norway. Monsen became God's instrument in leading the missionaries of Shantung Province into real revival.

After several fascinating decades of ministry in China with victories that could only be experienced during revival times, war erupted and the Communists took over Miss Bertha's China. The missionaries were expelled. It seemed to be all over for those devoted men and women of God. But not so.

The Communists expelled the missionaries in 1949 and 1950. (They had already gone through Japanese occupation and more hardships than most twentieth-century Christians can ever realize.) After the expulsion, Miss Bertha moved south and became the first Southern Baptist pioneer missionary to the island of Formosa, now known as Taiwan. There she lived out the remainder of her missionary days. Her life there also became a saga in itself.

When Bertha reached the age of seventy, the Southern Baptist Foreign Mission Board required her to retire. What could she do in a country like the United States with so many professing Christians? Why could she not remain in Taiwan the rest of her days where the needs loomed so large? A tremendous burden settled on her heart.

Then, God spoke to her most distinctly. She must "go home and tell." Tell what? Tell the story of how God awakens His people! God commissioned her to tell Christians in America how they must get ready for revival by having their sins "confessed up-to-date" and by taking in the fullness of the Holy Spirit. They needed to know how God uses anyone who understands that Christ resides in his or her life and that He is fully available to him or her. Above all, God called her to inspire American Christians to seek an awakening for their land.

When she went to China, the spiritual apathy on the part of Chinese believers was appalling. But revival came and transformed the entire spiritual scene. When Bertha came back to the United States, she found a comparable spiritual scenario in her native land. She must tell American Christians what she had learned, and she must seek an awakening for the country of her birth. Revival had come to China. Why not to America? Her ministry in the United States lasted another unbelievable thirty years, and in many respects proved to be as powerful as her years in China. Wherever Miss Bertha went, a touch of revival fell on the folk.

This author and his wife first encountered Bertha Smith during her American ministry when she came to visit our congregation. The week proved to be a spiritual high point, not only for my wife and me, but for many members of the congregation as well.

Bertha had a unique way of preparing pastors for her visits. She would say, "Be prepared, Pastor; the crowds will get smaller each night." True. By the end of the week, the only ones left were those willing to permit God to deeply search, revive, and empower their lives. What an experience it became for those who underwent the process of being genuinely quickened by the Holy Spirit through this unique woman of God. Wherever she went in America, few lives were left unchanged—one way or another.

Simply put, Bertha Smith lived most of her one hundred years seeking God in true revival and calling on others to seek with her. She was truly a "Woman of Revival." She breathed that atmosphere and exuded that spirit wherever she went. China received significant blessings through her ministry; America needed—and needs—a similar touch.

Let us now explore her fascinating life in some depth. It all began in little Cowpens, South Carolina.

2

Olive Bertha Smith Squeals Her First Cry

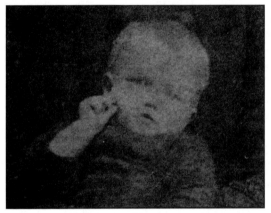

Bertha as a toddler. *Credit: Melten*

Little Olive Bertha Smith was born to John McClellan and Frances Thorne Smith on November 16, 1888. In that new life, God sent into the world a future servant who would make a far greater impact for Christ than her parents could ever imagine. The family was proud of their ancestor, Captain John Smith, one of the early settlers of Virginia. They would be equally proud of their little Bertha.

Early Years

The small town of Cowpens, South Carolina, can boast of housing the early home for Miss Bertha Smith—her first name, Olive, soon fell into disuse. Although she was born on a farm a few miles outside Cowpens, in March of 1894 the family moved into town, where father John built a beautiful home for his growing family. John McClellan Smith was a planter, a land owner, and a developer. He also engaged in the mercantile business and ran a sawmill. Owning a small store housed in a white wooden building in the center of Cowpens, he became something of an early entrepreneur. Cowpens served his business interests better than the farm and provided better schooling for the children. So into town he moved his expanding clan.

A growing clan it was. Bertha was the fifth of eight children. There were four boys and four girls in the family: Clinton, Lester, Claud, Broadus, Jennie, Pearle, Bertha, and Frances. As a middle child little Bertha failed to fill the stereotypical role given by psychologists of being insecure and non-assertive. She stood out as a leader from the start and was anything but retiring or insecure. These leadership traits apparent from childhood, served Bertha well through the missionary years. China demanded tenacity, determination, and a strong will. Bertha had it all, even as a child.

Bertha possessed a real streak of pride in her early years. She herself confessed she had a "naturally proud heart." Shortly after the family moved to Cowpens, on her very first day of school, she proudly walked down the street (a very confident seven year old) with other students and her equally proud father. A local merchant looked at the entourage as they marched to school and asked father John, "Why don't you send for a cradle for the little one?" Little Bertha said it "brought low" her proud heart, but not for long. She vowed to excel in school and show the merchant that neither size nor age could humble her. And excel she did. She was an exceptional student who would not be daunted by anything.

Family Discipline

Bertha was a disciplined child—self-disciplined and parentally disciplined. With eight children, the parents had to be in control. As Bertha put it, her parents' "yes" meant "yes" and "no" meant "no." Bertha admitted, "My mother did not spare the peach tree limbs." John and Frances Smith created a strict but very secure home life for their children. The security did not grow out of wealth, though the family was not poor as their lovely home, which still stands, testifies. The sense of acceptance and security in the home emerged from the love and discipline of mature, loving parents. Miss Bertha inherited a most happy home.

Discipline at home ensured obedience at school and fostered a love for study. Bertha always made the honor roll and she loved it. Pride still had her in its hands. She loved and deeply respected her teachers—and they her. They always said, as did all who knew her, that Bertha was a "good girl." And in her own words, she "knew no better than to believe it." She struggled to keep up the image. Later in life she admitted that she had reveled in the praise of her teachers. That praise became the spark that really ignited her passion to excel. And that passion is probably what made her somewhat intolerant of anyone who did not do everything to perfection.

School Days

The Cowpens school was a large two-story wooden building. The two rooms on the first floor housed the classrooms and they were referred to as the little room and the big room. Bertha said, "A large iron stove stood in the center of the big room, which kept us either too hot or too cold." The teacher stood or sat on a large platform that ran across the end of the room. A long recitation bench just below the platform is where the teacher heard the students recite their lessons. Students went forward to the bench as each class took its turn at recitation. Pupils were seated two to a desk. Bertha recalled, "A bucket of water with its dipper sat on one of the platform steps at the side of the room. A pupil could walk across the room for a drink of water any time that he was thirsty."[1] The alert and energetic pupils who completed their assignments at home "had the pleasure of enjoying all the subjects taught all day." They would learn subjects from two or three grades beyond their level. That arrangement delighted little Bertha.

School began at eight o'clock each morning with worship and singing. Bertha said, "We had our own little hymnbooks without musical notes. The principal read and explained the Word of God, assigned us memory work for the next day, and led us in fervent prayer."[2] Christian teachers required the students to memorize Scripture verses. Bertha put to memory the full chapter in which the required verses were found. Then she would proudly stand and repeat the entire chapter. It was not that she had a deep love for the Bible; she loved the lauds she received for the exercise. But that early memorization held her in good stead later when she came to salvation in Christ.

Bertha's Sunday school teacher also required Scripture memorization. Again Bertha excelled. Church, worship, Sunday school, and mid-week prayer meeting became her forte. She would not miss a service. She read her Bible and prayed every day, convinced that all the religious exercise made her very acceptable to the Lord.

Childhood Stories

One Christmas Bertha's mother was ill. Her father was unable to buy enough gifts for all the children. The three younger girls opened their gifts to find dolls made of sawdust with no clothes. Their oldest sister, Jennie, received a beautiful wax china doll. What a blow to proud little Bertha!

Bertha marched outside in a huff, put the doll on top of a log, and chopped its head off. After she told her two sisters what she had done, they proceeded to do the same. Later in the day her father explained ever so kindly and gently the problem. He said, "I thought you would understand that your oldest sister got a doll because she was the oldest and had the responsibility of taking care of all of you younger ones since your mother has been ill." When Bertha realized that her father could not afford a beautiful china doll for all the girls she felt horribly and desperately sought some way to attach the decapitated doll's head to the body. After finally managing to do so, she began to make clothes for her sawdust doll. Her loving father contacted a fellow merchant and secured a china basket for each of the girls. He simply could not endure the picture of three little girls with such disappointment written all over their faces.

One summer, in an effort to keep up with her older brothers and prove her ability to pick cotton, Bertha picked over 350 pounds of cotton in a day, thus setting a record for the number of pounds picked by any girl. She always set out to break records.

Bertha also loved to play. When she had to stay in and baby-sit for a younger sibling, Bertha would place the baby's face in the sun. This would make the child close its eyes, and soon sleep would follow. Then Bertha would go outside and play—rather ingenious.

Bertha's school dresses were made of flowered calico that cost five cents a yard. She also made dresses for her dolls. She said, "I was always busy with more plans for my dolls' wardrobes than I could possibly make for them. Sister Ethel and I used the back end of an upstairs hall for a doll house. I picked cotton and used some of the money to buy half a yard of beautiful red-hat velvet that cost fifty cents. With cardboard and cotton for a foundation I covered three overstuffed chairs with that velvet for the doll house."[3] Bertha's mother suffered from arthritis in those days and rarely got upstairs. One day she did go, and when she saw the furniture, she called Bertha in to give her a good "tongue switching" for cutting up the exquisite velvet upholstery to make doll chairs. Bertha's mother did not know Bertha was in hearing distance when she later told her father of the clever job she had done. She had the touch, always seeking excellence.

Spiritual Stirring

The Smith family worshiped at Cowpens' First Baptist Church. Services were held in a white wooden building where Reverend J. D. Bailey preached once a month for fifteen years during Bertha's childhood. It was what the Baptists called a "quarter-time" church. The deacons ran the Sunday school every week and conducted prayer meetings because the pastor lived forty miles away and served two or three other churches as well. The little congregation could only afford a part-time minister. Men and women sat on separate sides of the church. The young people sat in the center row.

A spiritual revolution began in Bertha's life when she was ten. This happened during what people in the Bible belt called a "revival meeting." She would learn the real meaning of "revival" later in her life in China. In those days, however, the term communicated a quest for conversions. Local churches would set aside a week or two—or maybe even more—for special evangelistic services. Often an evangelist would be called in to preach or perhaps the pastor himself would become the evangelist. Services were well attended and constituted something of the climax of a year's effort to lead the unbelievers of the community to Christ. Some people came to think that lost persons could be converted only during a revival meeting. That was its downside. However, during revival meetings many people would seek the Lord and come to regenerative faith in Christ. This was especially true in the smaller communities of the south.

Bertha came to a true saving faith in Jesus Christ on September 5, 1905. But it proved to be a long journey to Christ's redemption. She should be allowed to tell it in her own words:

> There were three classes of folk in the churches at that time: the warm-hearted Christians, the backsliders, and the class who were in those days called the "lost." Everybody went to church, the church being the social center, with nowhere else to go and nothing at home to keep one there.
>
> The grand old man of God preached, with tears rolling down his cheeks, pled with backsliders to confess their sins and come back into fellowship with Holy God. He pled with the lost to repent of their sins and flee from God's holy wrath to come, because it had been appointed unto man once to die, but after that the judgment! And while the man of God wept, preached the Word, and pled, saints prayed and the Holy Spirit moved.
>
> Baptist churches did not have altar forms as the Methodist's did, but for two weeks in the year, we had plenty of repenting space. Those sitting on the front rows of benches across the church moved when the invitation was given, knowing that people would come. They stood in orderly lines down the aisles next to the walls and continued their share in singing to the unsaved, such as: "Come every soul by sin oppressed, there's mercy with the Lord." As more came, more benches were vacated, and sometimes half the church would be turned into a "mourner"s bench!"
>
> Mourn they did, as the Holy Spirit used the Word, to show them the exceeding sinfulness of sin, and they realized that only their life breath

kept them out of an awful hell which had been made for the devil and his angels.

The backsliders were there too, like the prodigal of old, confessing to their Father their wandering away and doing as they pleased. They often wept sore as they realized what their sin had cost Holy God.

I was ten years old when, one hot July night as I sat beside the second window from the front, the Word of the Lord went to my heart! For the first time I saw myself, at least a little glimpse of what I looked like, in the eyes of Holy God. While people called me a good girl, I would not do in His sight, who saw all the pride of my heart—the selfishness and the wanting to be first in everything, just to be praised by teachers. I wanted to make a hundred on all of my examinations, but I did not want anyone else to make a hundred! I had to excel! What an awful human being, a chip off the old block, Adam, after the devil entered into him!

Praise the Lord that we had a man of God for a pastor who knew that every human being was just like that, and he knew the remedy: Jesus Christ had come and died and taken in Himself the sin of the human family; and that was what He proclaimed.

I wanted to go to the altar that first night, but on the evening before, a girl my age had gone and people said that she was too small, that she did not know what she was doing. Therefore, I did not dare go, but there was no peace of heart for me during the remainder of that meeting, or any other time.

The next year when the revival meeting began, I publicly announced myself a lost sinner by going to the altar and telling the Lord about my sins. In spite of the fact that I had been silently confessing for a year, that was my first chance to let other people know that I was conscious of my being one of the Lost.

No one was trained to do personal work at the altar. Only the pastor was at the altar to help people, and there were always so many older ones there, who took first place, that he never got to me.

I had to go on another year with my burden of sin, shedding many a tear in secret. Over and over again I told the Lord about my sins and pled for His cleansing.

About the third year, I was at the altar next to a woman whom the pastor came to help. It seemed to me that he talked with her a long time. He just stuck his head over toward me and said, "Just trust the Lord and He will save you." He was right, but I did not know what he meant by trusting the Lord. So that meeting came to an end with the cry of my heart being, "The summer is ended and I am not saved" (see Jer. 8:20).

When I went fifteen miles in the country to my grandmother's in the summer and attended their Big Meeting, I would just have to go to the altar. Occasionally we went to other nearby country churches for their summer meetings, and I could not but make my distress known. I went forward so much at my home church that I was afraid people would think that I was just going for the fun of it. I could have assured them that it certainly was not fun. Sometimes I would almost hold to the bench to keep from going forward but then I went home feeling worse then than when I went; and when I did go, it did no good! Oh, the wretched girl that I was!

After our pastor had been with us for fifteen years, he resigned and pastored another church in the community. When his revival meeting came, we went. I was among those at the altar wanting to be saved from hell. I was about fourteen by that time, and I suppose the pastor felt that I was old enough to have some attention. He said, "Bertha, if you will just trust the Lord, He will save you. Are you trusting Him?"

I replied, "Yes, I am trusting the Lord."

He said, "Well, you are saved then."

(Now, what about one human being telling another that he is saved when the advisor cannot see whether or not a miracle has taken place inside?) He went back to the pulpit and asked anyone who had trusted the Lord at that service to stand. I stood, but I went home just as much in the dark as ever. I knew a good bit about the Lord, but He was away out yonder and I was here, under the burden of what I was in the sight of God, with no connection between us.

Two more summers passed, with a pastor who did no personal work. Then one last Sunday morning, after I had gone regularly to the altar as usual, the pastor asked if any at the front were ready to come to Jesus Christ and take Him as Savior. For the first time, I saw that we come to the cross of Christ to be saved. Formerly I had not differentiated between God the Father and God the Son, and I did not know what was meant by "trusting God." Even though my advice had been right, all of the Godhead was God to me. I had been all those years trying to approach God the Father directly, no doubt even calling Him "Father," when He is only the Father of those who believe His Son (Gal. 3:26). I learned that what the preachers meant by trusting God to save meant to trust God the Son, who settled my sin and my sinful self when He took my sins and me in His own body on the tree.

I was on the front seat, having gone forward at the first verse. I knew that I would go; there was no use to wait. It was but a step to where the pastor stood. I took it, gave him my hand to signify that I trusted in Christ's death to save me. By the time I took the second step, which was back to my seat, my years of burden of sin had rolled away, and the joy of the Lord filled my soul.

I think sometimes if the Lord could ever save anyone the wrong way, He would have saved me! He must really have been sorry for me. I praise? Him that He never let go, but made that conviction stronger and stronger until someone said enough about Christ's death, or Christ being the Savior, for me to lay hold on what He had done for me. There is no direct road from the sinful heart to God the Father. I tried to make one, but it did not work! My sin was settled at the cross, and through Christ's death I at last came, which is the only way that anyone gets to Him.

I went home so thrilled, and so sorry for everyone else who was not in tune with the Lord, that I did not want any of that good Sunday dinner. My parents and two older sisters and both older brothers were church members and one brother and sister younger were old enough to be saved, so I just had to go to my place of prayer by the trunk in the walk-in closet in my room and plead with God for the family and for friends and neighbors.

But that joy wore off. Before many months I showed no more of the fruit of the Spirit in my life than the rest of my family, for whom I prayed that glorious Sunday when I passed out of death into life. I well knew to whom I belonged, even though at times I knew that I was not pleasing Him. When the visiting preacher, Brother Manness, asked, "Are you girls all Christians?" I knew that Sister Jennie answered right, but I longed for something more of the Lord whom I knew![4]

The Lord did not disregard that longing. In June of 1907, on a very warm Sunday afternoon as Bertha, her brothers, sisters, and mother were seated on the front porch of their lovely home enjoying what breeze was blowing, father John came down the street carrying the suitcases of three men. He ushered the men up to the front porch and introduced them to his family. They were Reverend Troy Manness and Reverend Luther Manness, evangelists, and Mr. McElrath, who served as the singer for the evangelistic team.

The Revival Meetings

The men had been in town for a few days and were living in the little local hotel. Arriving by railroad, they had hoped to secure a place in

Cowpens to put up a tent for an evangelistic crusade. They had difficulty in securing a place, and someone directed them to Bertha's father, suggesting he might be of help. Father John was very cautious, however. He did not want to have a part in any sort of evangelism that was not solidly rooted in good evangelical Christianity. So he talked with the men for some time. After considerable discussion, he decided they were probably trustworthy and had come to Cowpens to be of benefit to the community. So John went to the mayor and asked permission for the men to set up their tent in the vacant lot in the center of town, across the street from father John's store.

The meetings were set to begin on Friday evening and continue through the next three Sundays, a typical revival meeting in the deep south. The brothers did prove to be able men. Good preaching and music rang throughout the tent. As someone probably rather facetiously said, it was the "best show in town." Everyone turned out to see it.

Of course, Bertha and her brothers and sisters wanted to go right from the start. But their father said, "Wait until you find out what these men are preaching!"[5] Father John attended each service on Friday and Saturday evenings and Sunday afternoon. He had a few reservations at first, but by the time he brought the men to his home he was convinced they were sincere men and, as he expressed it, "They were there for the good of the town."[6] The children were then allowed to attend the meetings.

Bertha exuded excitement about the men being brought to their home that Sunday afternoon. So with her three sisters, who were all old enough to help and trained to do so, they soon prepared a sumptuous meal for the family and guests. They sat around the table with cakes and pies and all the good things of great southern cooking. That opened the door for the whole family to attend the Sunday night service. Sunday morning services were not held in the tent so the revival meeting would not interfere with regular Sunday morning worship in local churches.

The Spirit of God moved night after night. Many felt the meeting should not close, but only three Sundays had been scheduled for the center of town. So the evangelistic team moved to the Wesleyan churchyard eight miles out in the country. Every day the Smith family rose early, set about cooking and getting a huge picnic basket of food ready. The Smiths filled their buggies with family and folks to go to the three services that were held each day. As southern folk say, the crops were "laid by" and all the farmers had to do was to go to church. Go they did.

In that setting Bertha began to sense deeply the Spirit of God speaking to her heart. She had already been soundly converted, but she was far from satisfied with her Christian life. During the first supper the evangelists shared in the Smith home, one of them asked all the children, "Are you all

Christians?" "Yes," sister Jennie answered. Bertha confessed that she responded with the same reply but could not help but ask herself what kind of Christians they were. Thus began Bertha's journey toward a deeper spiritual experience. That pilgrimage forms a fascinating account of the work of the Spirit of God in the life of this vivacious young lady.

The Manness brothers were the sons of a Methodist minister in Greensboro, North Carolina. Their father was a well-educated man with a very fine personal library. His parsonage was filled with twelve children. With so large a family, finances barred the children from going to college. Consequently, the two evangelist brothers enrolled in Dr. Knapp's Bible School in Cincinnati. Although it was not on the same academic level of a college or seminary, they received good training. Bertha confessed that when her family heard the two brothers preach, they would try to decide which was the better preacher. She said she usually agreed that the last one they had heard proved best. Both brothers were very effective communicators.

The Manness team preached that people should be thoroughly and completely saved through faith in the Lord Jesus Christ. They further declared that God's redeemed people should acknowledge the total lordship of Jesus Christ in mind, body, and soul. Christians ought to live by that rule, confess all their sins, and remain in the constant cleansing blood of Christ as they yield themselves completely to the Spirit of God to be "filled with all the fullness of God" (Eph. 3:19). They declared that only the Spirit-filled Christian would be empowered with the strength of God to live a life pleasing to the Lord and be used significantly in His service. This "Spirit-filled life" presented a new idea to Bertha and her brothers and sisters. At that time, most Baptists had little grasp of the biblical doctrine of the work of the Holy Spirit.

Bertha's second sister, Pearle, had a gracious deepening experience with the Spirit of God in a strange way. While reading through a copy of a new hymnbook, the Holy Spirit moved powerfully upon her. Pearle came home with a testimony of having "gone all the way with the Lord."[7]

The entire family was moved by the meetings, particularly Bertha's mother. Almost immediately Mrs. Smith found herself at the altar seeking all that God had for her. Prior to the meetings the Smith family had practiced family prayers at home, but not on a regular basis. The pastor led a devotional when he spent the night in their home. Otherwise, there was no family devotional time. When Mrs. Smith knelt at the altar seeking complete surrender for all that God would do in her life, she felt deeply convicted that family prayer should be a regular part of their home. She was a quiet lady who had never given a testimony in public or even prayed aloud. She struggled over the issue. But that night she wept until her lovely lavender silk blouse was ruined as she yielded to God's prompting, and the change in her life was marvelous.

Then sister Jennie went to the altar, then brother Lester, a third-year student in college. He realized he had never truly been saved. He was baptized as a twelve-year-old child, but he never came to personally know Jesus Christ as his Lord and Savior. Down on his knees he cried out to God, repented of his sins, trusted Christ as his Savior, and found God's wonderful salvation.

This was too much for Bertha. Her time had come. God created in her heart a deep hunger for more. The Holy Spirit moved mightily upon her because of the experiences of her family and a sermon she heard on Romans 12:1–2:

> I beseech you, therefore, brethren, by the mercies of God, that ye present your bodies a living sacrifice, holy, acceptable unto God, which is your reasonable service. And be not conformed to this world: but be ye transformed by the renewing of your mind, that ye may prove what is that good, and acceptable, and perfect, will of God.

It began to dawn on Bertha that those whom God honored had to be bathed, and then clothed in white linen. After all, in Christ all believers are "priests" in that sense. In a word, Christians must present themselves to God totally and be completely cleansed of their sins if they are to be proper "priests" of the Lord. The message of Romans 12:1–2 so touched Bertha's heart that she realized she must make the sacrifice of dedication, without blemish, a perfect specimen of the cleansed life before she would be acceptable before God in service. For days Bertha had been confessing every sin that she could bring to mind. She recognized that the altar meant giving herself over completely to Christ and living for Him unreservedly. Everything came together and she knew what she must do.

When the invitation was given, Bertha went immediately to the front, fell on her knees, and as she later expressed it, had a "business transaction with my Lord." She surrendered everything in her life to the lordship of Jesus Christ, willing to receive anything He might lead her to do. She did not feel this to be anything special in her own experience; it merely fulfilled the Lord's requirement for all His people. It was "reasonable service." Surely that was not too much for the Lord to ask in the light of His grace and redemption. After she made the "transaction" with her Lord, she returned to her seat, determined she would not be conformed to this world but would be transformed in her mind day by day into the perfect will of God. She knew if she could discern the will of God for her life, it would be "good, acceptable, and perfect." She became utterly open of heart to the leadership and control of the Holy Spirit, and her life of obedience soon proved that the promises of God in the Romans passage were true. Whatever the Lord might bring or not bring to her life, she knew she would experience peace and contentment. She put herself on the altar to live for the Lord Jesus Christ and for Him alone. She later explained:

> Joy unspeakable was filling my soul! I knew that the Holy Spirit, who had come into my heart when I was saved and had wanted to fill me those two years, but could not unless I knew how to let Him. I thought the sin principle in me had been removed, eradicated, and I would never sin again. The Holy Spirit so magnified Christ that I did not sin for a good while! Or rather, I was not convicted of sins by the Holy Spirit. Certainly He saw much in me that grieved Him, but He would rule those things out as He saw me able to take it.[8]

A New Spirituality

Bertha's theology changed after her initial deepening experience. At first she thought the old sinful nature had been eradicated. But after a period, Bertha learned that sin, even for dedicated believers, can be a serious problem and must be dealt with forthrightly. What a blessing that experience afforded. Little did Bertha's father realize when he brought the Manness team to their home that the visit would result in such a deepening and enriching experience for his entire family, particularly Bertha. It set a new pattern of spirituality for the Smith home.

The results of being Spirit-filled were all but overwhelming in Bertha's life. The Holy Spirit so lifted up Jesus Christ in her daily experience that all worldly pleasure lost its attraction. She did not want to talk like the world, look like the world, or even have worldly thoughts. A dramatic change had come. She took off her jewelry, pretty clothes, ribbons, and flowered hats, and instead wore the plainest clothes. She did not want to attract attention to herself any longer. She picked up those ideas from the Wesleyans. That is the way they saw Spirit-filled people living out their experience of Christ. Later, as she herself said, she learned that modest, pretty clothes not only kept her from thinking about how she was dressed, but also it had the same effect on other people who had to look at her.

The Bible became a new book for Bertha. She began a correspondence course with Dr. Knapp's Bible School, and she thoroughly enjoyed it, even though her sister Jennie mildly rebuked her by telling her it would be too deep for her and that it was a preacher's course. Jennie was wrong. The Scriptures Bertha had committed to memory came alive as never before. All the verses of the Bible she had learned in school and Sunday school flooded in on her like a veritable tide. At school one day, the principal came into an unused room at recess and found Bertha sitting in the very cold room on the floor reading the New Testament. He turned up the heat and went out. Everyone appreciated her dedication.

As is always true when God touches a person with His Holy Spirit, a deep passion to see others come to Christ invaded the newly Spirit-filled believer. Bertha wanted everyone saved. The Lord laid on her heart twenty young people about her own age who did not know Christ. She prayed for them, daily naming each one before the Lord. Eighteen of these were saved that same summer. The nineteenth came to Christ some years later. The twentieth had moved away and Bertha lost contact. What a token of God's power on this Spirit-filled young woman. She had been given the spiritual gift of the "evangelist" (Eph. 4:11), as the rest of her entire life clearly demonstrates.

The key to Bertha's newfound relationship with Christ can be summed up in Bertha's own words, "Prayer became communion with God." This proved true in her private prayer life and in corporate intercession with others of like mind. She was gifted in evangelism, but her greatest power was prayer. She was only in the ninth grade, and all the kids said of her, "Bertha has religion."

Bertha felt that her own church was rather cold. Her real joy centered in attending on Wednesday afternoons a women's prayer meeting where the Spirit-filled women of the community would gather to pray and study God's Word. They had great times of prayer and intercession.

Spiritual Struggles

As time went on, young Bertha learned that the sin principle had not been eradicated in her life. All too often, she confessed, "It exerted itself and I really did not quite know what to do about it." She grieved deeply over even accidental sins. That which grieved the Holy Spirit grieved her. She prayed regularly, seeking to maintain fellowship with her Lord. She truly struggled for a sustaining intimacy with the Lord Jesus Christ. At times, however, there appeared to be no real power in her service and witness. Bertha had learned the principle of the Spirit's infilling and how to keep one's sins confessed; yet, she did not understand how to achieve sustained victory with Christ in His death and resurrection. So she threw herself into busywork at the church, but that did not satisfy. Even her personal witnessing appeared rather powerless at times, though she continually tried to lead others to Christ. She had to confess that during her four years of college, despite all the Christian work she was involved with on campus, she only led one classmate to Christ. Her heart broke over lost people, but she seemingly did not have constant victory in her life thus to win them.

Yet in all these spiritual dynamics, God was preparing His servant for a missionary ministry. Bertha had learned the secret of cleansing and the Spirit's infilling, even if the principle of victory eluded her at this stage of spiritual maturity. After one year at a small college in North Carolina, she was off to Winthrop College. A new chapter was opening for the young, vivacious, and committed Olive Bertha Smith.

3

An Unusual Servant for Unusual Service

Bertha as a young woman. *Credit: Melten*

With high school behind her, Bertha Smith faced the exciting days of college. Little did she realize at the time, but for all practical purposes Cowpens lay behind her, until her return from Taiwan many decades later. A new chapter unfolded for Miss Bertha, preparing her to become a "Woman of Revival."

Bertha embarked on a new adventure by attending Linwood College, a school for women an hour's drive by carriage from Gastonia, North Carolina, for one year. It had opened in 1882 under the name of Pruden Hall, named for the lady who founded it. From its inception it had Presbyterian ties. The small college had its early struggles, changing its name several times and having a succession of leaders. In 1903 it almost closed, but the governing board asked Dr. Lindsey to become president at this crucial time. The college was given its final name by him—and rightly so; he resurrected the institution. It became a boarding school for girls and then opened its doors in 1914 to boys as well. However, the school finally had to close its doors in 1921; its funds simply dried up.

After a happy and fruitful year at Linwood, Bertha transferred to Winthrop College, an all-girls' school. She chose the field of education for her major. As part of the physical education program, students were required to walk an hour each day. This walking became a valuable part of her training, for the discipline helped preserve her health while in China. One graduate, Miss Martha Franks, whom we shall meet later, said,

> Winthrop in the 1920s was a beautiful place, with attractive new buildings, wide expanses of manicured lawns and spreading trees just beginning to mature. The atmosphere was one of discipline, both physical and intellectual. The discipline was evident to the eye in the well-kept grounds and in the deportment of the young ladies who wore the same blue skirts and white blouses. There was a rigid core-curriculum followed by everyone. Every girl had to walk a mile every day and know how to swim before she was awarded a degree. Bertha kept up her walking regime throughout her life. The aim was to train young women for the maturing twentieth century, and discipline was a necessary means to that end.[1]

Although Winthrop was a state-supported school, it still enjoyed a robust spiritual atmosphere. Dr. Bancroft Johnson, the president during Bertha's days, was a dedicated Christian layman who believed that the spiritual as well as the professional life should be emphasized in college education. Bertha said, "He was like a father to me."[2] Winthrop had graduates serving around the world as Christian missionaries. The school was primarily a normal school, that is, a college designed to train teachers, named after the Honorable Robert C. Winthrop, chairman of the Peabody Educational Fund. It opened its doors on November 15, 1886, with seventeen students in the chapel of the disbanded Presbyterian Theological Seminary in Columbia, South Carolina. Then in 1895, it moved to Rock Hill, South Carolina. Following the move, Winthrop College grew tremendously, becoming one of the largest women's colleges in the country during those early years. Today Winthrop College rests on a beautiful four-hundred-acre site with a student body of over five thousand men and women, granting degrees through the master's level. It became Bertha's home and spiritual training ground for the next several years.

College Days

College days became growing days, a time filled with fascinating experiences and challenges for the young freshman. One such challenge centered in foreign missions. Bertha Smith had already begun to develop a keen interest in missions while still in Cowpens. Because of the exposure to the larger world that college inevitably brings, her interest in the Lord's service and foreign missions in particular, began to loom large in her expanding spiritual vision. Further, college became a place of discipline for Miss Bertha. She had a regularly planned "quiet time" with the Lord during the day in addition to morning and evening Bible reading and prayer. At first, she could not find a good place for her "quiet time." Then one day she discovered, as she said, "under the providence of God, that the room assigned to her in the dormitory had two closets," one for her, the other for her roommate. Her own closet could be arranged in such a fashion that it left enough space to keep her prayer vigils. So there she retreated daily. It was cramped to be sure, but she took the Lord literally when He said, "Enter into the closet and pray in secret." She said the closet was only wide enough for the clothes hangers, but fortunately she was not very wide herself in those days.

One day during her prayer time in the closet with the door closed, her roommate came in. She had planned her prayer time when the roommate would normally be in class, but on this particular occasion her roommate came in early with a friend. They sat down to talk. The friend asked Bertha's roommate what she (Bertha) was like. The roommate replied, "She is not very attractive, but she sure is religious. She reads her Bible before breakfast and says her prayers when she gets up in the morning just as at night."

The fact that the roommate said Bertha was not very attractive did not set well. The conversation, needless to say, disrupted her prayers. Bertha confessed her thoughts at that moment: "Now if she knew that right now I am in this closet praying in the middle of the day, what would she think!" But to Bertha's credit, she never revealed herself and saved the roommate considerable embarrassment. When Bertha related the story later, she made the quick comment that neither was her roommate particularly attractive either. Bertha's frankness, wellknown by everyone who knew her, at times got her into rather difficult situations, but it also served her well in helping people face the reality of their spiritual situation before Christ, and often led them into a deeper experience.

The Call to Missions

College days were filled with study and Christian service. Bertha met and became friends with some members of the Student Volunteer Band, a group of mission-minded students. Bertha had already begun to feel that she might be a missionary one day. When they recognized her deep concern for missions, members of the Band suggested that she join them. The Band met regularly for daily prayer and study. On Bertha's first visit, she was handed a declaration card that read, "I make it my purpose, God permitting, to become a foreign missionary." It had to be signed. This immediately threw Bertha into a serious quandary. Had God called her to foreign missions? How would this be realized in her life? What would it entail in future preparation? These and a thousand other questions flooded her heart and mind. She had to decide if she was going to join the Student Volunteer Band or not, for far more was involved than just joining a student organization. She realized the seriousness of making such a pledge; it meant dedicating her life to missions. She waited for quite a long time, attempting to discover God's leadership in her life. For the next few weeks, she prayed and prayed. But she could not find God's will or any light whatever on the subject.

Then on Sunday afternoon, January 9, 1910, during the required afternoon meditation time from two o'clock until four, while her roommate was in the infirmary, Bertha went before the Lord; she had to have an answer. She knew the climax had come and she had to settle the matter. She realized the radical difference between making a definite commitment to become a missionary and simply saying, "If the Lord calls me to become a missionary, then I will." Did God have His hand on her for such a task? She had to find the answer.

Bertha began to seek the Lord that Sunday afternoon on her knees in the closet. Other questions swept across her mind. Would her father be grieved over her decision and refuse to continue funding her college education? Would her brothers and sisters approve? It certainly would mean leaving home for a long time, perhaps even for life. She felt that if God did truly call her, she would probably live and work in Africa. Problem after problem disturbed her mind as the tension mounted. In her own testimony she acknowledged that she wept and perspired and perspired and wept. She was face-to-face with her Lord. She must have an answer.

Right then, light began to break through the clouds of doubt. It came to her that the Lord had given up all the glories of heaven and lived thirty-three years on earth and even died a shameful death for her. He did it because it was the Father's will. Surely, there could then be no holding back if the field of missions was the purpose of God for her life. Finally, it just burst forth from her heart, "Yes, Lord, if that is what you want." Then a deep, rich assurance swept over her that this decision truly was the will of God. She said, "All I could do was get on my knees and weep and thank God for the call."[3]

After the two-hour struggle, she came out from her closet and, with exuberance, signed her name to the pledge card. She testified, "A joy filled my heart which has never left me." The call had come and as a faithful, dedicated Christian, she had responded. Little did she know what was ahead in a life of ministry that would span over seventy-five years of effective, powerful service for the Lord Jesus Christ. China and the world would soon be blessed by the simple girl from Cowpens, South Carolina.

Bertha began to read all the books on missions she could lay her hands on. She read about many countries and tried to keep an interest in all of them, open to wherever the Lord would lead her. She trusted the Spirit of God to put her in the right place at the right time under His providential grace and leadership. She began to grow in her knowledge of the world and its multiplied needs.

In her senior year at Winthrop, Bertha led the Student Volunteer Band. She also served in the YWCA and taught a Bible class. Her days were full. Bertha was proud—in a good sense—of her college and all it afforded in spiritual matters as well as academic. She always carried her class pin through the years, but she never wore it. She said the clasp was too hard to fasten.

Early Service

While home for the summer break from college one year, Bertha organized a Young Woman's Auxiliary and a Royal Ambassador chapter in Cowpens. These were mission organizations for young women in their teens and for young boys, respectively, and were sponsored by the Woman's Missionary Union of the Southern Baptist Convention at that time. She threw herself into that work with zeal and enthusiasm. She also taught a boys' Sunday school class. A few years later, at the Missionary Training School in Louisville, Kentucky, her assignment in a practical missions course was to work with the Boys' Club at a Goodwill Center in Louisville. Through her service there, she developed a "special interest in boys," as she put it, and became quite effective in working with the lads.

Still Struggling

Back at Winthrop, not all was to Miss Bertha's spiritual satisfaction. She had a deep burden to win people to the Lord, but she seemed unable to do so. In those days she had something of that typical up-and-down, mountaintop-valley spiritual experience that many endure until they learn the secret of victory. She said, "I constantly prayed to get back the glorious experience of the first filling."[4] The Lord in His marvelous mercy did at times restore perfect peace and a measure of joy, but it was not continually sustained. This constant failure and restoration depressed her. "What to do with the old self I did not know," she exclaimed.[5] She would learn.

Off to Seminary

Bertha graduated from Winthrop College with a Bachelor of Arts degree in 1913. For one year she taught in a public school in Blacksburg, South Carolina. These days were also interesting and exciting times for the young missionary volunteer. In college she had learned the formal principles of teaching, but at Blacksburg she put them into practice and experienced firsthand what it meant to teach in the classroom. During this time she became an excellent communicator.

Bertha knew that she must have further biblical and theological training to receive an appointment by the Foreign Mission Board of the Southern Baptist Convention. Moreover, she wanted to be prepared more adequately for the years of missionary service that she devoutly trusted God to grant her. At this time, most women who aspired to a foreign mission appointment among Southern Baptists went to the Woman's Missionary Union Training School in Louisville, Kentucky. This excellent institution was modeled on the academic principles of a theological seminary and was located on the campus of The Southern Baptist Theological Seminary.

The Seminary, which was Southern Baptists' first such school, was organized in 1859 in Greenville, South Carolina. A great spirit characterized the institution in its early days. In 1865, just after the Civil War, the seminary seemed at an end. It had to be closed during the hostilities. Could it be opened again? Right then John Albert Broadus, one of the professors, stood up and said, "Suppose we quietly agree the seminary may die, but we will die first."[6] The seminary reopened with seven students.

In Miss Bertha's day the Training School had completely separate facilities, with a small valley separating the School from the Seminary proper. (The School became an official part of the Seminary in the 1960s.) Male students in the Seminary humorously called the valley the "valley of decision." The reason was obvious: Many male students went to the Woman's Training School to court young women preparing for Christian service, and many made the decision to seek their hand in marriage. Whether Miss Bertha had such suitors is unknown. She was attractive—regardless of what her college roommate said—and had a warm, outgoing personality. But she had dedicated her life solely to the Lord and never married.

Bertha studied the deeper, richer, critical realities of the Christian faith in Louisville. Miss McClure, principal of the Training School, influenced the young student. With her keen mind, Bertha excelled in academic life. She studied under scholars such as E. Y. Mullins, A. T. Robertson, and John R. Sampey.

The academics of the Southern Baptist institution Bertha attended have always been exemplary. The Training School was organized in 1907 by the Woman's Missionary Union (WMU) to provide theological education for women, especially mission volunteers. The school opened in October of 1907 with twenty young women enrolled. It began when a missionary to China, E. Z. Simmons, while on furlough in 1899, said, "When they [women] come to China, they readily learn the language, but they do not know how to teach the Bible for they do not know it themselves. There should be a school for training women."[7] Prior to 1907, women were only allowed to audit classes at the Seminary without credit. Simmons believed women should be admitted to class with credit privileges. The idea of a credited training school for women took years to develop. Many opposed the idea, but in 1907 female students were officially granted all the advantages of the Seminary's classes. Diplomas of the new Woman's Missionary Training School were signed by the faculty of the Seminary, WMU, and Training School officials.

Bertha Smith attended the Training School for two years. Her fervor for the Lord did not diminish as she immersed herself in graduate studies. She worked faithfully in mission work in the city of Louisville and made every day count for Christ. Two years later, in the spring of 1916, she graduated with a Bachelor of Missionary Training, confident that God had great things for her.

Mission Appointment

In 1916, the year of Miss Bertha's graduation, T. B. Ray, foreign secretary of the Foreign Mission Board, visited the seminary campus. Bertha had an interview with him. At this time she made her wishes known to the Board and sought appointment. But it was not to Africa she would go. An urgent cry arose for women teachers in China. Her vision shifted to the Far East, as the Spirit of God was leading in her life.

Bertha received tentative acceptance by the Foreign Mission Board. However, the First World War was raging and this made the appointment of missionaries very difficult. Travel problems abounded because hostilities sometimes erupted beyond Europe. The Foreign Mission Board asked her to wait one year before formal appointment and assignment to her designated place of ministry. She acquiesced reluctantly. She went back to South Carolina and served as principal and teacher of Cooley Springs School at Whitesburg in Spartanburg County, twenty miles from Cowpens. Her brother, who had just received the Master of Arts degree, had refused the post. Bertha taught grades three and four while her sister taught grade six. At her home church she taught a young men's Sunday school class and even led the services when the pastor could not get there due to high water on the nearby river. As she said, "The experience of the year proved very valuable in my work in China."

On July 3, 1917, Bertha Smith received her formal appointment by the Southern Baptist Convention Foreign Mission Board for service in China. On August 9, 1917, she left her beloved Cowpens. With a heavy heart over being torn from the intimate family circle that had been a source of joy and security through the years, she said good-bye. There were tears streaming down her cheeks and a lump in her throat that "just would not go down." Trying to console the family as well as herself, she said to her father, "Seven years will not be so long" (after seven years service in the field, the Baptist Mission Board granted a year's furlough). Bertha's father replied, "But I won't be here; yet, I know I can trust you, even if it is around the world." That brought a few more tears. So in sadness, yet joy, she boarded the train for Vancouver as she waved her good-byes to family and friends. Bertha found the comfort and strength that the Spirit of God alone affords. She knew she was following the leadership of her Lord and that His strength would be sufficient.

Bertha was on her way. As the train wheels clicked on the steel rails taking her to the port of embarkation, God reminded her of Matthew 10:39: "Whoever finds his life will lose it, and whoever loses his life for my sake will find it" (NIV). This verse brought special strength to her as she broke her family ties.

Now China opened its doors before her.

Part II
Revival Days
in China

Bertha along with a nurse in the Baptist Mission
Coumpound, Tsining, China, 1937. *Credit: FMB*

4

China Opens before Her

Graduation Day for some of Miss Bertha's students. *Credit: Melten*

God's strength and comfort continued to be Bertha Smith's companions as she sailed the Pacific on *The Little Empress of Japan*, a six thousand ton-steamer of the Canadian Pacific Line. Her cabin mates were Mary Nelle Lyne and Flora Dodson. They reached Yokohama, Japan, their first port of call, on September 4. Then on September 17, 1917—ten years before the great Shantung Revival broke—they arrived in Shanghai, and Bertha set foot on Chinese soil for the first time. China and the challenge of winning a nation to Christ lay before her.

Arrival in China

Shanghai is a fascinating city, and Bertha Smith got caught up in the excitement. She became the guest of two missionaries, Miss Willie Kelly and Miss Pearle Johnson. They showed her something of the work in Shanghai, then took her on a side trip to Soochow before she secured passage to travel north. Soon afterwards she began the long and arduous journey to Peking (now Beijing).

Language school—many long months of it—loomed before her, but she stood up to all challenges with zest. While awaiting the opening of the language school in Peking, she spent her first ten days in north China with Dr. John Anderson and his wife Minnie. Everything sparkled with a newness and fascination to Bertha. She remained in the capital city of China her entire first year, along with other young people in the College of Chinese Studies. Bertha and fellow missionary, Grace McBride, her roommate, gave themselves to learning the difficult Chinese language. The dialect they labored over was Mandarin, the official or main dialect of China.

Settling in Laichowfu

After the year of study in Peking, Bertha moved to Laichowfu, in Shantung Province, some seventy-five miles from where the famous Baptist missionary Lottie Moon had been stationed. It took several days to travel by mule litter with a speed limit of three miles per hour! Miss Bertha made it clear that the speed limit was never to be broken. Her arrival in Laichowfu increased the missionary force to eight, and in her twenties, she was by far the youngest. The others were at least forty. To Bertha, anyone of age forty seemed an old person, so she found it somewhat difficult to relate to her missionary colleagues at first. But she learned.

Bertha studied Mandarin for five hours a day with a private teacher in Laichowfu. She studied the Chinese characters and attempted to get the idioms and pronunciation of conversational Chinese just right. She had a heart to learn the language so she could share the gospel effectively.

She also taught English classes to Chinese students in the two mission high schools. This schedule set a pattern of hard work for Bertha. Missionary friend Martha Franks called her a "workaholic." Perhaps she was, but she intended to serve the Lord without limits or excuses. For the first time in her life Bertha began to suffer from loneliness—real loneliness. She cried out, "Oh, for a young person with time for frolic and fun when the work is done." She said she felt "lonesome and homesick enough to die," and that spiritual syndrome of feeling sorry for herself robbed her of joy in the Lord.

New Peace in Prayer

Miss Bertha had always been concerned for her physical health as well as her spiritual well-being. She continued the long walks from her Winthrop days, not only for her health and recreation but also for contemplation and meditation. The mission compound, located outside the city wall, gave her a place to walk in the fields and little pathways that divided the small patches of cultivated fields that the Chinese called their "little farms." She was somewhat apprehensive, however, and wondered if it would be safe to leave the mission compound and walk alone in Laichowfu. Her fellow missionaries assured her that there should be no problems if she kept in sight of the mission buildings.

The long walks were lonely at first and seemed to deepen her problem. Finally, the loneliness became almost unbearable for her. To ease her loneliness, Bertha began to draw upon the resources of the Word of God. During her first year at Winthrop College, she had memorized 615 Bible verses. For this achievement Mrs. Helen Miller Gould, the general secretary of the YWCA, one of her older friends, had given her a beautiful leather-bound Bible. She continued memorizing Scripture throughout her long life. On these lonely walks all of the memorized passages came to life as she repeated them day after day while strolling down the pathways. On those "Bible walks," God began to meet her problem of loneliness.

Bertha memorized hymns on some of her strolls. She found this little spiritual exercise a tremendous help. By the end of her Chinese years, she had memorized all the verses of scores of hymns. She would change the third person pronouns to the second. Instead of singing "about" the Lord, she would sing "to" the Lord. While seeking the Lord's presence through Scripture and hymns of praise, the wonderful presence of Christ began to grow and develop in her life. One day Miss Bertha recalled the Great Commission on one of her walks. She addressed it to the Lord by praying, "Now, Lord, you say that you will be with the one who goes with the gospel message to others 'always.' Always means now, you are with me here and now." Claiming the promises of Scripture characterized her whole approach to the Bible. Her favorite verse became 2 Corinthians 9:8: "And God is able to make all grace abound toward you; that ye, always having all sufficiency in all things, may abound to every good work." She would claim the promise to "abound," not "just get by."

Bertha confessed that when she began to practice reciting the verses of Scripture to the Lord rather than just going over them by memory, His presence became increasingly real. She came to understand that He did truly walk with her. When she "faithed" His promises, as she put it, the Holy Spirit made His Presence very real. What a change it effected in her life! Her walks through the little farmlands outside the mission compound became the most precious time of her day. Her spiritual life profoundly deepened, and she readily admitted that from then on she never had a lonely moment. She had learned to practice the presence of God. After discovering the significant revelation of how Christ can be genuinely real in a person's life, she longed for more time to spend alone with her Lord.

Those times alone with Him formed the basis of her spirituality and the profundity of her significant prayer life.

For two years Miss Bertha spent happy days in study and ministry. After finding the peace and comfort of the presence of Christ, she threw herself into her language studies with new zeal. She sought perfection. The drilling of pronunciation, learning the Chinese characters, and all the difficulties of the language no longer seemed a burden. Becoming quite adept in the language, she now felt increasingly ready for her charge. Her studies and her work with Chinese students took on a most positive tone. Her walks through the fields continued to be a time of great joy. She described it as "a joy to have an hour alone with my Lord in the fields where I talked aloud with Him, even though some Chinese occasionally walked up behind me and probably thought I was out of my mind. I not only talked with the Lord, I wanted Him to talk with me; so I carried my New Testament and memorized many choice verses, stopping long enough to read one and then to repeat it over and over to the Lord as I walked."[1]

After completing the second year of language study, she took charge of the girls' boarding school. She served there for some fourteen years, with the exception of a year's interruption due to a local war when she served as principal of the boys' school in Chefoo. Each day presented a new challenge and Bertha's incredible spirit enabled her to rise to all occasions. God's hand rested upon her.

All Was Not Easy

Miss Bertha's heart ached in seeing a country with no observance of the Lord's Day whatsoever. She found it difficult to adjust to the fact that all businesses stayed open on Sunday. People went to work in the fields on Sunday just like any other day. Of course, the Chinese people knew the convictions of Christian missionaries. When missionaries would not buy from the street vendors, they would always ask, "Is it Sunday?" At least the testimony of missionaries for the observance of a day of worship made some impression.

Even far worse than the lack of observance of the Lord's Day were the sights that greeted Bertha's eyes in the huge markets on temple days. She found the religious activities of the people to be appalling, and the pagan religions grieved her very soul. People would come from every direction in the surrounding countryside for the festivities, bringing handcrafts and wares for sale. Temple days were days of commerce as much as worship, and the commercial activities seemed to be a higher priority for the people. Grandmothers and children would go to the temple with the vendors for worship. They would leave an offering of some sort of gift at the temple. The gifts were usually commensurate with the financial status of the family. The offering would perhaps be a bolt of flowered paper or silk, which would be burned in the courtyard. The worshipers would then walk up the rickety stairs of the temple and bump their heads on the floor to an idol that could neither speak nor hear nor help. How Bertha prayed for them.

The more sophisticated high school students laughed at the superstition of their mothers and grandmothers who still believed in the gods. About four hundred students, eighteen of every twenty students in the public high school, were members of what they called the "No-god Society." And, of course, they were just as lost from the true gospel as the ardent idol worshipers. Miss Bertha saw them all as "sheep without a shepherd." She knew that their only hope rested in coming to faith in Christ.

A Deepening Faith

At this time, Miss Bertha entered into another deepening experience with the Lord Jesus Christ. She had asked herself whether God wanted her to marry. One of her cherished hymns was "I Surrender All," and in singing that hymn, God began to speak to her about marriage. She confessed that the Lord had given her something of a mother's heart, the depth of which she had not really grasped until she saw the difference in the lifestyle of the single women and those who were living with a husband and having precious children of their own. She began to reason: the married missionaries were in the will of God just as much as she. Why could she not have a husband and children and fill that maternal instinct so deeply ingrained in her heart? But what did God want of her? Did He want her single or married? The battle raged in her heart.

While going through this inner struggle, Bertha's father passed away during the influenza epidemic of 1918 in America. He had been right when he told his missionary daughter on her departure for China that she would not see him again this side of heaven. Upon his death Bertha had to travel to the seaport city of Chefoo, to sign legal papers at the nearest United States consulate. This trip required eight days of travel which proved to be difficult at best.

The "vehicle" used for travel was a two-mule litter which had a frame of two long poles forming shafts for the mules. Ropes were criss-crossed on the middle section of the poles, strung between the two mules. Over the ropes a bow frame covered with a straw mat provided something of a seat. The passenger would always provide a thick quilt-like cover to fit over the mat to protect from the heat in summer or the cold in winter. Pillows were used along with the make-shift mattress. Upon this the traveler had to make himself or herself as comfortable as possible. Bertha said that sitting and lying were both equally miserable. The mules could not be kept in step and one would jerk one way and one another until it was no more than a journey of joggling. Up and down, sideways, and every other way, one was tossed about until it became almost like a whirling washing machine. In other words, it was a dreadfully painful ride.

By the time Bertha embarked on the last leg of her journey back to Laichowfu, she had stayed with seven happy missionary families and their children. After leaving the last mission home before reaching her own station, Bertha traveled for two long days on a lonely road. She said loneliness caused misery, and "I can't stand misery!"

Something had to take place in her life. Could she live alone all her days? During the last hours of the journey, she walked on ahead of the driver and mule litter. She would often walk and not ride because local bandits who needed clothes would often accost traveling parties. It was wise to be away from the suitcases if such were the case. So she walked on ahead some distance, getting far enough away where she could speak aloud to the Lord. She had to get the matter settled before God, and she wanted to do it as verbally and as forthrightly as she could.

On the solitary road that ran along a mountain range between Laiyang and Laichowfu, she called on the nearby peaks to be the witness to a covenant she made with her God: "Lord, I want to enter into an agreement with you today. You called me to China and you gave me grace to follow in coming. I am here to win souls for you. The only thing that will take the place of my own children will be spiritual children. If you will take from my heart this pain, I will be willing to go through with just as much inconvenience and self-denial to see children born into the family of God as is necessary for a mother to endure for her children to be born in the flesh!"[2] Later she was to declare, "I was not disappointed."

No More Tears

From that moment, Miss Bertha said there were no more tears. The Lord met her every heart need and continued to do so throughout her life. Peace and contentment characterized her single-lifestyle ministry. She began to study the Bible and books on soul winning with a new commitment. Prayer became a more definite exercise as she began to intercede for specific individuals and needs. And, of course, she began earnestly to seek opportunities to speak for Christ and to seize every appropriate occasion to share the gospel.

Years later, she said that the transaction she had made with the Lord and the new zeal the Spirit of God planted in her heart to bring people to

Christ lasted from that day until the present moment. She could finally say after decades of missionary service that she praised the Lord for the privilege of being a single woman with other people's soul needs taking first place in her life. She remembered and empathized with the great apostle Paul in his travail for the Galatians to see "Christ formed in you" (Gal. 4:19). She rested on the promise of Isaiah that "as soon as Zion travailed, she brought forth her children" (66:8). She learned to permit the Holy Spirit to pray through her with "groanings which cannot be uttered" (Rom. 8:26) that specific persons might come to faith in Christ.

Bertha Smith's first years in China were packed with new adventures in the Spirit. God dramatically continued what He had begun in her early walk with Him. The principle of the Spirit-filled life had been firmly hammered down early in her Christian experience. Unfortunately, as she expressed it, "I was often filled today and empty tomorrow."[3] Something of the old struggle still persisted. At this junction, in 1919, God did a marvelous new work of grace in her life.

Victory on the Way

A saintly Christian in California, Milton Stewart, developed a burden for missionaries. He became vitally concerned about their spiritual life and deeply desired to see their effectiveness in service become all God would have it to be. Stewart left a sizable sum of money in his estate to build four summer conference resorts for missionaries in four different sections of China. These resorts were not only paid for by his grant, but also they were endowed in such a fashion that missionaries could go for spiritual refreshing at a cost to them of one dollar a day for a ten-day period. The spiritual life was the theme for all the retreats. Most conference speakers were from America and were often aided by Spirit-filled missionaries on the field.

The Foreign Mission Board of the Southern Baptist Convention had adopted a policy that allowed their missionaries to use their vacation time to spend a few weeks away from their fields of service every summer, in order to attend such conferences. Bertha said, "I always cooperated with the Board. I took a vacation every year. I went to a conference to get some spiritual food." It was there that Miss Bertha had another deepening experience with Christ. The principle of the infilling of the Holy Spirit first led her to the mission field. In the summer of 1919 she took another step forward. God began to show Bertha the secret of the long-sought daily victory her heart had cried for over the years.

That summer Dr. R. A. Torrey led one of the conferences in the resort town of Peitaiho. Miss Bertha heard him preach twice a day on the work of the Holy Spirit in the life of the Christian in achieving true spirituality. She exclaimed, "What a blessing!"[4] The Lord did a work of great grace in her life that summer by bringing her to a fresh infilling of the Holy Spirit that uplifted her tremendously. But even still, she confessed that the "old self" still occasionally surfaced. The struggle still failed to be fully resolved, but she set her heart like a flint to arrive at victory in Christ.

The next summer, Dr. Charles G. Trumbull, editor of the *Sunday School Times*, an evangelical periodical that helped Sunday school teachers prepare their lessons, came to speak at the North China resort Miss Bertha was attending. Along with Dr. Trumbull, Miss Ruth Paxon spoke. Through the years Miss Paxon had been mightily used of God. She became known as a "missionary to the missionaries." Her major work, *Life on the Highest Plane*, remains in print and has been a source of rich encouragement and blessing to a multitude of Christians around the world. A smaller volume, *Rivers of Living Water*, has also encouraged God's people in achieving victory. That summer Miss Paxon's address centered on the Word of God, particularly where the Scriptures expose the "old nature" of Adam and how a Christian can achieve victory over it. God profoundly spoke to Miss Bertha through Miss Paxon. Later Ruth Paxon spent two or three months with Miss Bertha.

Dr. Trumbull's messages focused on "Christ in you, the hope of Glory" (Col. 1:27). Miss Bertha knew through the Holy Spirit that Christ had abided with her ever since she had been saved; this was nothing new to her. Yet, how refreshing it became when it dawned on her that Christ lived *inside of her.* That was much more meaningful than Christ just "walking alongside" the believer. She rejoiced when this reality gripped her heart. Christ actually lived out His glorious life right in her human body! She soon discovered the "old self" was not nearly as bothersome as before; it had been dethroned through faith by the power of the redeeming Christ.

During the conference Miss Bertha had several personal talks with Dr. Trumbull on how Christ Himself becomes the believer's victory. Trumbull called her attention to the centrality of the word "is" in the Bible. For example, the Lord does not give strength; the "Lord *is* the strength of my life" (Ps. 27:1). "There *is* therefore now no condemnation to them which are in Christ Jesus" (Rom. 8:1). It *is* not so much that the Lord "gives" light and salvation, "the Lord *is* my light and my salvation" (Ps. 27:1, emphasis added). This wonderful truth helped her to realize that she had stood like a beggar outside the beautiful gate of the temple. Later she said, "It was a good place to beg." When the wonderful truths that Christ was her life and her victory, all she needed resided in Him, and He dwelt in her, she understood that Christ is adequate to meet her every need. She felt like the lame beggar at the temple after Peter laid his hands upon him, and she too jumped up and ran with joy, praising God. She said of this experience:

> When I saw the glorious truth that the Lord was at that very moment my victory over every sin, over every disposition, and over every circumstance, I was filled with thanksgiving. When I had praised the Lord, Dr. Trumbull wrote in his notebook by my name the words, "A five-thousand-dollar gift!" But that did not half express it. I so walked on air that it was a year before I was convicted of an old sin, and how brokenhearted I was then!
>
> Now I, "always having all sufficiency in all things, I may abound to every good work."[5]

Everyone at the conference received great blessings. Dr. Trumbull taught them to sing and to pray in the possessive mode. That is to say, not "I need Thee every hour," but "I have Thee every hour." Bertha said, "What a difference that does make!" One Presbyterian minister who attended the conference shared, "I will have to change my whole praying vocabulary."[6]

Conferences like this were turning points in Bertha's life, not to mention the other missionaries. And the message spread. Miss Bertha later influenced Watchman Nee as they fellowshiped and prayed together. Watchman Nee's writings have blessed countless people. He spent years in a Communist jail and was finally released as an old man, just a few months prior to his death. But his books go on, and Bertha had a real part in it all.

The Realization

Miss Bertha and these other missionaries learned that Christ in them was stronger than sinful human nature and that Christ Himself thus becomes our righteousness and victory. Not even the devil himself could stand up against the power of the indwelling Christ. Bertha discovered that her identification with Christ in His death and resurrection form the basis of righteousness and victory. She was in union with Christ; all He is and did, she shared. Therefore, she was crucified and resurrected with Christ. When Christ died, believers died with Him; and when He rose they rose with Him (Gal. 2:20). Each believer is to see himself or herself as dead to sin and alive to God. That is how Bertha learned to face daily temptations. As Paul said, "Likewise reckon ye also yourselves to be dead indeed unto sin, but alive unto God through Jesus Christ our Lord" (Rom. 6:11).

Bertha realized, as she expressed it, "When Jesus took my sins to the cross, He also took me."[7] A true Christian is *in Christ*. This is victory (Rom. 6:1–12). She learned, as she would say, "You cannot consecrate the old sinful self to God; you assign it to death."

After being enlightened with this spiritual reality Bertha said, "Life was never the same."[8] At last the long-sought victory was hers. She had learned how to deal adequately with what she called the "Big-I," her old self. One just claims death to it after being crucified with Christ. It is not striving to overcome the flesh. That struggle will lead to defeat. Faith in one's union with Christ in His death and resurrection is the key that became a central theme in Bertha's teaching through the years. Later she discovered a tract in a Presbyterian bookstore in Scotland on that theme. It is entitled *Not I . . . But Christ*. She gave away thousands of these tracts through the years. Many were blessed by her emphasis and moved into Christian victory over "self" as Bertha did. Throughout her life and ministry, she thanked God for those conferences.

As Miss Bertha and her fellow missionaries moved into this victorious truth, they had a deep desire for their Chinese Christian friends to experience what they had experienced. That, in turn, led them to gather together and pray at every opportunity. Consequently, a very definite burden to begin praying for the awakening of the churches developed. Their concern went beyond their own lives. They wanted to see renewal among their fellow believers. This was the first gleaming of the coming great awakening.

As their burden for prayer deepened, the awakened missionaries set aside the first day of every month to pray definitely and distinctly for revival. Their prayer meetings were simple. They would arrive at the church building at nine o'clock in the morning and pray until twelve o'clock. They would return at two o'clock in the afternoon and pray until five o'clock. No one preached. Each time they gathered, a different leader would choose a hymn, read a passage from the Scriptures, then direct the prayer. A deep consciousness that God would hear them pervaded the group as they were praying in the will of God. Claiming 2 Chronicles 7:14, they expected a true movement of the Lord in reviving strength.

Dr. Trumbull's motto through all those joyous days became theirs: "Let go and let God." Miss Bertha described these experiences of prayer as "joyous release."[9] The important truth of personal revival became very practical and saw her through all the spiritual warfare she engaged in. When it became necessary to seek victory over sin, Satan, and the world, she could victoriously face every temptation that assailed her. It was not "sinless perfection" she experienced—just genuine victory. In down-to-earth ways, Miss Bertha learned to claim the promise, "When He giveth quietness, who then can make trouble?" (Job 34:39).

Practical Faith

Shantung Province is a rather treeless plain in northeastern China that suffers from occasional dust storms. At midday the sky would turn yellow, and all the city shops were forced to close. People would rush home to seal the doors and windows. Yet even then the fine silt would creep in through cracks and keyholes. The houses would become coated with yellow dusty powder inside and out; the only place left white in the morning would be the spot on the pillow protected by the sleeper's head. Moreover, these dust storms often lasted for up to three days.

One evening at bedtime the wind raged and the inevitable infiltration of dust seemed destined to be Bertha's lot through the night. Sleep would be all but impossible. Then she read Psalm 127:2: "He giveth His beloved sleep". She prayed, "Thank you, Lord. I am your beloved because you see me in your beloved Son so I take sleep from you." In a moment she drifted off into sound sleep and slept soundly until morning, even though the wind howled through the night. From this experience she had learned to claim the peace of Christ no matter what sort of storms arose in her life. She had learned her lesson well.

Blanche Rose Walker, Bertha's missionary colleague, lived alone in a little Chinese house. One night Miss Walker had invited thirteen guests for a meal, even though hospitality and entertaining were not her greatest gifts. After the dinner was successfully over, she wrote to Miss Bertha saying, "The Lord is holding on to my nerves." Miss Bertha thought, "Surely, Lord, you are the one to hold on to a woman's nerves, for she can't hold them herself." So she turned over her own nerves to the Lord and He held them from that time on. She thanked God that He had not only taken her sins in His own body on the tree, but had taken her there with Him and she now could resonate with Paul, "I have been crucified with Christ." She prayed, "Lord, since you count me dead in your Son, I will count myself dead in Him, no matter how much alive I may be appearing!"[10] She simply took by faith her position in Christ, and the rivers of living water that Ruth Paxon spoke of flowed in and through her life.

Bertha's new spirituality, however, was never so "other worldly" that she forgot the more mundane things of daily life. In a letter to her sister Jennie, Bertha told of God's gracious material blessing provided for the missionaries by a friend:

What do you suppose we had last Saturday! All met at the Gaston's to have dinner together and eat deer sent by Mr. Leonard from Harbin. He and Dr. James and somebody else went hunting sometime ago and killed three. He wanted to send us this joint for Christmas but had no way to get it here, but a few days after Christmas he came in contact with a soldier in Harbin who was coming to Laichowfu so he sent it by him. It was frozen well so of course was still fresh. It was real good and I didn't say like Hattie, "This is not as good as I have eaten."[11]

Bertha was still "earthy Bertha." Nonetheless, the missionaries were now ready for God to work among them in new ways. The favorite hymn of the newly-revived group of believers was based on A. B. Simpson's poem, "Himself." They sang it daily as the first hints of the forthcoming Shantung Revival began to shine around them:

Once it was the blessing, now it is the Lord;
Once it was the feeling, now it is His Word;
Once His gift I wanted, now, the Giver own;
Once I sought for healing, now Himself alone.
All in all forever, Jesus will I sing;
Everything in Jesus, and Jesus everything.[12]

A New Task

After Miss Bertha had completed her formal language study and experienced the victorious deepening of her spiritual life, she took charge of a girls' boarding school. There she began to teach the Bible in Chinese in addition to English classes. Bertha felt she was doing one of the greatest works in the world now that she led the girls' school. The girls came to the school from country villages spanning more than five counties. Some were from Christian families but many came from non-Christian homes. Parents simply wanted their girls educated. Bertha exercised her gift of evangelism well, and a good number came to faith in Christ under her teaching. Often when a student who had come to know the Lord returned to her village, she would be the only Christian in the entire area. Her home would then become an ideal place for Bible study, and Bible women or missionaries would invite the neighbors in and share the gospel with them. Some of the school girls themselves became teachers, and a few entered full-time Christian service.

During the exciting years of teaching, Bertha continued to correspond with friends and family back home. The folks in South Carolina hung on her newsy letters. On June 1, 1923, she wrote a letter to "My dear Homefolk" saying:

It is certainly hard to realize that June is here, but with hot weather and strawberries and cherries, it must be that the sixth month is on us. And, too, I have all the June roses that one could wish. . . . When I come home (next year) I want to learn the names of all the roses I can so I will know the names of mine.

Miss Bertha's love for flowers opened many doors for witnessing. She set out fresh seedlings in the front yard of her residence, and when they grew and blossomed, she would cut the flowers and give them to non-Christians. She delighted in the beauty of the flowers, but even more over the conviction of sin and the many conversions that took place in her work.

Bertha continued her language studies on an informal basis. She studied Chinese grammar for three hours a day. During her second term she continued to study for two hours a day, and in her third stint in China, a teacher would come in to work with her twice a week for two hours. It is understandable that she became so adept in the Chinese language.

The first term of service for missionaries in China was seven years. Thereafter, nine years were required before they could enjoy another furlough. Many missionaries in China died on their first or second tour of service. As a consequence, all terms were later cut to seven years. So in 1924, after seven years of faithful service to the Chinese, Miss Bertha prepared to sail for home. Furlough time had come.

Preparing for Home

The missionaries gave Bertha a wonderful farewell party. They had a great time of fellowship, joking with her about how she loved to talk. Alice Huey, with whom Bertha had lived her entire first tour, suggested they cut out some donkey ears from paper, put them on, and let Bertha talk the rest of the night while they just listened. This drew a big laugh from all, even from Bertha. She had a great sense of humor.

Bertha longed to see family and friends, and a happy reunion it was back in little Cowpens when she arrived. The year was filled with activity. She spent one semester in study at the Biblical Seminary in New York. Her thirst for knowledge never ceased. A desire to be all God wanted her to be included all the education she could muster. Bertha was thrilled to hear G. Campbell Morgan, pastor of London's Westminster Chapel, who lectured that year at the seminary. Morgan said in one of his lectures that the Bible could be read in its entirety in sixty-five hours. This challenged Miss Bertha, so on a Monday morning she sat down to see if Morgan was correct. In fifty-three hours and twelve minutes she completed reading the entire Bible. After that, reading the entire Bible became a regular part of her life.

Bertha had exciting times in the States, one of which took place in Washington, D.C. The girls in Bertha's school in China had prepared a letter to President Coolidge of the United States that they sent by Bertha. It was a letter of gratitude to the president for a gift to China's educational fund. When the Boxers, a Chinese rebel group, were forced to pay an "indemnity fund" to the U.S. government for the destruction they had caused to U.S. property, President Coolidge gave the sum to the educational fund in China. So Bertha traveled to the capital and handed the letter to President Coolidge. The year of furlough passed all too quickly, and once again Bertha set sail to return to her work in China.

5

Sparks of Revival

Jane Lide *Credit: FMB*

Theologian J. I. Packer identifies four elements characteristic of revival:

1. Revival is God revitalizing His church.
2. Revival is God turning away His anger from His church.
3. Revival is God stirring the hearts of His people.
4. Revival is God displaying the sovereignty of His grace.[1]

In times of revival, the Church is revitalized, the community is touched and changed, needs are met, people experience renewal, longings are fulfilled, multitudes are saved, and great glory is ascribed to God.

The missionaries of Shantung Province prevailed in prayer for revival in China, a country in dire need of a spiritual awakening. To Miss Bertha and her missionary partners in Shantung Province, the need seemed particularly acute. So they devoted themselves to intercession for revival and they were not disappointed. Their prayers were heard. One glorious day God rent the heavens, and what is now called the Shantung Revival burst upon them. What a day it became in the life and ministry of Bertha Smith, all the missionaries, and China itself. In that inaugural year of revival, 1927, China experienced a genuine outpouring of the Holy Spirit that transformed multitudes.

First Signs of Revival

When Miss Bertha first arrived in North China, the missionaries were deeply grieved over the low level of spirituality and commitment among Chinese believers, as pointed out earlier. They began to fear that many church members had never truly been born again.

Miss Bertha had already experienced revival on a personal level through various missionary conferences and the enlightening of the Holy Spirit. She had learned well and her life exemplified victory in the Lord— the essence of revival on an individual level. Her heart, deeply moved by the plight of the Chinese believers, longed for a similar experience for all. Other missionaries shared this same longing.

Most great awakenings in history have begun with a mere handful of fervent intercessors staying before God until He opens the heavens. As revivalist Charles G. Finney put it, "The Spirit of prayer must be poured out upon God's people before an awakening will ever dawn on the land." Thus, God began first to stir the missionaries. They entered into fervent prayer for an awakening. The first day of each month for prayer continued for four years. As Miss Bertha put it, this monthly gathering became a "Little Bethel" for the dedicated believers.

Even after four years of fervent prayer, nothing of real significance seemed to happen. Deeper blessings did begin to fall upon their labors. Yet, the revival they longed for seemed to elude their grasp. That is not to say God was not at work. To the contrary, God was preparing China for one of the greatest movements of the Holy Spirit in Christian history. But the day had not yet dawned. That rested in God's sovereignty.

The Significant Move to Chefoo

In March 1927 the southern Chinese armies under Chiang Kai-shek burned Nanking. An American missionary died in the violence. The news was heralded around the world. Establishing a democratic government after centuries of authoritarianism was traumatic. Unrest broke out everywhere. The old warlords were not about to relinquish their power easily. China's history is one of turmoil and rebellion. The Chinese call it the principle of Ko-Ming. It had set itself in operation again.

The American Consulate in Chefoo sent an urgent telegram to all Shantung missionaries: "Proceed to the coast at once." The Consulate officials, seriously concerned about the safety of American citizens in Shantung, gave the orders. When the message arrived, the American missionaries heeded immediately. The Southern Baptist Foreign Mission Board had divided its work in China into four major geographical sections. Some fifty churches and forty-five missionaries were located in the northern peninsula section where Miss Bertha served. Those on the south side of the peninsula and in the western part of the province went to the seaport city of Tsingtau. Miss Bertha and others stationed in the northern sections of Shantung Province were sent to the port city of Chefoo. They did not expect the five-month stay from March to September, which the crisis precipitated.

Twenty-seven missionaries and all their belongings crammed themselves into the small Chefoo compound with only two residence homes. Included were couples with children and dogs, as well as single missionaries. "Humanly speaking it would have been a difficult time indeed, but we had the Lord!"[2] said Miss Bertha.

Outside the confines of the missionaries' homes, the "Red" influence brought ridicule and persecution against many Chinese Christians. In the city of Hunan, an old beggar in rags was labeled "God the Father"; a donkey was termed "Jesus"; an ox was called the "Holy Spirit." This caused much laughter among the pagans. Such incidents of ridicule toward Christians occurred all over China. And here were the missionaries, crammed together in Chefoo—cut off from their persecuted fold during a time of serious unrest. The situation fostered a deep burden in the missionaries for the Christians in Shantung to stand true if outright serious persecution from Communist influence should erupt. The huddled missionaries began to meet for an hour every morning after breakfast to pray for the steadfastness of their fellow believers whom they had left behind in the province.

The Spirit of God began to move in those prayer meetings. The missionaries were soon praying for more than one hour each morning; often the prayer meetings extended until midday. Not only that, and to their surprise, a dramatic shift came in the content of their prayers. They almost forgot the Chinese Christians they had left back home and began to pray earnestly for the Lord's blessings upon themselves. They recognized they had serious needs as well. The burden of their prayers revolved around the request that God would show them what He had in mind for them since permitting them to be torn away from the work they loved and crowding them into the little compound. They had to find the Lord's purpose for their own lives during that difficult time.

47

Days passed. The prayers and concerns of the missionaries deepened. In that setting Miss Jane Lide, a fellow missionary, was asked to share Bible messages with the group on "Christ, our Life." Miss Lide had been in a Bible study on the theme and was full of truths. These truths had become very real to her, as they had to Miss Bertha.

As Miss Lide gave her messages on the deeper life, the Holy Spirit began to move upon the missionaries. Slowly, they began to see themselves as "consecrated selves," to put it in Miss Bertha's words. They each received a clearer vision of themselves and the Christ who simply wanted to live His life in and through them. Bertha summed up the spiritual principles taught by Miss Lide:

- While we were weak, He wanted to be strength in us.
- While we were stupid, He wanted to be wisdom in us.
- While we were sinful, He wanted to be holiness in us.
- While we were easily aroused and intolerant, He wanted to be patience in us.[3]

The missionaries came to understand that they had to appropriate death to themselves and let the Lord Jesus Christ be their life, their power, their wisdom, their humility, and their all. They realized that they were prone to be rather proud of their talents, education, and years of experience. But they began to see, in a new and fresh way, that they must appropriate death to those manifestations of the self-life and let Jesus Christ live His life of meekness and humility through them. They must "go all the way with the Lord." Surely the Lord Jesus Christ would grant them the willingness to surrender all to His lordship.

The missionaries were profoundly convicted of personal sins as they dug deeply into the Word. The days became a time of probing by the Holy Spirit as the missionaries saw themselves as they truly were. They strove to get all their conscious sins "under the blood." Their lives were radically revived through honesty and broken confession. This move of God upon the missionaries created an even greater desire for revival among the Chinese people. On and on they prayed and prayed and prayed.

The Work of God Progresses

Miss Marie Monsen, a Norwegian Evangelical Lutheran missionary, also fled to Chefoo. The Baptists invited her to share her testimony with them. She told them about the unusual experiences in Bible teaching and evangelism she had experienced on her field and the many sick people she had seen physically healed by God's grace. This was all but revolutionary to the Southern Baptist missionaries. Many rejected those sorts of things as mere emotionalism, but Miss Monsen was a far cry from a mere emotion raiser. She only mentioned healing when missionaries asked her to share her experiences. Moreover, her words had the ring of authenticity.

Marie had seen some revival here and there during her years in the mission field. One day she told Charles L. Culpepper, president of the small Baptist Seminary in Shantung, that she believed a great revival was on the way, and it would come through the Baptists. "Why through the Baptists?" Dr. Culpepper asked. Marie responded, "Because you, more than any others, have fulfilled the promise of 2 Chronicles 7:14."

A New Understanding and Experience of God's Healing

Prayer for miraculous physical healing seemed quite unorthodox to Southern Baptists in those days. They only knew to pray for God to help the doctors. Some even believed that miracles had ceased in the first century. They reasoned that once the New Testament was available, miracles became obsolete. As they searched the Scriptures on the issue, James 5:14–16 came alive to them:

> Is any sick among you? let him call for the elders of the church; and let them pray over him, anointing him with oil in the name of the Lord. And the prayer of faith shall save the sick, and the Lord shall raise him up; and if he have committed sins, they shall be forgiven him. Confess your faults one to another, and pray one for another, that ye may be healed. The effectual fervent prayer of a righteous man availeth much.

They were moved by this promise. God had said it—they must accept it. At the same time, they became convicted that they must confess their faults so that healing could come.

Dr. Charles Culpepper was particularly pierced in his heart by his own personal need for the confession of his sins. His wife Ola said that God gave her a movie of her life since her conversion at the age of 15—and it was not complimentary. Ola even had to confess saying something clever and "cute" about Miss Bertha that hurt her. All the missionaries had some grasp of the truth of confession and revival because of the deepening they had experienced, but God had something special in store for the Culpeppers.

Dr. Culpepper was born on March 1, 1885. He graduated from Baylor University in 1919 and married Ola Lane the same year. The newlyweds attended Southwestern Baptist Theological Seminary where, in 1922,

Charles received the Master of Theology degree. He later received a Doctor of Theology from Southwestern.

In 1923 Charles and Ola were appointed as missionaries to China by the Southern Baptist Foreign Mission Board. During their years in China, they witnessed the defeat of the warlords by the Nationalist Army under Chiang Kai-shek, the invasion of China by the Japanese Imperial Army, and the overthrow of the government by the Communists in 1949 led by Mao Sei Tung. Through it all, they remained on the field and true to their calling.

Miss Monsen's testimony made a tremendous impact on all Baptist missionaries, especially the Culpeppers. Marie was a woman mightily anointed with the Spirit of God. As she began to talk about miraculous physical healings, the Culpeppers were touched. Ola, a beautiful, outgoing woman, had been suffering for years with optic neuritis—the decay of the optic nerve. Before traveling to China, a physician in San Antonio, Texas, had treated her. He had succeeded in reducing the pain and, to some extent, stabilizing the deterioration of her eyes. The vision in one eye was impaired permanently, but she could see reasonably well with the aid of glasses.

A few months before the Nanking crisis, however, Ola's eyes began to weaken again. Serious pain returned. An Austrian physician resided in a medical group at the Chinese Union Medical College, a Rockefeller Foundation hospital in Peking. Ola journeyed there for examination and treatment. The doctor told Ola she would lose her sight in one eye within three months, and in both eyes within six months. Blindness seemed inevitable. Ola's pain only added to their despair.

Yet after Miss Monsen's testimony, which significantly touched and challenged Ola Culpepper, the first real breaking of revival began. Dr. Culpepper tells the fascinating story in these words:

> As Miss Monsen gave her testimony, Ola began to be impressed with the fact that she should go and talk to her about the eye damage. We made an appointment and went to her apartment. As she met us at the door, Miss Monsen's first question was, "Brother Culpepper, have you been filled with the Holy Spirit?" I stammered out something less than a definite reply. Then, recognizing my uncertainty, she carefully related a personal experience fifteen years earlier when she had prayed for and received the promise of the Holy Spirit as recorded in Galatians 3:14. After visiting with her for two hours, we urged her to come to our home to pray for Ola's eyes.
>
> That night we were deeply troubled. Prayer for healing seemed unorthodox for Baptist people. But in private we read James 5:14–16 and were greatly encouraged. The words "confess your faults" particularly

pierced my heart. A consuming realization that our hearts must be completely open to God pervaded all our senses. I began to feel the Lord was going to undertake a great thing for us.

The next morning about 20 people came to our home for prayer. We felt an electric excitement, a feeling that God was preparing us for something we had never known before. After praying for several hours, we all seemed in a complete spirit of communion. Suddenly Ola took off her glasses and laid them on the mantle. Following the instructions in the Book of James, I anointed her with oil. Then we all knelt and continued praying. It was as though God had walked into the room. Everyone prayed aloud. We felt that Heaven came down and Glory filled our souls.

As we prayed, the male Chinese cooks from both missionary residences in Chefoo walked into the room. Their hatred for each other was common knowledge. But, as the power of God's Holy Spirit worked, they went to each other, confessed their hatred, sought forgiveness, and accepted Christ as personal Savior.

In the midst of our joy for the cooks' salvation we had completely forgotten Ola's eyes. Then someone remembered and asked her, "What about your eyes?" She replied, "They feel all right and the pain is gone."

It never returned. This was the most wonderful experience in our lives. We had never known such spiritual joy. The events surrounding those days in Chefoo were the prelude to the great Shantung Revival.[4]

Before Healing Comes Confession

As Dr. Culpepper read from the fifth chapter of James, God spoke to the hearts of all who were present. He did not explain the verses; he simply let the Word speak for itself. Then he put olive oil on Ola's head and invited everyone to lay hands on her head and pray for healing. At that moment God did a reviving work of grace in Bertha's life. She related:

I had gone into that room, so far as I knew, absolutely right with the Lord. I would not have dared to go otherwise. But when I stretched my hand out to Mrs. Culpepper's head, I had to bring it back. There stood facing me a missionary (Anna Hartwell) with whom there had been a little trouble. In her early years she had been head of a girls' school, but for several years she had been teaching illiterate women to read.

I had been asked to serve as principal in our boys' school in Chefoo while the missionary principal was on furlough. I had majored in education, and by that time had had ten years' experience in teaching and thought that I was "the last word" in education! I had recommended Miss

Hartwell to lead daily worship in that school. After a few weeks, I asked another missionary to tell her that methods for teaching old women were not appropriate for high school boys. She was hurt, of course.

But what about my proud self? I did not have a particle of sympathy for her. Right there before everyone, I had to say, "Miss Hartwell, I did not have the proper attitude toward you about that school affair. I beg you to forgive me!" My hand then joined the others and we prayed.

Had I refused to confess that sin, and joined in the prayer with it covered, I believe that I would have hindered the prayer of the others, and the eye could not have been healed.

Because all were right with God and of one heart, heaven came down! We did not have to wait to see whether or not Mrs. Culpepper's eye was healed! We knew in our hearts that she would never have another attack. The Lord had heard the prayers of such human frailty and had performed a miracle in healing one whom we so loved! She did not put her glasses back on. While the sight was not restored completely in the weak eye, both were strengthened and not once has she had any more pain, though using her eyes steadily for reading and needlework.

Walking around the room rejoicing and praising the Lord, we were all on a mountaintop of ecstasy. Then I had to be the joy-killer. There came over me such a sense of our inconsistency, that I had to speak of it.

"What kind of missionaries are we?" I asked. "We have gone through a week of heart-searching, humbling ourselves before each other and before the Lord, in order that we might be altogether right with him, so that he could hear our prayers and heal the physical eye of one of our own number. Yet we have never gone to this much self-negation for preparation to pray for the opening of the spiritual eyes of the Chinese to whom we have been sent." Our mountaintop of ecstasy suddenly became a valley of humiliation. We all went to our knees in contrite confession for having been so careless as to have gone along supposing that we were right with the Lord, while holding all kinds of attitudes which could have kept the Lord's living water from flowing through us to the Chinese.[5]

The physical healing of "one of their own" came with brokenness and openness, confession (Anna also confessed a wrong attitude to Bertha), forgiveness, and then a mighty outpouring of the Holy Spirit. If the real beginning of the Shantung Revival can be pinned down to one event, this was it. All the elements of a true awakening came together in Ola Culpepper's healing. The "glory days" were beginning. The revival was underway.

6

The Shantung Revival

Dr. and Mrs. John A. Abernathy in Korea, before they returned
to the United States in January 1960. *Credit: FMB*

A few weeks after the healing of Mrs. Culpepper, the cleansing of sin, and the deepened dedication of the missionaries, Miss Bertha and others were able to return to their various fields of labor. They returned, the men first and then the women, to teaching and preaching the dynamic and fresh new biblical message they had learned concerning the tragedy of sin in the heart and life of a Christian. Their evangelistic fervor did not slacken, but they realized that God must first revive His own people. Only then would the mass of unbelievers be warmed and drawn to Jesus Christ. And God met that need.

The Spreading Awakening

Revival began to permeate the work of the missionaries, although it would be three or four years before the full impact of the awakening would be generally experienced. It spread first among Chinese preachers and Bible-teaching women in the mission schools who were open to seeing themselves in the light of the holiness of God. One evening Miss

Bertha, while entering the school yard, met one of the Chinese teachers who asked to speak to her. They went to Miss Bertha's study, and as she started to light the lamp, the Chinese lady said, "Please do not make a light. I cannot look into your face and make this confession!" They sat in the dark as the Chinese Bible teacher suggested she bring her high school diploma to Miss Bertha because she had cheated on one of her examinations.

Miss Bertha, always sensitive to the probing of the Holy Spirit, realized that the convicting Spirit of God was seriously dealing with the woman. Bertha told the teacher to bring the diploma to her. She had signed it in good faith, thinking the Chinese lady had honestly done all necessary work to earn it. The convicted teacher surrendered the diploma. This meant little in comparison to the peace of God she received by doing so. Miss Bertha kept the diploma with her precious things until the Japanese occupied the house some years later and destroyed all her valuable keepsakes.

Later, the teacher, who had her heart thoroughly cleansed by the precious blood of Christ, received a call to another sphere. She went to North China Seminary for three years and became an effective, Spirit-filled Bible teacher with a full heart of praise for God's grace in forgiveness. As the life of this Chinese woman exemplifies, cleansing always precedes fullness, and the infilling of the Holy Spirit precedes joy and effective service.

A pastor in one of the city churches where Miss Bertha served shared that he saw himself as a fireplace with the wood all laid out and no one to strike the match. His testimony did not stop there. When he knew he had all his "sins confessed up to date" (one of Miss Bertha's well-known and favorite expressions), the Lord revealed Himself in a beautiful way. Then, "the fire blazed."

The early flames of revival did not flare up in Chefoo alone. Missionary refugees in Tsingtau were confronted by a preacher who spoke on the fullness of the Holy Spirit. Pearl Caldwell, a Southern Baptist missionary, was led by the Spirit of God into earnest heart-searching, deep humiliation, and seeking all God had for her in the fullness of His Spirit. Her needs were met. She was filled and from her heart flowed those joyous "rivers of living water." Bertha herself said if anything characterized the revival, it was the fruit of the Spirit Nehemiah called the "joy of the Lord" (Neh. 8:10). The preachers on the Tsingtau field began to hunger for the same power they saw in Pearl. They were not to be disappointed.

After the Chefoo episode and the return of the missionaries to their posts, missionaries in the city of Hwanghsien invited Marie Monsen to their city for a two-week meeting. They desired to receive a blessing similar to the one experienced in Bertha's station, Laichowfu. Martha Franks, a Baptist missionary and close friend of Bertha, said that Marie Monsen became the spark of the Shantung Awakening.

The Marie Monsen Story

Marie was a student at a Norwegian teacher-training college when God placed His hand upon her for mission work. But would she yield? At that time, a gospel preacher and friend of Marie's family by the name of Tormod Rettedal influenced her life tremendously. He reminded her of the story of Jonah, God's call to the prophet to go to Nineveh, and the prophet's refusal to surrender and its consequences. Rettedal said to her, "At first [Jonah] was allowed to go his own way, but God did not go with him on his self-chosen path. Don't be a Jonah!"[1]

Marie confessed that for three days the preacher's word haunted her. Finally, she yielded to God's will and responded, "Yes, Lord, I will go." Then God laid China on her heart. She never repented of that commitment. God had an incredible ministry for the young woman.

Scarcely a month after arriving in China, Marie fell down an iron staircase and lay unconscious for several days with a severe concussion. A missionary doctor gave the orders: "No language study for two years." All she could do was listen to Chinese people speak and hope to pick up some of the dialect. She remained in China and suffered with severe headaches for six years. Then the promise of James 5:14 came to her. She called the elders of the church to anoint her with oil and pray for her. She was instantly healed. Due to the ignorance in such matters of healing, she thought that physical healing could only occur once in her life. She soon learned differently.

Marie regularly suffered from attacks of malaria and dysentery. It wore her down until she almost fell into despair. Once again God delivered her from those sicknesses in answer to prayer. She was learning, and it soon became evident that the Lord was preparing her for great things in missionary service.

Marie grew in prayer and began to see great things happen. In turn, she taught the people to pray and claim God's promises. One Chinese woman set a wonderful example and prayed for the most incredible things. Even Marie thought her requests would never be answered, but the woman had a childlike faith and her prayers were answered.

Accounts of George Mueller's orphanage and Hudson Taylor's founding of the China Inland Mission by faith influenced Marie. She turned to the Book of Acts daily and claimed the promise of God's provision, care, leadership, and power to evangelize. God met her at every turn.

The first great revival in Korea broke out in 1907. This awakening grew into one of many mighty movings of the Holy Spirit that came into being through the fervent prayers of missionaries and Korean Christians. Marie, deeply inspired by the movement, prayed for money to travel to Korea to imbibe something of the spirit of revival. God responded to her prayers by saying, "What you want through that journey you may be given here, where you are, in answer to prayer."[2] In light of that tremendous challenge, Marie made the solemn promise that she would pray until a revival came to her life and ministry.

Marie's concern and vision for a great awakening continued to expand. She studied reports of revival on other mission fields. And she learned that long periods of waiting with much fervent prayer often come before a real awakening breaks. But revivals do come, regardless of circumstances. As Marie said, "In answer to prayers borne in deep anguish."[3]

Marie knew what she had to do. She continued to read, learn, and experience the Word of God, and to do the mission work she was called to do. Through it all, God continued to give her tokens of grace, glimpses of what would come when the awakening finally arrived. God truly was preparing her to be one of His key instruments in a great revival.

Off to Hwanghsien

During this time, Marie received an invitation to a conference for the Chinese Baptist churches in the Hwanghsien area. She immediately began to pack. In order to get to Hwanghsien, she had to travel from Peking to Tientsin, then by boat to Hwanghsien, about a day's journey overall. As Marie began packing and making arrangements to embark by boat from Tientsin, the Holy Spirit impressed her to buy some apples. Since the voyage was only a night's journey, this instruction left her confused. The Holy Spirit kept laying this impression upon her heart so inescapably that she finally bought an entire basket of apples. She reasoned, "Perhaps some sick person on the other side of the Gulf of Chihli needs them." She also took four boxes of chocolates she had received for Christmas from friends in Norway.

The Baptist meeting in Hwanghsien, Shantung Province, was scheduled to begin on April 22, 1929. But the boat Marie needed to take to meet the schedule was full. Humanly speaking, it would be impossible for her to make the journey as planned. But she said to herself, "If I am to travel by that boat, my Heavenly Father will see to my being given a berth, and if not, He must have some reason for my spending a few days in Tientsin."[4] God did provide. She received a message stating that the second mate would willingly give up his cabin to her for a certain amount of money in addition to the price of her ticket. She saw this as God's providence and paid the price. With apples, chocolates, and a few biscuits in hand, she prepared to embark.

At eleven o'clock on the morning of April 19, accompanied by an English missionary, Miss Monsen boarded the boat ready to sail at noon. When the English missionary saw the second mate's cabin, she said to Marie, "It is a good thing you will have to spend only one night in there." Little did she know it would be twenty-seven.

Marie had not taken along her normal bedding roll, thinking she would only have one night to spend on board. She could surely manage one night on the hard wooden boards of the second mate's bunk. She said, "It is undeniable that it felt hard that first night, but I had plenty of sound sleep on it later, and in the end it even felt fairly comfortable."[5]

As the ship maneuvered out of the harbor, Marie pulled out a duster from her case and cleaned the room. She dusted the wooden bunk and the little table that made up the furniture of the small cabin. A small cabin it was; an American friend who saw it afterwards said, "It looked like an old piano case."

Marie went out on deck, talking with passengers and handing out tracts. She could not help noticing some passengers who looked as though they might be thieves. Yet, she thought, surely in the midst of civilized Tientsin that could not be the case.

As they prepared to set sail, they were delayed in the harbor for a short time because of stormy weather, but soon made their way out to open waters, making good speed. They fully expected to see the Shantung coast the next day. However, as soon as they had put to sea, two bandits with loaded guns burst in on the helmsman giving orders. Instead of traveling southeast in the direction of their destination, they were going southwest.

Twenty pirates had secretly boarded the boat in Tietsien. Pistol shots, shrieks, and pandemonium broke out all over the ship. Marie knew at once they had fallen into the hands of pirates. At that moment the Spirit of God spoke to her heart: "This is the trial of your faith," and she became conscious of the "peace that passeth understanding" (Phil. 4:7). Her prayer was, "Oh, that He may succeed in keeping me close to Himself."

About the time the first shots rang out, more pirates came on board—sixty all together. They forced the cabin doors open and ordered passengers out on deck. They instructed the passengers to leave their possessions in their cabins. The pirates wrenched open Marie's door and commanded her to leave the cabin. She refused and just stood there. She knew she had been given that cabin in answer to prayer and trusted God to leave her in it.

Since Marie had not taken her bedroll with her, she was fully dressed. The pirates recognized her as a foreigner and a Christian at that. Every time they ordered her out of the cabin, the promises of God came to her "gently and refreshingly, like spring showers," as she expressed it. She thanked God for His promises, rested upon Him, and stayed put.

In the evening of the first full day at sea, a junk loaded with guns and ammunition came alongside the ship. These were taken on board along with the plunder the pirates had gained from pirating other boats. The pirates offered Marie all kinds of food: lobster, crayfish, tin goods of every kind, fish, and chicken. But they were stolen goods, so she adamantly refused them. She began to realize why God had her bring the apples, chocolates, and biscuits aboard. These provisions lasted nine days. Not once in all the time she holed up in the little cabin did the pirates ask for any of her apples or chocolates; they only asked if she had pears or oranges. God's providence works.

On the tenth day at sea there came a gentle scratching on her door. She jumped from her bunk remembering the Elijah story and her heart sang, "This is the raven!" The second mate stood there and asked Marie if she had any food. When she replied that she had none, he said, "Let me come in. I have a full box of eggs and a tin of cakes. You can have it all." He had bought them in Tientsin with honestly earned money. God continued His wonderful provision. The second mate had hidden the boxes of food under buckets of paint and old shoes. From that day on, when the guard patrolled the other side of the ship, the second mate would take two or three eggs from the boxes, put them in his pocket, and go away. Later he would return to Marie's cabin with boiled eggs. Her daily ration was one egg for breakfast, one or two for dinner, one for supper. She had a sweet cake at forenoon and in the afternoon.

The supply of food God provided lasted for the exact amount of time she was on board the ill-fated ship. She asked the Lord to transform the simple menu into all the nutrients her body required and testified that when she had eaten the small ration, she felt so satisfied that she could not have eaten more had it been available. God kept His promise to "supply all your need according to His riches in glory by Christ Jesus" (Phil. 4:19).

Miss Monsen had not packed any warm clothing for the trip because she thought she would soon be in a warmer area, but the weather was quite bitter. As she left Peking on the morning of April 18, a parcel came to her from Norway—a belated Christmas gift that should have reached her before Christmas. She stored it in her baggage with a bit of complaint because she did not want to carry it everywhere. Providentially, this parcel contained a heavy sweater and a pair of woolen stockings that, of course, proved tremendously helpful on the cold and stormy days on the Gulf of Chihli.

Every night one of the pirates stood outside Marie's door to prevent her from escaping. In a sense, this nightly watch protected her and she slept well and peacefully in the midst of all the difficulties.

After many miserable days on the Gulf, they sailed into an inlet on the Yellow River and dropped anchor. At three o'clock on Sunday afternoon, they heard the sound of guns. A great deal of confusion erupted on the ship and soon most of the pirates left. All the passengers understood this activity to indicate that the authorities had found them. They were right; a race up the river began with a gunboat pursuing them. Before long, the pirates left on board saw the gunboat gaining. Then a cannon shot screamed across the bow. In a panic, the pirates decided to take the foreigner with them as a hostage in order to help them escape. But one of the pirates said, "Under these circumstances, there's no use taking the foreigner. She has eaten nothing for twenty-three days; she can't walk much less run, as we must now." They fled the ship leaving Marie on board.

Marie immediately went out on deck. The captain turned the ship and went downstream toward the gunboat. The pirates, some of whom had made shore, were running across the sandbank for their lives. Others in the junks were likewise sailing away at full speed. The pirates did take twenty hostages with them, most of whom were women, but returned them before dark. All were rescued.

After twenty-seven long days the ordeal ceased and Marie finally made her way to the missionary conference. Needless to say, the Baptist missionaries were delighted and relieved to see her. In the conference, God blessed in a marvelous fashion. Hwanghsien experienced a taste of the spreading revival.

Miss Monsen employed a unique method that was powerfully used by the Holy Spirit to deepen the revival. She would stand at the door greeting everyone leaving the church after each service, take the hand of each one, look straight into the person's eyes and ask, "Have you been born of the Spirit?" If the person answered "yes," she would immediately ask, "What evidence do you have of the new birth?" If the person had less than a ringing testimony, she would say, "I'm uneasy about you. Ask the Lord to show you your position before Him." This approach impacted the lives of many and became the means of the conversion of multitudes. Miss Bertha made it clear that the missionaries never gave comfort to anyone with the slightest uneasiness about their relationship to Christ. They would urge each person to make a full confession of his or her sins and effect restitution when necessary and possible. Then they encouraged the believer to keep constantly before God so the Holy Spirit could continue to reveal needs. Marie's question, "Have you been born again?" became a key to the revival.

The theme and motif were set. And how powerfully God did use it!

Revival Methods

During the early days of revival, people were not invited to go forward to confess Christ by public invitation. Chinese culture would force them to go forward simply to keep the speaker from losing face. Thus, superficial decisions could easily be precipitated. However, as the revival spread, people were invited to come to the front of the church for prayer. By and large, inquirers were dealt with individually until they were absolutely clear about their conversion experience. They would then be assigned to a study group that explored the meaning of the Christian life, church membership, and all that is involved in walking as a true disciple of the Lord Jesus Christ. Every person was required to share his or her testimony before the church, before he or she could be received into full membership by Christian baptism. The missionaries exercised great care to assure that their evangelism was an evangelism for discipleship, the heart of the New Testament principle for bringing people into a true born-again experience. Miss Bertha would stress, for example, that salvation is not so much our receiving Christ as it is His receiving us as we truly repent and believe.

The spirit of revival continually deepened until many people could neither eat, nor sleep, nor hold their heads up because of the burden of sin. Peace, restoration, and joy only came when they learned to put all of their sins upon Christ, then make peace with everyone to whom confession and restitution were necessary. When they trusted and enthroned Christ, abounding joy flooded their hearts and they knew what it was to be "born again."

The Work Goes Forward

Miss Bertha held a special series of services in Laichowfu during those days. The Spirit of God probed many lives; one happened to be the Larsons' Chinese cook who had formerly been a warm-hearted church member and even conducted Bible classes for the other servants. During the meeting in Laichowfu, he became disturbingly convicted of his own personal sin and spiritual callousness. He found no rest or peace for days.

One morning at six o'clock the cook came to Miss Bertha. The burden of his sins had become so great that he had not been to bed the entire night. He first sought Miss Bertha's forgiveness for having said untrue and unkind things about her. Miss Bertha instructed him to go to others and tell them that the things he had said about her were not true. With tears streaming down his cheeks, he confessed what a hypocrite he had been and how blind he had become to his own sin and infidelity to Christ.

He went to the Larsons and confessed he had made money buying food for them on the market by pocketing the difference between the market price quoted to the Larsons and the price he had actually paid. He did not know how much he had stolen over a lengthy time, but he offered to work for two months without wages, believing that would probably put the matter square. They let him work without wages; they knew the Holy Spirit was doing a work in his life and he would have no peace otherwise.

When Miss Bertha saw the cook for the first time after his reviving experience, she said, "His face looked like that of an angel." In the churches in China a dividing screen separated the men from the women when the church gathered for worship. Miss Bertha confessed that she was often guilty of peeping over the screen to see how many men were in church. This is how she saw the angelic face of the cook. At a prayer meeting in Laichowfu, Miss Monsen asked someone thoroughly right with God to lead in prayer. The cook arose and began his prayer by saying, "Lord, I thank you that I am no longer I."

After the Laichowfu meeting Miss Bertha and Miss Monsen traveled together to Laiyang, the hometown of the revived cook. Traveling with the ladies were several other missionaries and the cook. There was no room in the car for the cook, so he rode his bicycle and arrived the next day. Miss Monsen once again asked for any brother who was right with God to lead in prayer. Again the cook rose and prayed. Such a volume of praise to the Lord poured forth from him that his old friends gathered around him wanting to know how such a change had come over him. The cook's transformed life became typical of what God did in multiplied ways as the revival spread.

A Preacher Saved

Mr. Chow, a preaching evangelist in the area, became uneasy about his own fellowship with the Lord. After every service he would seek out Miss Bertha. He wanted evidence that he had truly been saved. At last Miss Bertha asked, "Mr. Chow, what are you trusting in for salvation?" He straightened himself up and immediately replied, "You need not tell me that after I have walked for twenty-five years over this country telling people about the Savior, the Lord is going to turn me away from heaven's gate!" Miss Bertha immediately replied, "If that is what you are trusting in, you most certainly will be turned away!"[6] Bertha never hesitated to frankly tell the bare truth. God's Spirit arrested the evangelist, and he soon came to Christ alone for salvation.

A Great Outpouring

A year later, in November, missionary Larson returned to Laiyang to lead the annual Workers' Conference, a week of planning, inspiration, and Bible teaching for preachers and Bible women from the surrounding villages. Mr. Larson shared with his coworkers the wonderful theme of the Spirit-filled life. God created a real hunger within them. On Wednesday night at the closing session, he invited those who wanted God's best to remain in the church and join him for prayer that they might experience "all the fullness of God" (Eph. 3:19). Most went to their rooms, but a few of the hungry-hearted remained.

One of those who stayed behind to pray with missionary Larson was Brother Lai, pastor of the church. He had been unable to sing for several days, suffering from severe laryngitis. About midnight, the Spirit of God fell upon them, and Brother Lai rose from his knees to his feet and began singing in a clear, beautiful voice. Mr. Larson himself jumped up and exclaimed, "The Spirit has come." Suddenly both men were knocked to the floor as though struck by an electric bolt. Miss Bertha said of this incident:

> In a few minutes they were loudly praising the Lord while others were crying to him for mercy. The sleeping ones were aroused and rushed to the church, falling upon their knees in confession of their sins, coldness, and lack of power of the Holy Spirit in their lives. Loud hallelujahs and cries for mercy rang out through the rest of the night.
>
> Some were convinced of not having been saved, but by daylight they had entered into the joy of the Lord. Among these was Mr. Chow, the evangelist, for whom many had been praying. He refused to take a salary for further preaching, saying that he had already accepted too much for preaching without having known the Lord or the power of the Spirit. Now and then after that he had to sell a few acres of land to get money to support his family.
>
> Mr. Larson went back to his home in Laichowfu just in time for the workers' conference of that section. His burning testimony so moved the people that they continued in meetings through Christmas. Chinese leaders as well as missionaries so died to themselves that the Holy Spirit gloriously filled them. . . .
>
> Dr. Glass, Dr. Culpepper, Dr. Lide, and Dr. Abernathy were set on fire by the Holy Spirit. They, with Mr. Larson, were invited to church after

church in Shantung, where the Lord worked mightily. They then moved into Honan Province, where a great reviving began in the churches.[7]

The Revival Permeates the Area

Soon every church in Shantung Province began to feel the effects of revival. These effects were also felt at the seminary where Dr. Culpepper served as president. Before the revival, enrollment at the seminary had dropped to four students. The year after the revival began to permeate the area, the junior college building had to be taken over by the seminary because of increased enrollment. There were now 150 students—all the building could accommodate. Actually, a waiting list for an opening in the seminary was developed in every church. Hundreds felt called of God to the work of evangelism and preaching.

As can be imagined, the leaders found it disturbing to hear of those whom they thought were true converts that had never been genuinely saved. Yet, how they rejoiced over the abundant grace of God; they delighted over the many church members who came to true faith in the Lord Jesus Christ. Happiness, joy, and peace overflowed everywhere. One day little Nina Lide ran upstairs to her mother and cried out, "Daddy is down in his study just a 'Halleluin!'" Miss Bertha said, "We had come to the same place that Isaac Watts had come to when he penned his great hymn 'O for a thousand tongues to sing my great Redeemer's praise.'"

Many opium addicts found salvation and deliverance from the bondage of their narcotic habit. Quarreling, pugnacious women were transformed into loving motherly saints. Sick people were healed and demons cast out. These phenomenons, which may seem strange to many, are quite common in times of great revival—and they are genuine.

One of the most important results of the revival was in the transformation of the Chinese preachers. When they understood the principle of confession of sin, surrender, and the fullness of the Holy Spirit, the Word of God came alive to them as never before. They began preaching with power and wisdom beyond their knowledge. The seminary professors marveled.

Miss Bertha said that everyone became an evangelist of some sort. All desired to share the gospel. Many uneducated farmers became preachers. During the cold winter months when it was impossible for them to work the ground, they would travel by twos to preach Christ throughout the area. So many people professed salvation in Jesus that Dr. Glass (who followed Dr. Culpepper as president of the seminary) and pastor Kwan, (president of the North China Baptist Convention) felt constrained to tour a number of villages to help the numerous converts. Glass and Kwan were often kept up all night just reading the Word of God to the many new believers. Such was the spirit among those born again.

Dr. Glass immediately recognized the need for forming new churches for these new believers. He and his coworkers went to work in earnest. Revival time invariably becomes church planting time. For the work to progress and endure, it must be church-based. To this they gave themselves. Miss Bertha and her fellow missionaries were "church people." Thus, when new churches were established, the missionaries saw to it that full-time preachers were provided.

One born-again Chinese woman was illiterate, but lived in such close fellowship with the Lord that she knew when He wanted to speak to her. She would go to her bedroom and sit quietly and ask, "What is it, Lord?" The Holy Spirit, so very real to her, would give her a chorus of praise along with the melody. She had composed about three hundred choruses when a preacher visited her village and recorded them. She sang the songs and he wrote down the words and music. They were printed and sung all over North China.

Bertha and Lucy

Lucy Wright, a faithful, hard-working missionary nurse for many years, wrote a most surprising letter to Miss Bertha. Filled with the joy of the Lord, she just had to tell Bertha the good news. Nine years earlier, with only a head knowledge of Jesus, Lucy had come to China as a missionary. Miss Bertha had wondered why she had not experienced the same delightful fellowship with Lucy that she enjoyed with other missionaries. There seemed to be a barrier between them. Now Bertha understood; Lucy's letter was a testimony of her recent and glorious conversion. She had now been truly saved, and on the mission field at that. Needless to say, Miss Bertha rejoiced with Lucy in the Lord.

Lucy and Bertha's mission stations were sixty miles apart, which meant they only saw each other once a year at the mission meeting. When they met for the first time after Lucy's conversion, they hugged and kissed. The "wall" between them had dissolved in Christ's salvation and a spiritual kinship had been woven together by the Holy Spirit. Even missionaries were being born again.

At five o'clock one afternoon during the first mission meeting after Lucy's conversion, Miss Bertha asked Lucy to go for a walk and asked her why she thought she had not been saved until so late in life. The following experience unfolded:

The autumn before, when Miss Monsen was in Lucy's station leading meetings, Miss Monsen had requested all of the missionaries to ask each person whom they met whether or not he or she had been born again. . . .

In utter amazement she [Lucy] asked herself, "What does this mean? Can it be that I myself have not been born of the Spirit?" So uneasy did she become that for two days she sought assurance in her former works of church going, Bible study, tithing, singing, Sunday observance, and so on. But all to no avail. Then the third night she got on her knees alone before the Lord and prayed, "Lord, show me my condition before thee!" The faithful Lord, knowing the sincerity of her soul, brought before her the sins of a lifetime and revealed something of the exceeding sinfulness of her own heart.

For the first time, Lucy saw the meaning of Calvary. When she had taken refuge in the death of Christ, she became conscious of a cleansing and was filled with the joy of the Lord. For the first time, she came into a personal relationship with God.[8]

Miss Bertha came to understand why Lucy could not have been a child of God before her beautiful conversion during the Shantung Revival; she had merely joined the church at twelve years of age to please her teacher and some of her friends who had become Christians. Salvation comes only through Christ, not church membership.

Later, in 1944, Lucy moved to Wuchow, South China, to work in the Stout Memorial Hospital, a Baptist hospital that had opened in 1904. She almost died in Wuchow from a ruptured ulcer. But when she recovered, she began working with Dr. Bill Wallace, a Southern Baptist medical missionary who was a fine physician. Wallace had gone to China in September of 1935 and remained there throughout World War II. He carried on until the Communists gained control of the land and killed him because of his belief in Christ. Bill Wallace of China received the victorious crown of martyrdom. As exemplified in this man's life, the stalwart missionaries in those days went to their God-appointed fields to die if necessary.

Revival Fires Burn

The awakening began to engulf larger areas as the days, weeks, and months passed. Earnest prayer, along with personal witnessing, daily confession of sins, and Chinese Christians experiencing a new sense of commitment and surrender to the Lord Jesus Christ spread the flame. The Holy Spirit fanned the fires of zeal until they became a conflagration that began to spread across Shantung and finally into all of China. A great awakening had truly come.

Spiritual awakening is always characterized by brokenness over sin. This principle implies confession and at times restitution. Bertha said it would have been far more "face saving" if the Spirit had convicted her of her wrong attitude toward Anna Hartwell before the prayer meeting for Ola Culpepper's eyes. She could have then confessed it privately to Anna. But God spoke to her in the setting of the prayer group and she had to put it right with Anna publicly. The wisdom of God shone forth; others knew of Bertha's quick tongue and her confession served to deepen the conviction of everyone present. And after all, as Bertha said, she did not have any face to save because she was dead in Christ. Of course, one must be careful that God's Spirit is leading in such matters, but there are times and occasions when these actions are necessary. At times, issues may arise that took place years ago.

While a student at Baylor University, Dr. Charles Culpepper worked in the college cafeteria as a cashier. One Sunday a man and his family came in for lunch. They were the first in line to pay and Charlie had no change to give the man for a ten dollar bill. The man said, "That's all right, I will pick it up later." The man never returned, so Charles kept the money, thinking the man would come for it one day. Not long after that seemingly innocent incident, Charles' sister became critically ill. He had no money of his own to go and see his sister, so he spent the stranger's money for the train fare home. He had intended to give it to the man, but completely forgot about the incident. Years later, when Marie Monsen began to speak about confession of sin and restitution, the Holy Spirit spoke to him about the incident that had occurred years earlier. He knew he had to make it right with God and with the individual involved. Yet, he continued to argue with the Holy Spirit that he was too old and well-respected to bring up something that had been a mere oversight as a college student. The Spirit of God continued to impress the issue upon his heart. Finally, he wrote to the president of Baylor University, enclosing a check. He felt certain that such an act would bring criticism, if not disgrace, and he would lose the confidence of the Baylor family. It was several months before a letter finally arrived from the president of Baylor. The president wrote in his letter, "Dear Charlie, I think more of you than ever. I wish Baylor had more graduates like you." God vindicates His yielded servants.

The Culpepper children, as well as their parents, got caught up in the Spirit. Mary Culpepper, only five years old, was one day riding on a bicycle with her father while returning from a prayer meeting. She asked, "Daddy, if children die when they are very young, do they go to heaven?" Dr. Culpepper explained to her the meaning of sin and of the precious blood of Christ that cleanses all iniquity. Hearing this, little Mary said, "Then I wish I had died when I was very young, for I have so many sins."

That ended the conversation for the moment. But as Mary went to bed that night, her mother heard her crying. Ola went into her room and asked her little daughter, "Why are your crying so?" "Because I have so many sins," little Mary sobbed. Her mother invited the little girl to get on her knees and helped her to confess all of her sins and to accept God's forgiveness through Jesus Christ. She went back to bed but started crying again. She sobbed out to her mother, "Momma, I have thought of another one." This went on until she had exhausted everything she could think of that displeased God. Her mother shared with her the promises of God's forgiveness, and little Mary soon slept soundly for the rest of the night. Salvation came to Mary that very hour.

The seminary did not miss the blessing of the revival. The Culpeppers and other seminary leaders prayed earnestly for a deepening upon the many new students. Charles himself was moved by the Holy Spirit to confess his sins openly before the student body—not an easy thing for a president to do. This confession had a profound effect on the students. On a Tuesday at five o'clock the power of God fell upon the seminary. Confession and testimony continued for four full days and nights. On Saturday the glory of God fell (it normally comes in that sequence) and the entire student body praised God for five solid hours. If anything characterized the revival it was: "Woe is me" and then, "Praise the Lord," in that order.

Results of the Revival

It is important to realize that all this confession and restitution did not degenerate into morbid introspective psychological exercises. It was generated by the Holy Spirit in the light of God's consuming holiness. Those convicted were simply striving to be honest with God, others, and themselves. It was the only right thing to do by any ethical standard, let alone by the vision of the Holy God. Bertha and the churches realized that the "pruning" process must be grasped as a lifelong experience for those who walked with Christ.

Thus, the Shantung Revival, with its emphasis on confession of sin and restitution, brought in its wake a sense of genuine freedom in Christ's grace and forgiveness. The blood of Christ became a precious thing to all who were revived (1 John 1:7–9). Personal relationships that had suffered were healed. True fellowship among the believers became a glowing reality. They saw God for who He truly is. It gave the church a ringing testimony. People sensed and saw the sincerity of awakened believers. Consequently, multitudes of Chinese came to saving faith in Jesus Christ. That constitutes true revival.

7

A New Venture of Faith

Bertha Smith (2nd row, 4th from the right) pictured among some repatriates. *Credit: FMB*

In 1931, some four years into the awakening, the time came for Bertha to travel back to America on her second furlough. With both reluctance and joy, Bertha sailed home for rest, recuperation, and preparation for her next seven-year tour. While at home she studied at Columbia Bible College in Columbia, South Carolina. By 1932, the full devastating effect of the Great Depression was being felt. When Bertha prepared to go back to her work in China, the executive secretary of the Foreign Mission Board, Dr. T. B. Ray, wrote a letter to the thirty-five Southern Baptist missionaries then on furlough. He asked each one to look for other work until the economic situation improved. The Board scarcely had enough resources to keep on the field those still there. In a letter Bertha wrote, "What a blow." Yet she recorded the event by claiming the promise of Psalm 34:9: "There is no want to them that fear Him."

God Is Still Alive

Bertha found it hard to come to grips with this bad news. Did God want her to return to China? She must know. Early one morning she went to the church and sought a quiet place where she could truly seek the Lord's will. She spread Dr. Ray's letter out before the Lord and prayed like Hezekiah. She kept this vigil for two months and God met her. At the end of the period, she was convinced she should return to China.

Bertha's decision, of course, raised a question: How would she be able to go and be sustained in China? Once again God spoke to her through Isaiah 45:2–3: "I will go before you and will level the mountains; I will break down gates of bronze and cut through bars of iron. I will give you the treasures of darkness, riches stored in secret places, so that you may know that I am the Lord, the God of Israel, who summons you by name" (NIV). As she read that promise, her heart overflowed with assurance and joy. "Thank you, Lord!" she exclaimed. "The 'how' is now the Lord's concern! The riches are His secret. Since He knows, that is sufficient."[1] Now ready, she stepped out on pure faith. God had promised to care for her and to supply all of her needs. That was enough.

This step of faith would mean she could no longer work directly under the Southern Baptist Foreign Mission Board and she would probably be unable to serve with the missionaries she loved so well. Still, she felt no disillusionment with the Southern Baptists, for she was convinced that the Board's methods and policies were the very best approach to missions. And she had been working with the most dedicated missionaries with whom one could ever hope to serve. But she must respect the Holy Spirit and follow His leadership. She had friends who had gone out under independent faith missionary societies and she appreciated their work for Christ. She would simply go on her own. She knew that faith is always victorious.

Bertha continued to correspond with the Foreign Mission Board. She suggested returning to China and working under the same relationship to the Board, but with some definite stipulations.

- She would work on the same field in Shantung and serve with the missionaries whom she knew and loved.
- She would still be affiliated with the Chinese Baptist Convention but would not receive any funds from the Southern Baptist Foreign Mission Board.
- She would make no appeals to any churches in America for funds.

As the correspondence was sent off, Bertha approached the Lord in prayer, earnestly and fervently trusting that God would give the Foreign

Mission Board an agreeable mind. God answered. Dr. Ray was touched and agreed to every condition.

God's Care

The very afternoon that Miss Bertha sent the letter to Dr. Ray, a close friend from the Augusta Road Baptist Church of Greenville, South Carolina, Mrs. C. E. Hatch, drove over to Miss Bertha's home in Cowpens. She came to tell Miss Bertha that the Lord had revealed to her that Bertha must return to China. In a prayer service the night before, she had personally pledged gifts to help send Miss Bertha back to China. Mrs. Hatch further felt that God would have her to be Miss Bertha's secretary for the reception and forwarding of any funds that came in for her needs. Personal, individualized, and unsolicited gifts in no manner violated the principles of the Cooperative Program. The Shantung Awakening, far from over, needed Miss Bertha, and she surely did not want to miss any of the work of God going on in China.

Dr. Ray secured second-class passage on an American steamer across the Pacific at a missionary discount—it came to $300. That was a sizable sum to raise in the early '30s. Yet God provided and Miss Bertha soon had the money for the ticket plus enough to travel by rail to the west coast on a day coach. The Lord even provided enough funds for a railroad ticket from Shanghai to north China. Bertha said, "I praised the Lord indeed." Then, an additional amount came in for a Pullman coach ticket across America. A retired missionary from Los Angeles secured passage for Bertha on a Danish freighter bound to Shanghai for only $112. That gave her almost $200 over the original cost for crossing the Pacific. Blessings indeed.

Earlier in the summer, before Bertha sailed for China, she had been informed that a shortage of funds had reduced her girls' school in China to eight grades. The China Mission, therefore, asked her to transfer to the western part of Shantung Province and to work with her friends Martha Franks and Dr. and Mrs. Frank Connely.

Bertha and Martha

Martha Franks, like Bertha, was a native of South Carolina, born in the county-seat town of Laurens. She and Miss Bertha had degrees from the same college and from the Woman's Missionary Union Training School. The two of them had sailed to China together in 1925 when Bertha returned to the work from her first furlough in America and Martha sailed on her maiden voyage. Bertha said of Martha when she saw her for the first time, "She was about the prettiest thing I had ever seen in all my life. All dressed up in the prettiest clothes: witty, bright, warm."[2] They first met at the train station in Spartanburg. They traveled together for five days across America to the West Coast. Martha had a thousand questions to ask Bertha, and, as Martha reported, Bertha had two thousand answers. Then they spent one month on the ship together. By that time they were well acquainted.

Yet the two women were very different. As Martha's biography states:

> As unlike as they were, it is a wonder that they were able to stand each other's company. Bertha was a very strong-willed brigadier general, a real disciplinarian; she believed in a place for everything and everything in its place. Martha said one of Bertha's favorite words was "proper." She also labeled Bertha almost a "workaholic." It must be admitted Bertha was opinionated and frank, sometimes to the point of appearing rude and may have worked too hard at times. But it must also be said, when Bertha saw herself wrong, she always deeply apologized and restored fellowship. And her criticisms she did mean constructively. She did have real love, even if it was tough. Martha, on the other hand, was a little flighty and somewhat lacking in discipline, but they liked each other. In time the two "generals" came to respect the strengths of each other so that they could live and work together with the greatest joy.[3]

When Martha returned to China after a six-month furlough in 1929, she was unable to secure permission from the American Consul to return to Hwanghsien. "Consequently, Martha stayed at Bertha's station for a period. The two women, thrown together for several months, began to study in greater depth the Holy Spirit. They rested, prayed, studied, talked, laughed, and learned together."[4] They came to love and appreciate each other.

Before Bertha sailed back to China on her faith venture, Martha Franks wrote, "We need you. If you can secure passage money, come back and live with me; and we will get along the best we can on my salary, going fifty/fifty with it."[5] Bertha's problem found God's solution in her faith and Martha's devotion and sacrifice. That gesture spoke of the spiritual depth of Martha Franks, one of the sweetest Christian women this author has ever met.

Bertha wondered what Dr. Connely would think of her arrival on the field with no money for living or for the work. But she simply gave it all over to the Lord in complete trust and God continued to meet Bertha's needs. Before Bertha left America, Frank and Mary Connely, not knowing that Martha had made the sacrificial gesture to Bertha, wrote, "Come back and live and eat with us. We will stretch two salaries to do for three and manage some way. You shall have everything that we do." Dr. Connely even sent a check for one hundred dollars to help on her passage.

Off to China

Bertha fixed her eyes toward China in the joy of faith. Miss Alice Huey, "Heavenly Huey," sailed with her. Like Bertha, Alice had not been reappointed by the Board either; her passage and support were provided by the Woman's Missionary Union of Alabama.

Alice and Bertha arrived on the west coast of America and made their way to the steamer in Los Angeles harbor; a host of friends gathered to see them off. Bertha said that the very joy of heaven filled their souls at this moment. The friends commended them to the keeping of the Lord Jesus Christ and prayed that they would be a blessing not only in China but also to those on board the ship.

The Danish ship pulled out of Los Angeles harbor and set its bow westward. Along with the Danish crew and officers, five different nationalities made up the short passenger list of twenty-seven. Bertha had been praying for some time that God would lead her to the exact ship she should travel on as she returned to China. Bertha and Alice Huey began to pray for every person on board and began to seek opportunities to witness for Christ.

A young Russian woman aboard was married to an American Marine stationed in San Francisco. She was on her way home to visit her parents in Manchuria. She had a vivacious personality and became the center of attention to everyone on board, especially Bertha and Alice. They prayed that Lueba would soon come to know the Lord. One evening out on deck, Lueba nestled close to Miss Bertha to keep warm. It was December, and they were sailing the North Pacific. Bertha slipped her arms into Lueba's and asked if she had been born again. This puzzled Lueba. She unleashed a torrent of questions on Bertha. Apparently, for the first time in her life, she had begun to come alive to spiritual realities.

The next day Bertha and Lueba had another long conversation as the Holy Spirit began to speak to her heart more deeply. After a few days, Lueba began to demonstrate a genuine concern and desire to be saved. A problem arose, however. Lueba's roommate on the ship was a Jew. Moreover, another Jewish lady and her husband were on board. Lueba had been brought under the influence of the three and felt very fearful she would be ridiculed if she professed faith in Jesus Christ. The situation rocked on as the waves rocked the ship for a period of days. Bertha and Alice continued to pray.

The Storm That Brought Salvation

God acted on December 31. The ship sailed into a tremendous storm. The vessel tossed mercilessly from side to side and from stem to stern. Bertha exclaimed, "My heart thrilled with the thought of the God of such power being my own loving heavenly Father and actually living inside me."[6]

As the hours trudged on, the storm grew more violent. About noon of the first day, a huge wave struck the ship. Fortunately the ship avoided the complete impact of the water. Had the full force of the wave come down upon the ship with its tons of water, the vessel would have disintegrated. God was merciful. Inside the ship, pandemonium broke loose. Dishes and the dining tables went smashing on the walls and the floor. Sideboards fell and food was strewn all over the galley. The meal had to be prepared three times that day because of the violence of the storm. Even some of the sailors could not eat.

Throughout the day and night, the captain and the chief engineer stayed on the bridge to guide the vessel safely through the pounding waves. The first officer was assigned to passengers for their welfare. Bertha said he looked like death itself as he went from one person to another doing what he could, giving them sedatives to calm their nerves. When he came to Bertha and Alice, he saw that they did not need any. By the miracle of prayer, Bertha did not feel seasick and actually relished her meals. And she was prone to seasickness.

The first twenty-four hours of the storm saw the ship make only ninety-three miles, and not in the direction of Shanghai. The ship could only do four or five knots per hour and dare not face the storm head on. When the storm first hit, Bertha and Alice made their way to the lounge to see if they could be of assistance. There they saw Lueba, wringing her hands and begging for someone to pray. Her Jewish friends sat helplessly beside her, unable to pray or comfort; they too were terrified. Bertha, putting her arms around Lueba, began to pray earnestly. Bertha, absolutely calm and restful, had the deep assurance that God would see them safely to Shanghai.

In the height of the storm, as Bertha and Alice shared the truth of Christ with Lueba, they spoke loud enough for all the passengers to hear. The storm raged on. Bertha said, "Words cannot describe the feeling in my heart! It was more than assurance and rest of mind. It was a joy unspeakable bubbling up and filling my soul! God, the all-terrible God, the Creator and Controller of all the forces of nature, was in tenderest love surrounding me, His child. In fact, from His Word I knew that I was with Christ, so hidden in God that I was just as safe from the power of the angry billows as if I had been in heaven itself! All I could do was to rejoice in it and praise Him!"[7]

Lueba and all the other passengers sat quietly while Bertha and Alice spoke of the love of the Lord Jesus Christ as God's sacrifice and how He could save. Their testimonies came with such spiritual power that many of the passengers—Russians, Chinese, Scots, Americans, and the Danish first officer himself—said the expression on their faces confirmed the testimony. Lueba asked Bertha to go with her to her stateroom and teach her how to pray. Miss Bertha pointed out that before God could hear her prayers, she must completely repent of her sins, place her whole faith and trust in the Lord Jesus Christ, and find the new birth she had spoken of in their very first spiritual encounter. Lueba opened the door of her heart to Jesus Christ. In the days that followed she began witnessing to other passengers and officers about what the Lord had done in her life. The turbulent sea had turned out to be a tremendous victory!

God's Provision

The remainder of the journey brought pleasant weather. It had been a very dangerous experience, nonetheless. The first officer confessed to Miss Huey and Miss Bertha that he had expected the whole deck floor to blow off, which would have meant the ship would have gone down almost instantly and taken them all to a watery grave. But they made the journey safely and arrived in Shanghai relieved and thankful to God for all the events they had experienced.

When the ship docked in Shanghai, Miss Bertha went to the American Oriental Bank and deposited the two-hundred dollars she had saved by taking the Danish freighter rather than the American passenger ship. Then Bertha and Alice made their way on to Tsining. Martha Franks and the Connelys were stationed there and joyously greeted them. Bertha handed Frank Connely the check he had sent to her. Ministry under a new principle lay before her; she would serve Christ completely on faith without Board support. And God had already put two hundred dollars in the bank for her to live on. That would last for some months in China; in those days an American dollar went far.

The Connelys graciously opened their home to Bertha and gave her a bedroom. She decorated a little study in a small shed in their backyard and took her meals with Martha Franks. God provided wonderfully according to her faith. Every month, without fail, she was able to pay her share of the expenses.

Bertha knew she could not subsist on the fare of the native coolies. That would not give her enough strength to do her work. But she did not have to eat as a king. Upon her decision to return to China, she told the Lord that her food would be left to Him, whether good or bad. God once again spoke to her heart through the Word. In Proverbs 30:8 she read, "Feed me with food convenient for me." Bertha found, as always, that God keeps His Word. Martha and Bertha fared well.

A New Step

Miss Bertha made a further commitment to Christ. She said she would never take time in prayer begging God to supply her needs. He had promised to meet every need and she, by faith, would simply claim it. She devoted her prayer time to pray for the Chinese, leaving the "bread and butter to Him." She confessed that only once during the two years she lived by faith did she backslide. By the second year, her funds were getting very low and she prayed for money. She felt so ashamed when later she learned that contributions to the Foreign Mission Board had significantly increased, and they were planning to appoint new missionaries, but not before resuming the support of those already on the field living by faith. She asked the Lord to forgive her. All of her friends admired her for her faith commitment. But Bertha responded by saying, "To me it was not by faith, but by the living Lord."

Bertha lived without support from the Board for two years, but it required no more faith than in former years when the Board fully supported her. She said the only difference was that funds were channeled to a committee that divided them wisely among the missionaries. This process required faith on the part of everyone involved. How God provided through the Foreign Mission Board was truly miraculous. Ninety-three cents of every dollar the Board received made it to the field. Thus, the missionaries received more than if the individuals had sent their gifts directly with all the problems of postage and foreign exchange rates.

Even so, the personal faith of the missionaries was often tested. The spring after Bertha arrived, she traveled to the city of Chefoo for the annual mission meeting. She had saved a little money for some new summer dresses, so she went a few days early in order to go into town and purchase the necessary cloth. She chose two pretty patterns of blue silk material. Blue was always her favorite color. She wrote a check and took the material to a tailor. The next day she went to town to buy some other things, and began to write a check as she had done for the blue silk the day before. However, the clerk would not accept the check. Miss Bertha asked why. The American bank in Shanghai stood behind the check, she explained. The clerk replied, "You just go around to the bank and cash your check and bring us the cash." Miss Bertha left her package and walked up to the bank in confidence. After all, it was an American bank, she reasoned. But there she discovered that the American Oriental Bank in Shanghai had closed the day before. It had gone broke.

The situation did not disturb Bertha at all. True, she had to find funds for the check she had written the previous day as well as for what she had already committed herself to buy. But she had absolute confidence that the Lord would completely vindicate her. In a letter to her family in America she wrote: "As I had some checks out I was not only left with nothing, but worse, I had debts. What difference did it make? Well, it made none whatever with the bank of heaven and not so much with me, other than give me a chance to see what the Lord would do for His child away out here with only a few coppers."[8] And He did provide.

Dr. Williams, the mission treasurer in Shanghai, was leaving his office for the bank to deposit the month's salaries for each of the missionaries when a caller arrived and detained him until after the bank had closed its doors. The bank did not open the next morning, so Dr. Williams arrived for the mission meeting with a briefcase full of Chinese money, a month's salary for each of the North China group. Miss Bertha was able to pay all of her shopping bills and get back home.

Miracles like that occurred regularly among the faithful Shantung missionaries. Miss Bertha confessed, "The two years without a salary had so completely delivered me from money that I just committed the situation to the Lord, knowing that I would get along some way until the next month."[9]

Later Miss Bertha decided to go with a Bible woman to visit some Christians who were hospitalized two miles away from where she was stationed. Bertha did not have a single penny for ricksha fare. Not embarrassed, she simply told her Bible woman companion that she had changed her mind about going. But it soon got around the mission compound that the missionary had no money. The next morning Bertha found only one egg on her breakfast plate, and she was accustomed to eating two eggs. When the cook came in, she asked why she was only receiving one egg. He replied, "Don't you know that American bank in Shanghai has failed! How can you afford to eat two eggs!"[10] Then Brother Hoh, a wheelbarrow man, came in and said, "I have heard that the American bank has failed, leaving you without money. Not even enough for ricksha fare. I have a friend who has a ricksha, and when you want it to go anywhere, just let me know and I will borrow it and take you without charge." What a sacrifice, for wheelbarrow men only have food when they get a load to carry. Then the poverty-stricken wheelbarrow man looked at Bertha and added, "I have a dollar, and if you need it you may have it!" The spiritual depth of the Chinese believers spoke of the dynamic experience of the great revival.

A nearby Presbyterian missionary had fifteen dollars she had saved to buy a new afternoon dress. She sent the money to Bertha, and as Bertha said, "I ate the dress."

Christmas Blessings

At Christmas, Bertha's sister sent some dress goods in her regular Christmas package. One of the pieces of material was a beautiful pea-green color. The Presbyterian missionary lady who had been so gracious to Bertha was blonde, and Bertha thought a pea-green dress would be much prettier on a blonde lady than on herself. She gave the Presbyterian the material. It made a beautiful dress, far more attractive than anything she could have had tailored in one of the fine tailor shops. The dedicated Presbyterian missionary wore it for one summer, went home on furlough, then sent the dress back to Bertha. She then in turn passed it on to a red-headed missionary. Bertha said it looked so beautiful on her that "it must have been dyed in the beginning just for her. No one had been denied in order to share with me, and I had eaten two eggs."[11] The revival continued on in the selfless spirit of the believers.

On her birthday in 1933, Bertha wrote the following letter to her friends:

> Today is my birthday, but what does it matter to anyone here that I was born! Would that the fact that I was born a second time might impress them! But, the Good News, which I am spending a week here to bring to them, seems to make no difference. No, not even the fact that the King of Glory was born.
>
> There are many Mohammedans in this country, as all over China. The Bible woman asked how such a religion could spread from Arabia all the way here and get such a hold. Is it because the followers of the false prophet are more zealous for him than Christians are for their Lord? Or is it that the sinful human heart more readily accepts the false than the true? Perhaps it is both.[12]

Bertha remained true to the gospel and to her calling despite problems, hardships, and all of the enemy's obstacles. She had learned that faith overcomes the world and she determined to be an overcomer.

8

The Revival Broadens

Charles Culpepper *Credit: FMB*

A true revival rarely dissipates as rapidly as it begins. To the contrary, it normally deepens and broadens as it reaches out to engulf new areas to the glory of God. The transformation that people experience during awakenings almost defies description, even though the spiritual journey to God's fullness may be a rocky road filled with dangers. Such is the case of one product of the Shantung Revival, Dr. John Sung, who served with Bertha Smith.

A Great Chinese Evangelist

Dr. John Sung, a child of the broadening revival, became known as the "Billy Sunday" of China. Billy Sunday, the well-known American evangelist at that time, had something of the image and reputation of earlier American evangelists such as Charles Finney and D. L. Moody. Dr. Sung, destined by God, filled the role for his native China.

Sung received his higher education in the United States. In that setting he had become something of a skeptic. But God spoke powerfully to him.

One day while in school, he fell to his knees in his room and cried out, "Lord, I believe that you are God come in the flesh, and you came to die for my sins! I put my sins and my simple self upon you! Come into my heart and be my Lord!"[1] God heard that heart-rendering cry. John jumped to his feet and ran down the hall of his dormitory, praising God and telling his fellow students that he had been gloriously saved. As strange as it may seem, he had never truly been born again before this incident. The revival had even reached America, at least in this one significant instance.

Back to China—a New Man

Fear gripped John Sung on his return voyage to China. He felt God leading him to preach but his father wanted him to go into teaching, using the Ph.D. science degree he had earned to help support the family. Aboard ship, he unpacked all of his diplomas and threw them into the Pacific Ocean. He wanted to have no evidence that he had passed his examination and qualified as a professor.

When John embarked on China's coral sands, he immediately went home to share with his parents all the wonderful things God had done in his life. They understood. He then arranged to marry a young lady to whom he had been engaged in early childhood. He became a field evangelist with the Bethel Bible School of Shanghai. He and six other Bible School graduates formed what became known as the "Bethel Band." They traveled all over China preaching and singing the gospel, thus spreading and broadening the awakening.

John Sung and Bertha

Dr. Sung held a great series of meetings in Tsining, where Miss Bertha served with Martha and the Connelys. Prior to his arrival, the missionaries had been praying for a certain Dr. Hou, a druggist and medical man who had been educated in a mission school but had followed the early skeptical pattern of John Sung. He stopped going to church and began to ridicule those who did. In the first service, Dr. Hou was present to hear the scientist/preacher. All the missionaries, including Miss Bertha, kept their eyes fastened on Dr. Hou. He began to show interest that soon deepened into concern. After a few days of hearing Dr. Sung, Hou sunk into absolute misery. The missionaries were thrilled when they saw Dr. Hou walk down the aisle, get on his knees, and give himself totally to the Lord Jesus Christ.

At the close of Dr. Sung's crusade in Tsining, Dr. Hou volunteered to be a leader of one of the crusade's twenty-four evangelistic bands. He became burdened for a church some six miles from the city. The church suffered without a leader, and the members had grown cold and apathetic with no one to lead them. They had even stored their harvested crops in the church building. Dr. Hou left his drugstore and clinic. Together with the pastor of a large church and another church member, Hou went to the little congregation and attempted to revive the people.

Dr. Hou led the first service testifying to what Christ had accomplished in his life on that wonderful night when he surrendered all. The small group stayed for three days testifying, praying, and preaching until late in the night. Miss Bertha said, "By the last day people had become so heart-hungry for the Gospel that they were willing to come by the way of repentance and confession of sin."[2] Several were converted. A new dedicated group formed from the little congregation and became a dynamic witnessing band. They began to hold regular church services that reached many people for Christ.

In the church where Bertha served as a member and teacher, a young lad began to attend. He was the twenty-seventh child in the family. Twenty-five of the children had died of starvation. Then the father died and the young boy had been sent to a mission school. One day he stood up in class to recite and fainted. Upon examination, the teacher discovered that he had had nothing to eat for three days. After hearing Dr. Sung in Bertha's church, he soon went forward and, on his knees before God, another miracle of grace occurred.

In the same crusade another medical man became the center of prayers. He had been a slave to cigarettes and opium and had a very mean disposition. After hearing Dr. Sung for just a few days, he was gloriously converted and delivered from every addicting habit. He had a ringing testimony and threw himself into Bible study and service. All the missionaries were filled with praise to the Lord.

Healings

Dr. Sung was a man of prayer. Often people with physical ills would come to him to pray for healing. He would share the promises of the Word of God and then pray for their healing. However, he would pray for healing only on the condition that they wanted help in order to serve the Lord more effectively. God honored that depth of dedication and the prayer of faith precipitated many genuine physical healings. This still baffles some, but in revival, God does miraculous things.

Bertha shared a fascinating testimony of God's power to heal:

Joseph, son of deacon Chiang, developed tuberculosis of the bone in a lower limb, when six or seven years old. He spent years in the children's ward of the mission hospital in Laichowfu, where he was loved and tenderly cared for by Dr. Jeannette Beall and Alda Grayson, superintendent of nurses, and their staff.

When Joseph was about fourteen, Dr. Sung was leading meetings in Pingtu. Sinners were turning to the Lord, and saints were seeing the Lord work wonders.

Mr. Chiang, Joseph's father, wrote a letter to Dr. Sung describing Joseph's condition and asking prayer for his healing. Dr. Sung read the letter to that congregation, who were in tune with the Lord. Then, laying the letter on the lectern, he put his hand on it and said, "We will all now pray in unison for the Lord to heal Joseph."

A volume of sincere prayer went up to the throne from cleansed hearts. Joseph began improving immediately; little pieces of bone worked their way out through the flesh and skin. Within another year he was working on the farm.[3]

Some Aberrations

As the years unfolded, Dr. John Sung began regular healing services during his campaigns. Hundreds came seeking healing but a weakness crept in. Often the spiritual state of individuals was left unattended. Human nature being what it is, many exaggerated their illnesses and healing experience. Others gave all the praise to Dr. Sung, even though Dr. Sung would not take one iota of glory. Miss Bertha deeply regretted this turn of events that did not aid the awakening. Yet, there always seems to be some perversions in revival. Satan is shrewd. Thankfully, Miss Bertha saw this and did all she could to keep the movement on solid biblical ground.

While Dr. Sung was at the pinnacle of his ministry, he developed intestinal tuberculosis. Many prayed for his healing, but God saw fit to take him home; he died at the age of forty-three. Miss Bertha raised the question relative to the deterioration of Sung's healing ministry: "Could Dr. Sung's closing years explain why we do not now see more people definitely healed?"[4]

An Investigative Tour

The devil stirs up opposition in great revival movements. The first attack came, strangely enough, from the new secretary of the Southern Baptist Foreign Mission Board, Dr. Charles E. Maddry, who visited China accompanied by Dr. J. P. Weatherspoon, well-known professor of homiletics at The Southern Baptist Theological Seminary, in Louisville, Kentucky. Dr. J. T. Williams, Baptist missionary in Shanghai, traveled with them as an interpreter. They went to North China to investigate the situation there. It was clear that they were skeptical about what they would find.

The first city the American group visited was Tsining. Frank Connely met them in his car at the railway station for the twenty-mile trip to the station. Dr. Connely began to explain to the group that he and the other missionaries were convinced that the revival was a genuine outpouring of the Holy Spirit.

In the Connelys' home that night, Dr. Charles Maddry made a remark in passing to the several missionaries who had gathered: "I hear that Katie Murray is casting out demons in the name of the Lord over in Honan Province!" Bertha Smith replied, "Yes, we often come in contact with demon-possessed people among the Chinese. The Lord used Dr. Connely to cast one out here last Sunday!" This startled the American group. It seemed foreign to the rather restrictive theology and experience of the visitors; they did not know what to make of it. They turned and gazed at Dr. Connely at the head of the table. In a very humble manner he related the following story:

> Brother Chang, a church member from a village a few miles away, and Brother Liu, a new convert, had come to church bringing a stranger who could not speak.
>
> Brother Chang asked the pastor to request the brethren to remain after the services and pray the dumb devil out of the neighbor whom he had brought. Some of the loudest testifiers picked up their hats and went grinning toward the door as if to say, "That is too much for me."
>
> The pastor, one old church member, and Dr. Connely went to the prayer room with the three men and got on their knees.
>
> After each had prayed, they asked the dumb man to say, "Praise the Lord." Though trying his best, he could not get his lips open. For a week he had been in that condition, having been seized suddenly.
>
> After having prayed for some time with the same result, Dr. Connely turned to the man and, with the voice of authority, said, "In the name of the Lord Jesus Christ, I command you dumb devil to come out of this man!" Immediately the man opened his mouth and started talking.[5]

Bertha then told the story of Mr. Liu. Everyone who had a sensitivity to demonic activity knew Mr. Liu was possessed by a demon which had absolute control over him. At times it would even throw him into the water or fire just as in the incident in our Lord's ministry (Matt. 17:15). The Chinese pastor had asked Miss Bertha to go with him and pray to cast the devil out of Mr. Liu. She went, and when they arrived the pastor asked her to lay hands on the demon-possessed man as she prayed. Miss Bertha, with her keen spiritual perception, consented to pray, but stated that she would not lay hands on him since Jesus never put his hands on demon-possessed people. They gathered around the man and prayed. God answered with a mighty deliverance. The demon departed, and most glorious of all, Mr. Liu became a Christian. Then Mrs. Connely told about a number of sick people who had been healed in answer to prayer.

As Maddry's tour of mission stations in north China continued, the visitors heard continual testimonies of those who had been delivered from all manner of bondage, physical and spiritual, of people being healed, and of demons being cast out. They saw the churches packed with people eager to hear the message of Jesus Christ as multitudes were brought to saving faith.

After the tour, Dr. Maddry held a conference in Shanghai of representatives for the various mission groups. He confessed he had been skeptical when he arrived, but he had become completely convinced that God was at work and doing a marvelous thing. He said he felt he was reliving the Acts of the Apostles.

The Deepening
Experience of the Missionaries

Not only did Chinese believers continue to be deepened in their commitment to Christ, but through the earlier years of the awakening, the missionaries continually experienced similar blessings. The hunger to know and experience the deeper spiritual life pervaded the entire mission. Dr. Culpepper, for example, could not escape the question Marie Monsen had asked, "Have you been filled with the Holy Spirit?" This question began a spiritual quest that lasted for four years, even after Mrs. Culpepper's miraculous healing of optic neuritis. Dr. Culpepper confessed, "It influenced every moment of every day and led us through a spiritual wilderness of internal turmoil and crisis."[6] "But he found victory at last." As the spiritual movement spread and deepened over the area, many Southern Baptist missionaries attended the Peh Ta Ho Conferences to hear the esteemed missionary, Dr. Jonathan Goforth—"Goforth of China," as he is known. God used him powerfully in His work not only in China, but also in Korea. At this soul-searching conference, he shared a series of messages entitled, "Christ Is My Life," based on Colossians 3:3-4. Many were deepened.

In those years, one of the women missionaries began teaching the Book of Acts to a high school class. As she prepared the lessons, it became clear to her that one of the central themes of the Acts of the Apostles centered on, as one put it, "The power of the Holy Spirit in soul-winning." God began to speak to her heart about her lack of spiritual power to lead others to Christ. It set her on a spiritual journey, and by God's grace she was blessed with a newfound faith and strength and power for witnessing. When her testimony reached the other missionaries, it kindled a like desire among many. By June 1932, twenty-four Southern Baptist missionaries and many Chinese leaders had experienced a mighty infilling of the Holy Spirit. They rejoiced as their ministries were blessed with an effectiveness they had not previously dreamed of.

A Mature Approach

For the most part, the revival did not take on any seriously bizarre forms. The churches scrupulously strove to avoid sensationalism. Miss Crawford wrote, "Miss Monsen herself is one of the quietest speakers I ever heard. There was very poor singing, no invitation for public decisions, only the quiet question, 'Have you been born again?'"[7] Everything was done "decently and in order" (1 Cor. 14:40). Another missionary wrote, "Everything otherwise has been so quiet. Were it not for a wonderful spirit of prayer and an occasional testimony, no unknowing visitor would believe we were in the midst of a revival." It became self-evident that the Shantung Awakening was dominated and led by the Holy Spirit. The missionaries were most careful to keep it balanced and biblically centered.

Wherever the missionaries went, Miss Monsen in particular, the revival spread. Preaching was an experience of great joy. The pastors and evangelists found the many listeners so eager that it was easy to preach to them. A newly converted missionary nurse who taught in the mission school said, "In 23 years of life I had never been so happy. My feet could not stay on the ground; my heart was so light. I knew that Jesus was the Living Lord who frees sinners."[8]

Barriers Overcome

Resistance to the gospel continued, but the Holy Spirit continued to break barriers. For example, a young worker in the church tried to deceive others by insisting that he was saved. But he could not deceive the Holy Spirit. One night he was suddenly struck down in the courtyard of the church. He lay there cold and stiff as though in some sort of catatonic trance. Friends gathered around and knelt by his side praying. As the missionaries knelt praying and urging him to confess his sins, he feebly opened his mouth and confessed his need for Christ. He stood up, a forgiven and new man, his life radically transformed.

An older, hardened man in the congregation could not remain seated one evening during the service. He stood, walked to the front of the church, and confessed a life of sin. However, his confession did not appear to be real or sincere, and the atmosphere seemed permeated with evil. He remained hard, cold, and seemingly untouched, even by his own words. Christians earnestly prayed for him, and later the same night he was gloriously converted. The next day his countenance radiated his new life in Christ. Tears streamed down his face as he testified he had been set free by the power of God.

One of the male teachers in a girls' school, a teacher of classics, had joined the church but lived a nominal Christian life. He had the reputation of being a good scholar, having studied both Chinese and Western history extensively. He read his Bible regularly but thought he had no sins. One morning, however, he woke up at 2:00 A.M. and began to pray earnestly. The Holy Spirit revealed his sins to him one by one. He grabbed a piece of paper and wrote down each one of them. As he went over the list, he began to doubt that all this conviction could really be the work of the Holy Spirit. He felt that perhaps his own psyche had stirred it up. But he wanted to be sure, so he fell on his knees and prayed, "God, if you are God . . . and if the blood of Jesus shed on the cross can wash away my sins, and if these sins brought before me are the conviction of the Holy Spirit, then I will confess all and ask you to give me peace, then I will know that you are God."[9] The saving peace of Christ came into his heart with the full assurance of God's reality and presence.

One of the most profound manifestations of the revival was the experience of a deep conviction of sin that in turn precipitated deep repentance on the part of those coming to faith in Christ. A missionary from Laiyang wrote, "You who have been praying for the meetings in Laiyang will be happy to know that the Holy Spirit is present and powerful in convicting and saving these people." In Laichow, a Mr. Li found some of his friends rejoicing in the new birth. He knew their liberty and joy was something he had never experienced. With a sad heart he wept and prayed through much of the night. The next day he journeyed to nearby Laiyang a miserable man. He attended the services there, which just increased his misery. On the evening of the second day, after having honestly laid his sins before the Lord, Mr. Li found peace.[10]

Continuing Blessings

At Hwanghsien, the North China Mission had established a seminary, a hospital, and a boys' and girls' school. One morning a number of missionary doctors, nurses, teachers, and seminary professors held a prayer meeting at 5:00 A.M. They met again at 10:00 A.M., 2:00 P.M., and in the evening. They prayed to prepare their hearts for an upcoming series of services that would be led by Mr. I. V. Larson. The missionaries were mightily revived during that meeting. One missionary confessed,

> The Holy Spirit and God's Word continued to probe until I believed I would die under the searching, accusing finger of God. . . . I went upstairs, called my wife and asked her to come downstairs and pray with me. We prayed for the meeting. Immediately upon arrival at the meeting place, I asked the leader to let me make a statement. I don't remember all that I said, but I know the Lord enabled me to tell my inner feelings to the group of about 40 gathered there. I told them how God had made me realize my spiritual impotence. I told my missionary colleagues that their praise of me as being a good missionary had made me proud. I told my Chinese coworkers that in their compliments of me as an effective worker, I had stolen God's glory. My heart was so broken I didn't believe I could live any longer. While I was speaking, the Holy Spirit so deeply convicted those present of their own sins, we could not bear it. I watched their faces grow pale. Then they began to cry and drop on their knees or fall prostrate on the floor. The missionary, sitting on the front seat, dropped to his knees and began to weep. When he got up, he went across the chapel to a Chinese preacher and said to him, "Mr. Kiang, I have hated you." The Chinese gentleman answered, "Yes, and I have hated you, too." Missionaries went to missionaries confessing unpleasant feelings toward one another. Chinese preachers, guilty of envy, jealousy, and hatred confessed their sins to one another. . . .The Holy Spirit had brought such conviction upon the group that none could keep from it. It was so unexpected and unpleasant that no one realized what was happening.[11]

The meetings became so powerful that they would sometimes begin in the morning and last through the night. No unwholesome confessions ever surfaced in all of this heart-brokenness, only a genuine spirit of contrition before Holy God in the light of His convicting Spirit. People would walk into the services and immediately be convicted of their sins. The missionaries would simply follow the direction of the Holy Spirit and pray for those needing help. Informality characterized all the meetings. Anyone who wished could speak or pray or confess or make a request.

One Thursday morning the principal of a boys' primary school came to the prayer meeting. His eyes were wet with tears as he shared with the people that he had not slept the night before. He had not even gone home from school but had stayed in his room and read the Bible and prayed all night. He said,

> You people know me on the outside. You know me as a leader of our church. You have selected me to serve as a deacon. You also know that I

have a wife and three children who are not members of the church. What you do not know is that my home life is miserable. My wife has sneered me, has sneered my soul! When I want to give a tithe to my church, she is opposed to my giving anything. So I have deceived her by telling her that I am making only $18 a month when I am actually making $20. I have lied to her and deceived her so that I can give $2 a month to my church. In doing this, I have displeased God. Also, she does not want me to go to church on Sundays. She says if I go she will follow me, and when we get into the church she will jump up and down and scream in order to disgrace me. I know her, and she will really do it. On Sundays I tell her I am going to the market to buy something for the school. I go a roundabout way to the church, attend worship, then go back by the market and buy something before I go home. In doing this, I have lied to her and deceived her. I thought I was justified because I did it to attend church. Last night the Lord showed me, through . . . the Bible, that I have displeased Him. He showed me that the only way to escape is to confess my deceit to Him and to my wife. I want you to pray for me while I go home and confess my sins to my wife.[12]

The believers fell on their knees and prayed for him and his wife. He went home and soon came back to church with tears running down his cheeks, but not tears of contrition and conviction. He said to those gathered, "When I got into the yard gate (Chinese homes have a yard wall around the house), I had to knock because the gate was fastened on the inside. I heard my wife start out of the house, raving because I had not come home that night. I told her to be quiet because I had come home to confess my sins to her. She heard the words 'confess my sins' just as she opened the gate. Her eyes popped wide, and her mouth flew open. For once in her life she stopped talking, and I began telling her what had happened. I told her I had not slept the night before because God had convicted me of lying and deceiving her, and He had made me come home and confess how I had wronged her. When I finished, she was stunned. Finally she said, 'Well, if Jesus Christ can make you confess your sins to me, then I want to know about Him too. I have a lot of sins myself.'"[13] A few days later his wife accepted Christ and became a faithful Christian.

Such incidents occurred repeatedly. Missionaries and Chinese Christians were embracing one another as God dealt with their pride, envy, jealousy, and criticism. A fascinating incident took place in the life of Dr. W. B. Glass. Dr. Glass had a large nose and Chinese Christians called him "Dr. Big Nose" behind his back. When the revival broke and the convicting Holy Spirit gripped the hearts of the Chinese believers, they had to come to Dr. Glass and confess calling him Dr. Big Nose.

Dr. Culpepper said, "It seemed as if my heart would burst with love and compassion for others—my wife, children, coworkers, and the unsaved. For the first time I realized the true meaning of Romans 8:26–27, 'Likewise the Spirit also helpeth our infirmities: for we know not what we should pray for as we ought: but the Spirit itself maketh intercession for us with groanings which cannot be uttered.'" Dr. Culpepper went on to say, "Suddenly it dawned on me what a wonderful privilege it was to be a Christian—one to whom such unbelievable power is committed. Then I grieved because so few of God's children ever experience the full extent of blessings available to them. I knew that to receive that blessing one must dare to believe and accept the promise of the Holy Spirit."[14]

A School Converted

A great work of the Holy Spirit took place among the young men and women in the mission schools. In one area, a girls' school with 600 students had only 120 professing Christians, and it was doubtful that many of them had a genuine experience of Christ. But the Holy Spirit fell mightily on the girls. One afternoon the principal sent word to the nearby Baptist seminary, asking that the teachers come over and help in leading the girls to Christ. When the professors entered the school, to their amazement they found virtually all 600 girls in groups of two or three in a large room deeply under conviction of sin, not knowing what to do. This was not just a generalized feeling of guilt. The girls were under the conviction of cheating on examinations, stealing peaches from the school orchard, lying to parents and others, stealing pencils, pens, and money—very specific sins. The seminary professors worked with them, prayed with them, talked with them, and pointed them to Jesus.

Then the boys' school felt the touch. The principal called for a Chinese pastor and a missionary to come and help. The school chapel seated some 1,500. Between the girls and the boys who had been moved upon by the Holy Spirit, they filled the entire chapel. Doctors and nurses from the nearby Baptist hospital also came. Scripture was read, the plan of salvation outlined, and an invitation given. Everywhere in the chapel people were kneeling and confessing their sins. The conviction ran so deep that tears streamed down their cheeks as they prayed.

The meetings lasted for ten days. At the end of this tremendous moving of the Spirit of God, all 600 girls had made a profession of faith. The boys' school boasted 1,000 attenders. Of that one thousand, 900 came to faith in Jesus Christ. Those who did not come to salvation left the school; they could not endure the spiritual atmosphere without receiving Christ.

Dr. Culpepper tells of a fascinating incident that occurred in that setting:

About the middle of the first week of the meetings, as I was closing a night service, one of the teachers told me a boy under a bench at the back of the chapel was calling for me. I turned the services over to one of the Chinese pastors and went back to the boy. He was very upset. I got down beside him and heard him say, "Mr. Culpepper, you don't know me. I'm a Communist. We have a secret Communist cell here in the school. I've threatened to kill you and all the missionaries, and I've sworn to wipe out Christianity and burn your churches. When I heard about this revival, I thought the missionaries were just hypnotizing the students and that the concept of God was foolishness. I decided to come tonight to expose you. But when I heard you preach and ask those students to go forward and accept Christ, and when I saw them go forward and get down on their knees to pray, I said in my heart there is no God, that you were just hypnotizing them, but that you couldn't hypnotize me. I started to stand up and challenge you, but something struck me and knocked me under this bench. I know it was God. I know that you Christians are right, but I can't believe. I have gone too far. I can't believe."

We dismissed the students, but several of the teachers stayed and prayed for the boy and pleaded with him to give his heart to God. He kept insisting he had gone too far. The next morning he left school, and one week later we heard he was dead.

The next night Pastor Wang preached and a large number of students were converted. When we stood for the benediction, I felt something brush my back. I looked around. A boy lay on the seat where I had been sitting. I knelt beside him and asked what was the matter. He gritted his teeth and flexed his fists. He said, "Take me home! I am going to die."

I answered, "No! Let's pray."

By that time the crowd had been dismissed, and the teachers gathered around the boy for prayer. He kept saying, "Take me home! I'm going to die."

But we kept praying. After several minutes he suddenly screamed out, "Oh God! If you won't crush me to death, I will confess my sins. . . ."

Then he screamed even louder, "Oh God! You know I have said that when I have destroyed all the Christians, I would like to climb up to heaven and kill You! . . ."

90

When the boy ended his confession, he became completely limp. By holding his arms, we stood him on his feet and walked with him around the room. After a while he returned to normal, and we took him to his room. For several days he seemed dazed, but he finally accepted Christ and was saved. We discovered the Communist cell in the school consisted of eight or ten members, including these two boys. About half of the members were saved during the meeting, and the others left the school. The cell was destroyed.[15]

Like the school, the mission hospital became a revival center. Doctors and nurses banded together in witnessing and evangelistic teams and worked among the patients. When they had time off, the doctors and nurses would go to nearby villages to share the gospel with needy people. Many came to the Lord Jesus Christ. The burden for the lost weighed heavily upon them all.

The Spread of Blessings

The revival spread as far as Honan Province and Manchuria, then into Anhuei Province. Not only did the work spread to other provinces where Baptist missionaries worked, but also it mightily influenced the work of missionaries of other denominations. Of course, there were some who opposed the work, fearful of emotionalism, but they could not subdue the impact of the Spirit's work. The movement was simply too great! One missionary wrote, "We have experienced a revival during the past week that I would never have believed possible. I heard confession of sin until my ears and heart hurt as I thought of them. My own heart was deeply convicted, and I was brought so low that I would have despaired if I had not had the blessed hope in Christ."[16]

A missionary's wife confessed, "No missionary ever went to a foreign land with a more shallow experience with Christ than mine. I realized I wasn't prepared to come, yet I didn't know how to change. People mistakenly think one has reached the depth of consecration and the height of devotion when he or she goes to a heathen land. But after being in China a short time, I realized I had run into a stone wall and had no power to scale it. I didn't even know how to claim God's power. I was happy with my surroundings and had great joy in my home and with my children. But the unrest and need in my life increased."[17]

Soon after this statement, revival broke in her province. Prior to that she had read a book on the fullness of the Holy Spirit that affected her life; then she began to pray earnestly that God would touch her heart. In her prayers she sincerely told the Lord she would follow Him regardless of the cost. The Spirit showed this woman things in her life, from her childhood to the present, that she must correct. As one missionary expressed it, "She was stunned." At first she found herself unwilling to make the needed changes, even though she had pledged her devotion to Christ. The Holy Spirit continually probed her conscience with the question, "Aren't you willing to walk for a little while a road you thoroughly deserve, when I walked to Calvary for you and for your sins?" Suddenly she realized she had been deceiving no one but herself. She stripped off her spiritual veneer and confessed everything that God had laid upon her heart. And like the morning dew, peace and joy gently settled into her life.

However, that was not the end of her spiritual journey. After some time had passed she said, "I entered a depression that completely engulfed me. Even my desire to pray suddenly disappeared. A spirit of rebellion entered my heart; and I know now it was Satan making a last, great effort to restrain me from Christ."[18] During this time her husband moved into the fullness of the Holy Spirit. This experience of her husband created a barrier for her; she could not rejoice with him. Finally, she threw herself upon God and prayed, "Lord, I just want to surrender it all to you. You only can answer it." Suddenly, the great event occurred. She was filled with the Holy Spirit and the joy and presence of Christ all but overwhelmed her. She said later, "The world is new to me, and never has God's Word been so precious as it has been since that moment. I could never praise Him enough for His loving goodness to me."[19]

Similar spiritual experiences were taking place among the Chinese leaders in the church. For example, Pastor Kuan, a leading minister and a man of great ability, experienced a profound move of God on his life. He had become so eager for the fullness of the Holy Spirit that he knew he must give his life totally into the hands of Christ. As he studied the Word of God, he became convinced that the promise of Acts 2:38 was for him: "Repent and be baptized, every one of you, in the name of Jesus Christ for the forgiveness of your sins. And you will receive the gift of the Holy Spirit" (NIV).

He grew so spiritually hungry that he prayed through the night. One day, while kneeling in the church, the Holy Spirit came upon him with such power that he knew God's promise of the fullness had been fulfilled in him. Overflowing with joy, he praised the Lord for days. One of the missionaries said that he had been a good pastor, but now he was a pastor of power and prayer and soul winning. Soon the entire church was moved. These glorious happenings continued as the revival expanded and broadened across China.

9

The Expanding Work

Ola Culpepper *Credit: FMB*

The Shantung Revival had been ablaze for some years and the inevitable expansion of the work followed. It was a demanding but glorious time. The missionaries threw themselves into the work with great zest and zeal. Although a small measure of spiritual depression and gloom continued to be sounded at the mission meetings in 1930 and 1931, everything was radically different by 1932. More people had been saved in Tsinan than in any other year in the history of missionary work in that area. The churches reached a new spiritual plane; preachers, teachers, and missionaries had all moved into a deep experience with Christ. Buildings were not large enough to care for the large numbers of people coming in from many different areas. The report from Laichow-Laiyang read, "This has truly been one of our very best years in China. The sheer joy and rapture of this new, marvelous, intimate fellowship into which we were brought with the glorified Redeemer Himself is beyond the power of human expression."[1]

Encouraging Words

A most encouraging word came from Pingtu. A missionary at that station wrote, "God has been adding daily to His church. We estimate that 3,000 have been saved this year. There have been about 900 baptisms with others waiting. The 'Acts of the Holy Spirit' are being re-enacted in a very remarkable way right here in our midst."[2]

Perhaps the most significant work revolved around the Chinese preachers. One revived preacher said,

> I want to tell you that I have been preaching for 30 years and have not been worth my salt. I was so lazy I could not walk a mile and a half to tell people about Jesus. Since the revival, I go to prayer meeting at 5:00 in the mornings, go home and eat breakfast, take a little bread for lunch, and walk 25 miles witnessing in villages, then come home and go to prayer meeting at night. The next morning I am ready to go again. When the revival began, we had about 50 members in our little church. Now we have at least one Christian in each of the 1,000 homes in this town. Dozens of villages surround us and we have witnessed in all of them. There are hundreds of Christians in them.[3]

Evening Bible classes would sometimes last for nearly two hours. Verses would be read, then the questions flew. The classes culminated with a wonderful prayer meeting in which everyone present would pray. The prayers so scintillated with life and dynamic that it seemed as though they were talking face to face with the Lord—which, of course, they were. Spirit-filled Christians would then sing, and as one person expressed it, "It sounded like heavenly music."

New Methods

New ministries began for Bertha as the spirit of revival spread throughout the area. She began traveling from Tsining over a five-county area and said, "I knew that I had been promoted."[4] She developed an effective method of evangelism and church growth. When she went into a town, she would put up a large poster announcing the meeting. Then she would spend a week in Bible study with an organized church. This always attracted the people, Christians in particular. Miss Bertha's teaching style proved most effective. She did much teaching on Old Testament events as types of New Testament truths and often employed what used to be called a "felt-o-graph," a large poster made of flannel or felt material that pictured various biblical principles or scenes. She would place figures of Chinese words on it (they stuck on the flannel) depicting people or truths. It formed a simple visual illustration of the message being taught. For example, she had a felt-o-graph lesson on the Tabernacle in the Wilderness that pictured a type of heaven and the coming of God through Christ. Her favorite lesson—or so it seemed as she used it so often—made use of a felt-o-graph upon which she placed the Chinese character for "man," some red, some black. The red men represented those "washed in the blood"; the black, the man lost in sin. In this way she graphically illustrated the necessity of being born again. Bertha used the felt-o-graph in China and in America as well. This teaching tool was used before modern audiovisual aids were available, and it could be carried to the remote, primitive villages. It was especially appreciated by those who were illiterate.

Bertha centered all her teaching on the Holy Scriptures. She was blunt and frank in presenting the truth, cutting no corners. She denounced sin forthrightly and specifically, naming sins one by one. She would often say, "I do not know how the Lord stands us." Then she insisted everyone make out his or her "sin list" and get their sins confessed up to date. At times she offended people; her hearers either loved her or turned away. Perhaps at times she was too blunt and did not understand all the circumstances of the folk. She could be quite dogmatic, at times rather judgmental. But if she did offend unjustly, she would always apologize. Through it all, many lives were transformed.

Martha Franks said Bertha did not know how significant her ministry was. People would come from all directions. Many times only one or two people from a village came, bringing their bedding roll, a few steamed rolls, and a little jar of turnips pickled in brine. The church would provide a drink of hot millet broth. The men slept on the brick floor of the church. The women would be housed with the pastor's wife next door. Despite the hardships, the people flocked in and they testified to a glorious time in the Lord. After the week of study in the church, usually in the county seat of the area, Miss Bertha would then travel to smaller, more remote villages and minister in the little chapels. At times she would spend an entire week in a village, especially if it had never been visited by a missionary before. In villages with no chapel, meetings would be held on the threshing floor.

During the protracted meetings, which often lasted a month at a time, she would never hear one word of English, except what she spoke to the Lord. Even though the meetings often came in the middle of winter, she would never see a warm fire. The weather required her to carry up to thirty pounds of clothing just to keep warm during the day. At night, with good warm bedding and a hot water bottle, she would manage to keep comfortable. Each new day she would face bitter cold mornings. She exclaimed, "Oh, the transfer time from the warm bed to cold room in the morning!" It was not easy. Bertha groaned under the ordeal of getting into three suits of "long-handles" under the covers in the dark. She put on eight pairs of stockings that invariably twisted. She literally had to break ice in the basin to wash her face. That woke her up, needless to say.

Despite the physical hardships, Bertha found it tremendously satisfying to share God's Word with these rural churches. Often she would take a short New Testament book and teach it for a week. Sometimes she would take a topical approach; at other times, an exegetical approach.

Miss Bertha always combined her Bible study with evangelistic work. In the evening those attending the Bible study would go from house to house, witnessing for Christ and inviting the unsaved to attend evangelistic services. That is, those who had been blessed by the teaching would return to their villages and share what they had learned. This method of witnessing became a key to spreading the work.

Spiritual Discipline and Ministry

Faithful to her calling and enduring hardship as a good soldier of Jesus Christ, Bertha would rise early to have her quiet time with the Lord. She had to complete her prayer time before the community arose because she was "always on exhibition" when away from her station and home. In one village on a typical evangelistic Bible study journey, her prayer closet was a frosted haystack down the street from the home where she was staying. There she would kneel before God early in the morning, the only one awake for miles around, and look to her heavenly Father and worship Him in deep and sincere intercession. Bertha said she never "practiced" the presence of the Lord; that might be a self-conjured-up experience. Rather she "faithed" the presence of the Lord and that always brought Him close to her. She would take God at His Word when He promised: "My presence shall go with you, and I will give you rest" (Exod. 33:14, NASB). Such disciplines were indicative of the significant work of the Holy Spirit in Bertha's life and ministry.

One autumn day, a man walked twenty-five miles to the city of Tsining to find someone who would go with him to his village to tell the people about Jesus. Tragically, no one was free to go. A few months later he came back again; still no one could be freed up to go. The third time, Bertha, so moved by the man's commitment, said, "I am going." Regardless of other obligations she felt constrained to accompany the earnest Christian. She put together her regular camping outfit and food supplies, packed them into a wheelbarrow, and along with Mrs. Han, a young Bible woman, they made their way to the small village in rickshas. It took an entire day of travel to reach the town. They were wheeled into the village just as the sun was setting. The entire populace turned out to greet them. Bertha said, "It was like going through a receiving line. The day had been hot, and little boys were dressed accordingly—'In their skins.'" The enthusiasm of the crowd all but overwhelmed them. However, some of Bertha's enthusiasm cooled when she saw her accommodations, a room with an ox tied to one end.

Mrs. Han said, "If the King of Glory could come down to this earth and be born in a stable for us, we can endure this room for ten days."[5] Bertha had to agree. So they praised the Lord for the opportunity to present Christ to hungry hearts, and believed He would enable them to endure the smell of the ox.

The room measured about eight by ten feet, and the ox got his share of the space. A very narrow wooden bed frame stood in the middle of the room along the wall. The mattress was made of Kaffir corn stalks. Mrs. Han put her bedding on that. The other bed was across the end of the room. Bertha had brought along her camping cot but found no room to put it up except on top of the bed. On the wall opposite Mrs. Han's bed, sat a little table where they did their cooking and eating, and beyond that stood "Mr. Ox." He could have swished his tail in the soup but they had no soup. If they had, "It certainly would have been ox tail soup," Bertha facetiously said.

The women of the village had never seen an American woman. They stood and stared at Bertha with her white skin and blue eyes. One of the natives said, "She is just as pretty as an egg shell. What made her white?" Someone else replied, "I know, I know. She drinks cow's milk!"[6] That first evening they did not get to bed until eleven o'clock because of bystanders who wanted a glimpse of the white woman. Bertha was so exhausted she could not follow her habit of falling asleep in two minutes after getting in bed.

Not only that, the room was filled with what Dr. Jeannette Beall, a fellow missionary called "China's millions": lice. They were all over Bertha, biting as they crawled. What could she do? Tempted to be upset, she remembered what her Lord had suffered for her. She prayed, "Lord, I am not here on a pleasure trip; I am here to tell these people about you. I cannot see them tomorrow unless I rest. Down in Egypt you sent the very small animals scampering at your rebuke. Now just turn the heads of these lice in another direction and let me sleep."[7] She closed her eyelids and immediately fell asleep. She never saw another critter in her bedding in all the days she spent in that room.

The next morning, right at the break of day, the daughter-in-law of the host family came into the room with a basket of straw and wheat bran and a pan of water. She stirred the food for the ox for quite a while; then her mother-in-law came in to help her feed the old ox. Of course, what they really wanted was a good look at the American missionary while she slept. The ox, a lazy old thing, just stood chewing his cud all day long. Bertha asked if he couldn't be fed a bit later in the morning, but the lady of the house said he must be fed at the same time every day to stay fat. Some excuse! But understandable. During the entire stay of Bertha and Mrs. Han, the old animal only got put out once or twice to plow.

Wherever the missionaries went, the crowds followed. Bertha found it difficult to find a place to pray. But they had to pray. So Mrs. Han and Bertha would close the door and appoint someone to stand guard. They would then seek the Lord in prayer and ask His blessings upon the Word and to work in people's lives. But Bertha still had a problem. She loved to pray out loud. Even though this arrangement allowed her a quiet time, she felt she had to find a way to call upon the Lord vocally and in secret. Finally, she found the shade of a big tree out in a nearby field. Much to her surprise, the curious people left her alone there. But later she found out why. The Chinese women thought a god lived in that particular tree.

Before the week ended, as Mrs. Han and Bertha faithfully proclaimed the Word, people began coming to Christ. Miss Bertha and Mrs. Han would go from one courtyard to another during the day. They would normally find the women sitting on straw mats taking apart quilts and winter clothes for washing—a yearly task.

The winters in Shantung Province were very cold. Everyone has a quilt, something like a sleeping bag. At night they would slip into it, then take off their padded clothes and spread them on top. It was the only way to keep warm. The poorer people of the area had only one set of clothing. They had to take their winter clothes apart in the summer, not just for washing, but because the top and lining were used as summer garments. Before the cold weather set in, the cotton would be cleaned, fluffed, and put in again. Many times a raging cold front would sweep through and catch the families unprepared. They would be miserable.

As the women would sit on their mats, Bertha and Miss Han would sit beside them and explain the gospel. They would point out the sinful state of all people without Christ and their failure to glorify God and worship Him. They always presented the message with an emphasis on the love of God and what Jesus Christ had done for them in taking their punishment. But the replies they often heard were, "I can't read; I am just a pan of starch, too stupid to understand anything new."

Bertha encouraged the women by pointing out the fine abilities they had. They were very adept in managing their homes. They knew how to buy an exact amount of cloth for garments for their children. They could play very intricate gambling games with great skill. Still, the women would try to sidestep the issue by saying they could not understand anything. But Bertha continued to faithfully share the truth.

Each night after all chores were done and supper had been eaten, a large group would gather for a meeting on a threshing floor. Bertha's kerosene lantern would be hung on the mud wall along with Bible verses written on strips of paper with pictures and posters, all held in place by thorns from nearby bushes. Soon attitudes began to change. An openness to the gospel began to emerge.

The first night they met for one hour. But the Chinese wanted at least two hours of teaching. Since the men worked in the fields until sunset and had to eat after they returned home, the services began at around nine o'clock. Bedtime became quite late. One day Mrs. Han asked the lady of the home in which they were staying if she would keep the family quiet in the morning so the missionaries could get extra sleep. Early the next morning, the hostess woke her up to tell her that she would keep the daughters-in-law and children quiet so she could go right on sleeping.

Traveling marketers selling vegetables and millet would come to the village every fifth day. But the fifth day fell on Sunday that week and Bertha and Mrs. Han would not buy anything. With the next village being too far away to shop on Monday, they found themselves with no food. Finally, they found a Chinese woman who would sell them a rooster, but they could not boil it tender. Mrs. Han put a piece of salt-peter in the pot to make the rooster tender, but Bertha still could not eat it.

Whenever Bertha and her companion began to cook, flies would arrive in droves. The flies got even worse when it rained. Big black and green flies invaded the little room. The ox, of course, provided an extra attraction to the flying menace. Bertha again remembered what God had done in Egypt. She prayed,

> I am one of your spoiled children. All my life I have been accustomed to screened houses and clean food. Now, I just can't eat with those flies all over my food. Down in Egypt you had flies come and go at your word. You are the same today and you are ready to work in the same way if my situation demands it. Now please do one of two things for me: Either take the flies away, or enable me to just go ahead and eat and not mind them. You then take care of any disease germs which they may put in my body. Just whichever you wish to do will be good enough for me![8]

If it concerned Bertha, she reckoned it concerned God. It did; He heard her prayer. Not one more fly flew into that ox stall while they were there. What a testimony to the power of prayer! It was nothing short of a genuine miracle. With a twinkle in her eye, Bertha would say, "I have an even bigger one than that to tell":

We missionaries did not teach the Chinese to pray. We just told them that anyone could approach the holy God if he came to Him through His Son, the only mediator. I urged those men to open their mouths as well as their hearts, in confession of sin and in thanksgiving for Christ's death for them.

What a volume of prayer in that undertone! I could only distinguish the words of the one at my feet as he thanked the Lord for taking the punishment for his wine drinking, opium smoking, gambling, and bad disposition. Eight or ten had previously come to our room one by one and knelt at the foot of the cross in humble confession and faith and gone away rejoicing.

If those people were born of the Spirit, that was the greatest miracle of all earth's wonders. "Cooties" and flies have no enmity against God in their nature; but when a human being realizes that he is deserving of hell, admits his guilt, and willingly turns away from sin and chooses Christ as his Lord, that is a miracle.[9]

When Bertha and her faithful Chinese Bible women went out to share the Word, they found life in the villages to be challenging, mixed with joy and excitement. God honored their witness by granting many converts— Bertha's covenant children. The covenant she made with the Lord in 1918 was being kept.

Bertha's Healing

In 1933, Bertha began to experience a buzz in one ear. Fortunately she was able to go to the Peking Union Medical College Hospital, a fine medical facility (the one Ola Culpepper visited before her healing). An ear specialist diagnosed Bertha's problem; the eardrums were becoming concave. He told her that she would gradually lose her hearing. Medical science had not yet found a way to prevent the malady once the degenerative process began. When she returned home, she said to the Connelys, "When I can no longer hear, I will not annoy my friends by pretending I can. I will just be honest and admit deafness and use a hearing aid."

A visitor from America came to China and learned of Miss Bertha's diagnosis. He said, "If I were you, I would not accept deafness like that. If I were a missionary called to do the work that you are, I would take my ears to the Lord and ask Him to heal them, now!"[10] Bertha began to realize she had not really turned the matter over to the Lord, as she thought she had. So she began to pray daily that the Lord would heal her ears if it were His will. Yet, she seemed to get no word from God and would have been surprised had she been healed. This situation continued for two years.

At that time Bertha was working alone in Tsining and the church had no pastor. She had heard no preaching for more than a year except, as she said, "my own and that which a few laymen could do, which was even poorer than mine!" Miss Bertha confessed that she did not believe in women preachers. However, when no one else could preach, she could take up the challenge and preach an incredibly effective sermon. Still, her hunger to hear good preaching grew.

The church invited Pastor Fan Wei Ming, pastor of a large church in the city of Hwanghsien and vice-president of the North China Seminary, to preach for a week. When the series of sermons began, Bertha's ears buzzed and irritated her mercilessly. The buzzing would start in one ear, then move to the other. She knew Pastor Fan had prayed for the sick many times. The very first day she asked him to pray for her ears to be healed. He put her off.

"Christians Should Live Holy Lives" was the overall theme of the week. Pastor Fan preached from the Old Testament about the Feast of Unleavened Bread, urging all to search their hearts for any leaven (symbolic of sin) in their lives. Miss Bertha loved good preaching and did everything she could to cooperate with the meetings. She began praying that the Lord would reveal to her if there were any "leaven" in her life. The Lord spoke to her about several matters, but one issue that loomed large was her use of money. She had been a faithful tither for decades, but God showed her that she needed to consult Him about the other nine-tenths. God taught her a vital lesson.

People gathered at the church and experienced the power of the Lord twice a day. The Spirit of God continued to deepen Bertha's own conviction that she would be healed of her illness. One day, while they were sitting at a table, Bertha burst out crying and exclaimed, "I have said that if the Lord willed for me to be deaf, I was willing. But I did not know what I was saying! I do not have to hear conversation that belongs to this world, but if I cannot go to the house of God and hear His Word preached, I cannot live. I just cannot be deaf!"[11] Pastor Fan looked at her and admonished her to turn her ears over to the Lord. He continued preaching with power and urging everyone to keep searching their hearts.

After some days Bertha began to realize something of the exceeding sinfulness of her natural nature and cried out to God, "Take out the leaven? I am nothing but leaven! I cannot take out my very self. The poison of the devil is in my nature!"[12] She saw herself as a sinful sight before Holy God. She was at a place where she could neither eat nor sleep, and tears streamed down her cheeks. She confessed that the thought of what she was in her old Adamic nature gave her a physical backache. During three services in a row she was the first one to respond to the altar call, deeply convicted that she had used her ears to sin. "All my life I had reveled in compliments," she confessed. The old sin of "the pride of life" had haunted her since childhood. Then, in deep dedication, she presented her ears, her all, to the Lord for cleansing, just as Isaiah presented his lips when he saw the Lord high and lifted up in the temple (Isa. 6:5–7).

In the afternoon of the last Sunday of the meeting, several gathered in Bertha's living room. She said all were "so heart-hungry that she could not let the meetings come to a close without a new uplift from the Lord." God met their cry and opened the heavens and poured surpassing joy into their hearts. Bertha said that all she could do was kneel by her chair and laugh as one wave of joy after another came over them.

Then Pastor Fan asked Bertha if she still wanted prayer for her ears. Bertha replied she did and they read Exodus 4:11, "Who maketh the dumb, or deaf? . . . have not I the Lord?" While reading, Bertha felt a physical sensation on each side of her face as if a tight tendon were loosening up. Then Pastor Fan read from the fifth chapter of James and prayed. She knew that God had heard and she would be healed.

Yet, while Bertha continued rejoicing in the Lord, her ears kept buzzing. Even days after the prayer, one ear would buzz and the other ache, then both would buzz and ache. They had never hurt before. Bertha thought that perhaps the devil was trying to make her doubt her ears would be healed. The pain became all but unbearable, and after about a month, she cried out again, "Lord, you know that these ears are not mine! They were definitely given over to you, and since they are yours, they cannot hurt unless you let them hurt. Now if you do, it will be for some purpose and you will enable me to stand it."[13] By the end of another week or two the pain and buzzing completely stopped. She had been healed, despite the testing time.

Moreover, Bertha's healing received a wonderful confirmation. Two years later, while at home on furlough, she had the complete physical examination required by the Board. An ear specialist examined her thoroughly. Bertha asked, "Are my eardrums growing in?" "Why did you ever think that?" replied the specialist. Then she related the story about the diagnosis of the specialist in Peking. The doctor said, "I cannot understand such a diagnosis! Your eardrums are in perfect condition!"[14]

She took this opportunity to share with the doctor what had happened through prayer. Further, she openly confessed that it was not merely their faith that wrought the miracle, but the loving Lord making it possible for her to continue to go into His house and hear His Word faithfully preached.

The Mr. Huang Story

In 1933, soon after Bertha had been transferred to Tsining, she met a Chinese man by the name of Mr. Huang, a city councilman for the Tsining section. He was known among the Chinese as "the street elder." He would visit the mission station several times each year to collect quarterly taxes and communicate any new city council regulations the households must observe. Bertha always saw Mr. Huang's visits as opportunities to share Christ with him. He was of the ancient Chinese school that taught men should never look at women. Proper etiquette among the older generation demanded such. So, he would sit with his eyes focused on the corner of the room and completely exasperate Bertha by saying, "All religions are good. Buddhism is good; Taoism is good; Confucianism is good, Mohammedism is good, and Christianity is also good."[15]

A Presbyterian friend had sent Bertha some tulip bulbs. She planted them and the blooms became the delight of the Chinese as they passed by. Bertha always shared them, especially with the Christians. She became noted for her generosity. One day Miss Bertha saw Mr. Huang walking through her yard dressed in tan satin brocade, a sign of wealth. He exuded the air of "possessing the universe." As Mr. Huang walked through the garden and saw the tulips, it was obvious that he admired them very much and asked about them.

Miss Bertha, sensitive to his position and his system of etiquette, could not tell the proud Mr. Huang that she would be glad to give him some. But after he left, she put three of the prettiest tulips in a pot and sent them to his house with her card. Bertha also had a beautiful lily of the valley in her garden that Mary Connely had given to her when she left for the States on furlough. Bertha tenderly nurtured it and in the early days of May it began to bloom. When the blooms began to pop out, Mr. Huang came by to express his appreciation for the tulips, as Bertha put it, "strutting through the yard in peacock fashion to see what else had bloomed." He spied the lily of the valley. He so loved flowers that he humbled himself enough to smell it and ask many questions.

After Mr. Huang had gone, Bertha said aloud, "I am after Mr. Huang's soul, and if it is going to take Mary Connely's lily of the valley to win him, it will have to go."[16] She put the blooming portion in a pot and sent it to his home. Mr. Huang immediately returned to her yard, expressed his appreciation, and began to act like an old friend. Bertha invited him in. This time he actually sat and looked at her as she told him of the wonderful good news that Christ forgives sins. He listened attentively, then went home with a copy of a Gospel and some tracts Bertha had given him.

The Spirit of God was obviously at work, for the following Sunday Mr. Huang came to church. He sat on the back seat on the men's side with amazement written on his face, amazed at himself that he would actually be there. He began to attend regularly, and every Lord's Day he sat closer to the front. By the end of summer Mr. Huang was sitting on the second bench from the pulpit. He had also visited Bertha's home many times and heard more of the truth of Jesus Christ.

The church had no pastor or preacher at that time, so Miss Bertha led the services. One Sunday evening in September, Bertha spoke on Amos 4:12, "Prepare to meet thy God." When she finished her message, she invited anyone who wanted to be ready to meet God to come forward. One of those who came to the front and fell on his knees before the Lord was Mr. Huang. The victory had been won.

The next week Mr. Huang started attending the early morning Bible class and prayer meetings. After a few months of reading the Scripture, praying, and getting a full grasp on his own salvation, he made his public profession through baptism. His life began to blossom as the flowers with the wonderful fruits of the Spirit. He sent his children to the mission school and they too came to Christ. The two eldest children, a son and a daughter who were in the high school, volunteered for Christian work. His wife and many other near relatives soon accepted Christ. Miss Bertha capped it all off by saying, "Hooray for the lily of the valley!"[17]

The work expanded in a multitude of ways. The revived churches became the incubator of blessings that grew into multitudes of conversions. Victories abounded on every side, the signs of a refreshing revival in progress.

Part III

Chinese Ministry Continues

Bertha Smith (right) with fellow wheelbarrow-traveler and missionary Inabell Coleman in China.
Credit: FMB

10

Village to Village

Frank Connely *Credit: FMB*

Bertha liked to minister in the villages, despite the hardships. She had learned that no sacrifice looms too large if it brings people to faith in Christ. With that spirit and commitment, a significant portion of her work centered in village-to-village, itinerant ministry.

The Work Goes On

While in a village one winter, Miss Bertha and Miss Hu, a Chinese Bible woman, gathered into a little room some young single and married women, plus a few older women to study the Scriptures. They stood to pray because the ground was too cold to kneel on. As they got ready to pray someone asked, "What shall we do with our hands?" Bertha put her hands together under her chin as children are taught to do, and everyone followed her lead. She said, "As I viewed them in their earnestness bowing reverently before the true God for the first time, it was well that I was not the one leading the prayer for the fountains in my head had broken loose."

Miss Bertha always considered the Week of Prayer for Foreign Missions an important yearly occasion. She wrote home: "Miss Hu and I, with our faithful servant, and Mr. Chou, the evangelist from the nearby county seat, knelt out in the yard in the sunshine while Miss Hu read the prayer guide item by item in Chinese, and we prayed around the world."[1] That sort of praying made the Week of Prayer a powerful event in Baptist mission service and helped to keep the missionaries going.

When the team held open-air meetings in the villages, children often came early to sing while the others assembled. Once, a little girl leading a lamb, fearing she would not get on the front row, picked up the lamb in her arms and, as Bertha said, "came as fast as she could with such a load, the lamb bleating every breath." If only all would be as eager as little children!

Speaking in the cold outdoors did havoc to their throats. As a consequence, on one occasion Miss Hu developed serious pain in her chest, so they had to return home a week earlier than expected. Bertha said, "With three big mules [hitched] to the cart we bumped along so rapidly that we made the fifty miles in fifteen hours. I was too tired to sleep soundly that night and every time those . . . bed springs moved I thought it was the bumping cart wheels and kept wondering if we would never reach Tsining. But the next morning when I got really awake I was here, and how thankful for a clean little house and a chance to forget the desperate need of folks."[2] After she retired, Miss Bertha used to tell folks in America that she never went to bed at night without thanking God for her bed and clean sheets.

After returning home from a tiring trip just before Christmas, Bertha and Martha Franks started making candy. Bertha said, "I was so tired I was not interested in it and wondered if I was getting so old that I could not be interested in Christmas candy." She went to bed soon after dinner and slept through the night. The next day she "got up rested ready for candy making and thoroughly enjoyed it." They shared their candy with several friends.

On Christmas day itself, the missionaries had a great program that Mary Connely had put together. But Bertha had to say, "I can't say I enjoyed that for I had to do police duty in the balcony where the youngsters sat and they were crowded and noisy." Two days later she traveled to Tsinan at the invitation of the Abernathys in order to visit the Dawes, another missionary couple who had recently returned to China. She stayed long enough to travel back with Mary Connely, who had taken her children to school in Tsinan.

An Eventful Conference

In her March 1936 letter to friends and family Bertha wrote, "The time since my last quarterly letter has been taken up with country trips. The most interesting of the experiences was an unexpected sixteen-day trip to Anhui Province where I took a Bible Conference appointment for Mr. Connely, who was kept at home by the illness of Mrs. Connely."

Miss Bertha had only twenty-four hours to prepare to speak to the Chinese preachers and Bible women at the conference. She admitted she was tempted to tremble over the thought of giving two messages a day to Chinese workers and highly educated missionaries. But she had learned that one cannot tremble and trust at the same time. And, of course, she dared not go without trusting the Lord. God had been faithful to meet her every need; surely He would supply all she required in this present situation.

Mr. Tai, a young preacher, was to be the other speaker at the conference. Bertha confessed that perhaps the reason she felt uneasy about speaking at the Bible conference was because she feared that her ability in the Chinese language would not be as good as the older missionaries. Mr. Tai exclaimed, "Mercy on us! May the Lord save us from going over there with the sin of pride in our heart!" Then Miss Bertha, who always strove to keep her "sins forgiven up-to-date" fell to her knees and settled that issue immediately.

The trip to Anhui Province involved a change of trains. At the first railroad junction, Bertha and Mr. Tai went into a small inn to wait for the next train. They got on their knees and began praying for the conference. A young man appeared at the door and asked, "Are you ready for cigarettes?" When he noticed they were praying and hardly ready to "light up," he left them alone. Most Chinese people respect religion, even if they are not Christians.

The team traveled another five hours to Hsuchow railway center, just over the border of Kiangsu Province, then on to Kweiteh for Sunday. After another five hours of travel west into Honan Province, they climbed aboard the mission's old Model T Ford which took them the last forty miles to their destination. They had traveled through four provinces, which had taken some thirty hours, not counting the Sunday spent at Kweiteh. The cost: $2.50 each in American money. It took very few dollars in those days to move about in China.

Moreover, the missionaries were conservative with God's money; that is how they saw their finances: as God's money, not their own. They traveled third class. The coaches on two trains were like box cars with long benches running along the side. By making this sacrifice, they saved three-fourths of the first-class fare. Regardless of the inconvenience, they had a great trip.

The conference opened with a heavy snowfall and a bitter chill. The cold wind rattled every door and window in the unheated church building. They could not let the weather deter them, however. Bertha said, "Like

Nehemiah, those in attendance were doing a great work and could not be disturbed, not even by the weather."[3] Physical comfort blew out with the chilling wind, but the Lord blessed the meeting in a marvelous way.

Prayers were heard as the Word of God went forth. People responded. Several who attended were saved. Others were revived by bringing their sins to the cross. Many Chinese coworkers received a new vision "of their opportunity to serve the Lord," as Bertha put it. At the close of the ten-day conference, praise from overflowing hearts ascended to the Lord for His mercies. Bertha's apprehensions were laid to rest.

Going Home

The trip home had its share of the unexpected. The Model T wouldn't start, so they had to take a bus. Snow-covered roads meant mud in the middle of the day when things began to thaw. A flat tire, an overheated engine, and wooden benches along the side of the bus that caused them to feel like "Humpty-Dumpty" as the bus bumped over frozen roads, were experienced during the days of travel. Bertha said, "Mr. Tai and I were able, by the Lord's abundant grace, to keep a patient, Christian spirit."[4]

They made twenty miles the first day, stopping at an inn for the night. While sitting in the courtyard that evening, Bertha and Mr. Tai had the opportunity to share the gospel. The next day, while the men were changing another flat tire, Bertha walked up to an opium-smoking official and said, "You do not have to be bound by sin. The Lord Jesus Christ can set you free!" Then, she walked away. Later the official asked Mr. Tai what she meant. He answered the man's questions and soon another "covenant child" was born into the Kingdom. Each time they stopped during the tiring trip by bus, God opened another door to witness.

When Bertha and Mr. Tai finally reached home, too tired to hold up their heads, they said, "We were grateful, beyond words to express, for all the ways in which the dear Lord had smiled upon us."[5] How did Bertha Smith remain in passable health during such physical ordeals? Her willing spirit and right attitude had much to do with it, not to mention God's grace.

Continued Travels

Before her summer vacation one year, Bertha was off as usual teaching tirelessly in the villages and helping with the Bible Institute at her own church in Tsining. When summer finally came it "brought refreshing rest in the beautiful port of Tsingtao along with opportunities for teaching the

Bible to Chinese who were thirsting for the water of life." The weather turned extremely hot that summer. Bertha said, "We were fortunate to be in a cooler atmosphere, for about seventy Chinese and three German Catholic priests died in Tsining from the extreme heat."[6]

In August 1934 Martha Franks transferred to Hwanghsien to teach in the North China Baptist Seminary. Miss Bertha said the mission force had become so small that all of them had to be ready to leave their work and fill in where most needed. Mrs. Connely was confined to her bed with a bad heart as a result of rheumatic fever she had contracted in the winter. This left only two missionaries to look after the work of four counties. Even the weather did not cooperate. Miss Bertha was restricted to Tsining during August and September because of heavy rains that made it impossible to travel. It resulted in a serious flood over the area. After she could at last get out, she took a nineteen-day trip and said, "Miles and miles of farm land are still under water."

Bertha began her trip in a car, but she had to abandon it and take rickshas; then she had to walk a good portion of the way. During the trip several Chinese evangelists, Bible women, and two pastors gathered at the church where they were based for a conference on Bible study, prayer, and consultations concerning the work. Mr. Connely led the conference. Bertha said, "We sat for six or seven hours a day on backless benches that were four to six inches wide and too high for a six foot man." She commented, "A week of cabbage and bean curd for breakfast was enough for me, and when it came to peppergrass soup—well dear old Paul didn't know how much he was saying to me when he wrote, 'I can do all things through Christ who strengtheneth me,' and I suppose the soup strengthened too, for it had a little flour stirred in it and a few beans which were not done." But the blessing of the Lord more than physical comforts is what they wanted, "and He did meet with us."[7]

Miss Bertha and Mrs. Han (who accompanied the missionaries on the trip) remained with the church eight days conducting Bible study during the day and evangelistic meetings at night. Bertha said, "We found a wealth of teaching for everyday living as we studied First Peter." The theme of the study was "Be ye holy for I am holy." All were filled with a longing to be holy in all manner of living. The Holy Spirit brought conviction of sin. One church member who had been "more interested in making money than in living as a Christian came to see that he had been traveling a road of mud for twenty years when a beautiful golden road had been prepared for him."[8]

One evening during the evangelistic service a particular man was called upon to lead in prayer. He cleared his throat and hummed and hawed and repeated his opening words until the school boys began to giggle. Miss

Bertha said, "In response to the plea of our hearts the Holy Spirit seemed suddenly to show the man why he could not pray and he broke forth in such confession of his sins to God that the rowdiest youngster who knew nothing of what prayer meant was silenced."[9]

During those days Bertha met a Mr. Pi (pronounced Be), a teacher in the high school. He was about sixty but only two years old in the faith. Bertha said, "He was a joy to us." During the study Mr. Pi prayed, "Lord, you know that I have read everything that Confucius and the other sages of China ever wrote, but never have I read anything that has the flavor of what that fisherman Peter wrote."[10] Mr. Pi, a highly educated man, had the admiration of many. A few years before, he had attended services at the county-seat chapel, but it failed to impress him. Then God sent an unusual man into his life, a wheelbarrow pusher. One day Mr. Pi made a trip of several miles by wheelbarrow. His pusher, Brother Ho, who did not know one Chinese character from another, witnessed to him all along the path. Brother Ho had memorized only one verse of Scripture, which he recited. He then told Mr. Pi what Christ meant to him since he had been born of the Spirit. And God used the weak to confront the wise.

This gentlemanly scholar was impressed by the simple testimony of Brother Ho. At the end of the journey, the scholarly Mr. Pi purchased a New Testament and began to read with an open heart. He soon "passed from death to life." He testified that many had talked to him about his need for salvation, but a simple wheelbarrow man pointed him to the Lord. Brother Ho's personal relationship with the Lord had touched Mr. Pi.

When Bertha and Mrs. Han finally left the village, they traveled some twelve miles to another village where Miss Bertha had spent a week the previous winter. She said, "Every village in that country had its gambling den, a big cellar on a vacant lot. When the ground is frozen so no farm work can be done men spend their time there."[11] They scheduled an evangelistic meeting, and one day as Bertha walked to the services, she saw the men going to gamble. When Bertha and Mrs. Han rose early the next morning to go to their prayer meeting, the gamblers were at it. One man gambled away everything he owned, even his home. The spiritual needs of the people broke their hearts.

Bertha was on tour from village to village so often that she had little time to keep in touch with those on the homefront. Even her quarterly reports at times went unwritten. But finally in April she penned a letter to "My Precious Mudderkins" (her mother). She mailed it early so it would be received in time for Mother's Day. In it she indicated her appreciation to God for "His goodness in sparing you to be with us still." She visualized the May flowers blooming in the yard at the South Carolina home and wrote: "Just to look out at the beauty growing fills one's heart with praise and should make us all bow before God in thanksgiving. These are the extra things which He gives us to enjoy in addition to the gift of His Son . . ." She closed this letter by thanking her mother "for all your thoughts of love during the years that I have been your child."[12]

The same April, Bertha began two Bible classes for young men who were either saved or seeking the Lord. In the autumn she opened them to any man who wanted to come. At the same time, she began classes for women: one for those who could read and one for those who could not. These classes were taught by Mrs. Han and Miss Hu. The men met at Bertha's house. She said, "At times I have been embarrassed when the men kept a'coming and the house done full! Don't get too big an impression; my study and living room combined holds only about forty."[13]

Work at the Station

On September 21, 1935, Bertha wrote to her family asking them to contact publishers that produce tracts, hoping they would make a contribution of tracts to her work. Unfortunately, one firm sent a large lot of unusable tracts. Another sent only a few thousand good ones that were soon gone. The missionaries used the tracts during street meetings. Bertha said, "We just go anywhere and sing a song and all the folks get quiet to listen, then we pitch in and such attention!"[14]

About forty thousand refugees fled a flood during excessive rain that year and crowded into the locale. Serious floods were common. Bertha joined the victims and shared Christ. They were good listeners. In order to paint a clear picture for her family, she exclaimed, "Imagine the State Fair with all the folks huddled together as close as they can sit, on their bedding, what little they escaped with, no rest rooms, no towels, no wash basin, no nothing!!!"[15] Bertha seized the opportunity. She had a "captive audience" as she shared Christ with them.

September was the traditional month for making pickles. She wrote, "I have just been over to the kitchen and salted down some cucumber pickles for the night, which will be made into delicious sweet pickles after they take the salt." Bertha crammed the pickle-making in between helping a Chinese teacher with a letter that had to be dictated and written "sentence by sentence there being no Chinese short hand to save time." That same evening she entertained the Connelys in her backyard for dinner. The cook prepared the meal—with a little extra instruction from Bertha. They were having chicken croquettes made with leftover chicken and potatoes. After seventeen months in bed and seven months recuperating, Mrs. Connely was almost well, and she thoroughly enjoyed the evening.

On the annual Woman's Missionary Union Day of Prayer that year, the women invited the men to pray with them. Bertha described one of the attendees at the prayer service as a man who had "reached the gates of hell, but God in his mercy brought him back." He had served as a military official at Nanking in 1927. Due to illness, he had spent eighteen months in the hospital and came out an opium addict with a wooden limb. Being a lawyer, he soon found a job making thirty dollars a day by working only a few hours writing accusations for trials at the Higher Provincial Court in Tsining. That was an excellent salary, but he spent most of his earnings on opium. A military official who had recently been saved shared the gospel with him. The lawyer was soon converted, ceased to be a dishonest counselor, and gave up his opium habit. The power of Christ transformed him.

Some Difficult Days

Soon after the "old year slipped away," Bertha sat down to her ancient but faithful typewriter and composed a letter to friends and family. She reflected on the promise God had given her for the year:

> "Unto him that is able to do exceeding abundantly above all that we ask or think . . ." (Eph. 3:20). She told of a recent correspondence she had received where one of her prayer warriors had prayed that she be kept from loneliness. Her response was, "I praise God that before he called that prayer had been answered, for never do I know a lonely moment. Eighteen years ago on starting to China for the first time I received a letter from a missionary on the field stating that I was entering a life of many tears and joy, but how true her statement has proven and the longer I stay and the deeper I go into the work the more the tears, but praise the dear Lord, I can add, the greater the joys. Never have I known such genuine heart joy as the past year has brought even though I have been faced with more heart-breaking circumstances.[16]

One of those heartbreaking circumstances, which was due to the floods, was "freight train loads of human cargo, men, women, and children, sick and well, packed as thickly as they could sit on the floor of the box cars, tagged and being shipped off; they knew not where, but to some dry county in the Province." In one city she saw "tens of thousands gathered in the vicinity of the railroad station awaiting their turn to be shipped. The government was giving out daily bread but not enough, and two or three big sheds had been built to protect them from the sun and rain, but the majority were out in the open with no protection. Thirteen babies were born in one day there in the midst of the crowd."[17]

Another most difficult circumstance was hearing that Broadus Smith, Bertha's brother, had died of pneumonia in January just three days after she had mailed her annual letter to friends and family. She received comforting letters from missionary friends. Two other brothers had died earlier in the 1930s, William Clinton in April 1931 and Lester in October 1934. Facing these losses proved difficult, and being on the other side of the world made it even more trying.

The following March (1936) Bertha attended the Shantung mission meeting. There she had the privilege of hearing Miss Ianbelle Coleman speak. She said, "That would have been enough of a treat," but Dr. George W. Truett arrived on Tuesday and the missionaries got to hear the great preacher and pastor of the First Baptist Church of Dallas, Texas. Bertha was thrilled to make his acquaintance. The more the missionaries heard Truett preach, the greater their admiration. Miss Bertha remarked to fellow missionary Pearle Todd about the blessing of getting acquainted with "great people" while serving on the field, people they would probably not have the opportunity of knowing back home. Pearle said, "That was part of our reward for leaving home and living in a strange land."

Several missionaries, including Dr. Truett, rode together to the station to catch the train to Tsinan. When they got out of the car, Doris Knight said to Bertha, "I envy you getting to sit by Dr. Truett." Miss Bertha wanted to tell her that "she would not envy me long if she knew how I felt." Dr. Truett was a large man and Bertha was sandwiched between him and another missionary. She said, "Dr. Truett was embarrassed because he knew he was crowding me, but we survived it." Such was life in the midst of China's need.

Mary Crawford invited Miss Bertha to stay with her so she could host Dr. Truett and Dr. Rushbrooke, general secretary of the Baptist World Alliance. Bertha told the following story about Dr. Truett:

> It was a bit cool all day and that night Dr. Truett found an aluminum hot water bottle in his bed and said, to himself, "For this once today I'll get my feet warm." He was so worn out that he was asleep in a few minutes and lo, the next morning there was a huge blister on each heel. He had to go to the hospital for treatment and really suffered a good bit with it all day. Fortunately he did not have to stand that day and by going back to the hospital again Sunday morning for treatment he was able to stand for his two services Sunday. The afternoon session was an informal meeting of the Baptist workers of Tsinan where he sat down most of the time.[18]

Miss Bertha returned to her mission station in the early hours of Monday morning. Frank and Mary Connely were leaving on furlough on Tuesday afternoon, and Bertha had house guests who had come to see them off. She spent the remainder of the week getting accounts in order, writing and answering letters, and preparing to lead, as she wrote, "Our foreign service on Sunday and as yet I do not even have a text. This is unusual for me for I like to think over my subject for several weeks."

On Wednesday, just as Bertha finished closing up the Connelys' house and eating a light supper, an American gentleman arrived. He was employed with a Texas oil company and had come to China on business to check on their fields in the flood areas. He asked if he could stay with her. She gladly gave him housing. He had a conference in another town but would return that evening. He asked if he might take dinner with her when he returned.

When the oil company businessman arrived at 8:30 P.M., Bertha served him dinner and sat and talked with him while he ate. She learned that his wife had recently given birth to twins and one had died. The other weighed only two and one-half pounds and took up much of his wife's time, so they had stopped going to church. Miss Bertha spoke to him of what it meant to be converted and it touched his heart.

Later, after returning from another trip out, he asked, "What do you mean by being converted?" When Bertha explained the new birth, he confessed that he had never had an experience like that. For the next two hours she shared the gospel with him. When he left the next day he had a New Testament in modern English, which he promised to read. He paid her two dollars in Mexican money for entertainment and gave her five dollars for the work. She sent him on his way with a letter of recommendation to Mrs. Dawes, a fellow missionary, feeling confident that Mr. Dawes would "lead him on the rest of the way."

Such were the varied and wide experiences this "Woman of Revival" had in her ministry of the Word in China. God continued to lead and use her life in unusual and significant ways.

11

The Japanese Invasion

Wuchow Pooi Ching High School after Japanese bombing in which ten students were killed. *Credit: FMB*

The political situation in China began to erode and soon the country was in a serious upheaval. China has always languished in the throes of revolution. This time the threat came from Japan. The giant nation of China stood to face the greatest crisis it had encountered for centuries. In September 1931 the Japanese army launched its first sortie into Manchuria. The Chinese regime there was quickly wiped out. In 1932 fighting broke out in Shanghai, and great destruction ensued before a temporary peace could be restored. But it was to be only temporary. In July 1937 the Japanese army struck again. The most severe fighting took place in the lower part of the Yangtze Valley, in and around Shanghai and north toward Nanking. The Japanese slowly drew their cordon around China's throat, cutting off contact with the outside world. And there was Bertha—alone.

Bertha Is Alone—Yet Not Really

The Connelys had sailed to America on furlough in 1936 and because of poor health were compelled to stay in the States for two and a half

117

years. Miss Bertha was the only Baptist missionary left in Tsining. But as usual, she found God's guidance and strength for all she would soon be called upon to endure. She was not truly alone; God stood by her side.

In April 1937, Bertha wrote to wish her mother a happy Mother's Day. She enclosed some Hollyhock seed with the letter. She wrote, "I hope [the seeds] will be blooming by Mother's Day 1938. They will be pretty all around the fences and back next to the barn, wash place, and so on. I sent enough for you to get a good variety of colors."[1] Bertha then reminisced a bit: "I like to think of you these warm spring days being out seeing to your flowers and wee chicks with the fruit trees all in bloom and the farmers in the distance saying 'Gee-Ha.' Just two more springs until I will be there when the blue flags bloom."[2]

A New Helper

Missionary Olive Lawton joined Miss Bertha in the spring. Bertha deeply appreciated human companionship as well as the divine presence. Olive and Bertha planted a vegetable garden. Soon they had a good diet of cabbage and fresh greens. However, Bertha had a gardener who knew little of gardening. She asked the gardener if the asparagus tips had shot up; he brought in a weed and asked her if the weed was asparagus. Bertha said, "Evidently there was plenty of that kind in the bed." But they thoroughly enjoyed the vegetables and ate the last of the celery in a chicken salad.

After eight months of delightful fellowship in the work, Olive and Bertha went to the mission meeting in Chefoo, then on to the Young People's All China Conference for ten days in Hwanghsien. Olive left from there to visit with her parents, who were also missionaries in China. Bertha returned to Tsining for a two-week meeting in the Tsining church conducted by Mr. and Mrs. Wei of Chengchow.

A Shock and God's Providence

Late in July 1937 Bertha received a call from the United States Consulate insisting that she proceed to the coast because the political situation was rapidly deteriorating. Right then the providence of God struck. On the morning of August 1, an earthquake rocked all of East China. Taishan, the city where Bertha was resting, began to "jerk and quiver." The damage was extensive, especially back in Tsining. Therefore, it became absolutely necessary for her to return to her station to assess property damage and make arrangements for repairs. Her trip to the coast at the urging of the United States Consulate did not take place.

Returning to Tsining by rail, the train had to sidetrack at every station in order to permit long troop trains to pass. Bertha said, "How my heart was stirred at the sight of these young men. Hell had enlarged herself, she had opened her mouth wide to receive the young men of China. I knew that Chinese manhood could not stand against steel. Oh, if I could have gotten on a train and gone along with them. It would not have mattered what would happen to me if I could only have told a few of them about the Saviour."[3]

When Bertha finally arrived in Tsining, the city was in a state of alarm, and not just from the earthquake. The Japanese armies were on the move. Even before Bertha could complete the plans for repairs of the mission property, the Consulate sent another urgent call, advising her to proceed to the coast at once before railway lines were cut, making escape impossible.

There was no pastor in the Tsining church. How could Bertha leave those "sheep without a shepherd?" She confessed she felt such a burden for the inexperienced Chinese workers that she just could not leave. Not only that, those in the surrounding counties would have no one to consult about the work. She said, "The consul had estimated the time of our remaining away from our work from six months to three years. Many of our church members are but 'Babes in Christ' and, alas, I fear others have not been born into the kingdom, while the strongest Christians among them still need teaching and encouragement. Were they all mature Christians the ache in one's heart over the thought of what might overtake them in the future would have been enough."[4] But as she assessed the entire situation, she realized she had no alternative other than to leave, as difficult as it was. So she packed to be gone indefinitely.

On the day of her departure, the Chinese Christians gathered in the yard while Bertha stood on the steps of the Connely residence and read Psalm 46 to them. The more mature believers understood why she was leaving, as she put it, "in order to cooperate with my government." Yet she felt as if she was pointing them to the Lord for protection and then going to a safer place for herself. One Christian remarked to her at the station, "We may not all be here when you return." She left with much pain in her heart.

Bertha boarded the train and headed to the seacoast. On her way she saw train after train loaded with people fleeing to the interior. The entire country was in turmoil. When Bertha arrived at the seaport city at Tsingtau, the city appeared to be coming apart. Many shops had closed their doors. The price of food and commodities was skyrocketing. In Tsingtau she met fellow missionaries Alda Grayson and Mary Crawford. They rented rooms, set up housekeeping, and began ministering to the folk in the seaport city, as best they could. Soon the consulate advised them to leave for the United States. Even the daily newspapers ran articles stating that President Roosevelt had urged all Americans, without exception, to leave China immediately. The United States government adamantly refused to be responsible for the protection of any who chose to remain. What to do?

It seemed most wise for Bertha and her missionary friends to leave at once. But what about the Chinese? What would become of them and the work? Well, Bertha reasoned, the president of the United States had not sent her to China. Not only that, twelve years earlier, she had requested the Foreign Mission Board to accept a statement she had written requesting that nothing be said if she should lose her life or any of her earthly possessions in China. In faith, she believed that the Lord had carried her to China, and during the coming months and years China would need missionaries as never before. Should she not therefore stay?

Of course, to remain in China meant that those who chose to do so would find themselves in great danger. Already nearly one thousand people had been killed by just one bomb dropped by Japanese planes on Shanghai. Such would surely be the situation all over China as the invasion progressed. But Bertha reasoned that Chinese hospital workers were expected to remain at their posts. Should she desert her work? She remembered that military chaplains were permitted to remain in war zones. But chaplains were men and trained for the military. Women on the mission field often had to do the work that men did because there were no men around. What was God's will?

For two and a half months Bertha and her colleagues remained in Tsingtau struggling over the issue. One day several missionaries and one Chinese Bible woman sailed across the bay to an island six miles away. They visited and ministered in three villages. On the trip, the Chinese Bible woman said, "All of these villages may be destroyed, so we must hurry and witness to them for it would be terrible for them to be blotted out without having had a chance to be saved." On the way back she said, "We may not see them saved now, but when the trouble comes, they will know there is a true and living God on whom to call."[5] Bertha continued, "It's not the three villages that breaks one's heart, but the tens of thousands of them! To meet you in the air—what glory for us, but what tragedy for these people should our Saviour come before they hear that he came the first time!"[6]

In that context of inner turmoil, the conviction grew in Bertha's heart that the Lord wanted her to remain in China and return to Tsining to stand with the suffering people. Bertha went to the American Consulate and reported that she was returning to Tsining. God's answer had come.

When Bertha prepared to return to her beloved Chinese Christians in Tsining, she had to travel at night. The trains only ran after dark to avoid being bombed. It was an eleven-hour trip from Tsingtau to the capital of the province, Tsinan. She described the overnight travel as "a long night of joyful praise to the Lord for the privilege of returning to the Chinese Christians, to stand with them in their dark hour, and take what they would have to take."[7] She spent the day in Tsinan with Mary Crawford and the Abernathys, then that night took another train to her field. The night travel proved to be providential; she could not see the bombed-out trains along the way. The devastation was terrible.

Back to Tsining

When Bertha arrived in Tsining, she found pandemonium and panic in the city. Men and women rushed from shelter to shelter, hoping to escape the Japanese bombings. Some Chinese women lost their minds. Children were screaming in terror. But the believers were overjoyed to see her. Bertha related, "Never did one receive such a welcome!" The Christians said to her, "Since you were not afraid and can trust the Lord and come back, we will trust Him and quit being afraid."[8]

Bertha went right to work and immediately opened the church for services every evening. People who had resisted the gospel and had shown no interest in the things of Christ began to attend. Not only that, the city became inundated with refugees from the northern cities that had already fallen to the Japanese. Many of these refugees also attended the services and at times the church could not hold the crowds. The revival of 1927 continued, this time given tremendous impetus by the invading Japanese armies.

Bertha did not labor alone in the work. Two teachers who had returned home to Tsining from Hwanghsien Seminary took turns in leading the services. Each evening they gave an invitation for those who wanted to receive Christ. People were asked to come forward, then take part in an after-meeting where the gospel would be fully explained. Bertha was concerned that those making decisions would make an intelligent and full commitment to Jesus Christ. She knew that many of the people would soon be moving west to escape the Japanese armies. Therefore, she wanted to see as many as possible clearly established in the faith before they left.

One evening Bertha invited any who wanted personal help to come to her home the next day at the noon hour. To her surprise, thirty-five people came. She immediately enrolled them in the regular daily early morning Bible class. This program had been in existence for ten years and had borne much fruit.

Sacrificial Labors

The hospitals in Tsining overflowed with the wounded. Soon the authorities had to take over the mission high school and large private homes to provide bed space for those who had been injured on the front lines. Even commercial businesses had to turn their buildings into make-shift hospitals for the injured. Miss Bertha visited the hospital in the afternoons. She found it an open door to share Christ. The hospital itself was two miles away but she never took a ricksha. She walked both ways. Bertha realized that many of the people she would pass as she walked back and forth from the hospital would probably be dead the next day. She handed out gospel tracts to everyone she met.

For eight busy weeks, "trying to make every moment count for eternity," as Bertha said, she fervently shared Christ with the poor, distraught people. Yet she never lost sight of the fact that she must stay in close fellowship with the Lord herself. She guarded carefully her own time for prayer and devotional Bible study. She said, "I know that no matter how busy I might be for the Lord, I would soon become useless unless I took time for my personal fellowship with Him day by day."[9] Apart from that, every ounce of energy was spent for others.

One Saturday afternoon, a Mr. Wang asked to see her. He had been attending the Bible class for some time and he wanted to be saved. Miss Bertha and the seeker both got on their knees before an open Bible as she walked him through many verses of Scripture on sin and its consequences. She wanted to be sure he understood what sin was. She asked, "Mr. Wang, what is the greatest sin you have ever committed?" To her utter astonishment, he replied, "Murder." Miss Bertha said, "What a glorious message I had for a murderer!" She showed him that according to God's holy law he should have forfeited his life, but the Lord Jesus Christ had done that in his place. Two hours later Mr. Wang was rejoicing in Christ and the wonder of forgiveness. His whole countenance changed. Miss Bertha exclaimed, "That one trophy would have been sufficient reward for all that I endured during the war, had I been looking for rewards."[10] Someone has said, "The day of trouble will prepare many hearts to find the salvation of the Lord." How true!

The Lord's Leading

After this exciting experience, it was too late for the daily visit to the hospital. So Bertha dropped to her knees and asked the Lord what she should do with the two hours before the evening meeting. The Lord impressed upon her mind a young couple who had shown some spiritual interest. She felt the Lord leading her to visit them. But Bertha reasoned that such an impression could hardly be of the Lord since they lived as far away as the hospital. Not only that, it was Saturday afternoon. Bertha reasoned: "What person from South Carolina would not want to have Saturday afternoon off, and for the past month I haven't sat down to rest even for five minutes."

Bertha had been wanting to read a little book by L. L. Legter on the fullness of the Holy Spirit. She rationalized, "I know that it would please the Lord for me to sit down and relax and read this little book."[11] She sat down to enjoy the book, but she had no flavor for it, and her heart disturbed her. So she started off to visit the young couple. When she reached the end of the first block, she had a strong feeling that she should go south rather than north. The young couple lived to the north, but to the south she turned. In the middle of the next block she met a man in a civil service uniform and handed him a tract. He was startled to see an American woman in China at such a time. Bertha told him about the services in the church and invited him to come.

By the time she reached the next corner, she felt she should no longer continue south. She started walking north outside the city gate to make her call. She contacted the couple, then on her way home handed a tract to everyone she met and invited them to the evening service. She passed another man in a civil service uniform. He took the leaflet and said, "I approve of this! My wife's people in Tsiensin are Christians." When she returned to the church, the first man in the civil service uniform she had met on the street was on the front seat. Later the second uniformed man came. Both men waited for the after-meeting and in a few days they both came to new living faith in the Lord Jesus Christ.

Through the years Miss Bertha had learned the importance of seeking direction from the Lord in every detail, then listening for His answer. She knew that merely looking around to sense needs was not the way to find God's will. Needs alone could lead one in a thousand different directions. Bertha sought distinct direction for every move she made. Of course, like anyone, she faced the temptation to rationalize, but her sensitive heart did not let her fall into that trap, at least not too often. She knew victory in Jesus Christ.

Bertha was never able to get around to all the men in the wards when visiting the hospital each day. This dilemma left her with the disturbing thought that every day some would die without ever hearing of the Savior. On one occasion, she stopped outside a large ward on the second floor where she intended to go. She earnestly sought the Lord to find exactly where He would have her visit for the next three hours, and felt led to return to the third floor where she had been the previous day before. In obedience to the Spirit's prompting, she climbed the stairs to the third floor.

When Bertha walked into the ward she saw a fifteen-year-old soldier visiting a wounded friend. She discovered that the boy knew nothing of the gospel, so she invited him to attend the church meeting that night. He informed her that he only had one night in the city because his company was just passing through. She urged him to come that night. There was a problem, however. The city gates were closed at dark and the young soldier did not know whether his company would be billeted inside or outside the city walls. Yet, he promised that if he could possibly make it he would be there. In the few moments Bertha had, she shared the gospel with the young man, then left him with his wounded friend.

When the evening service opened, she looked everywhere for the young soldier but could not locate him. He was there though, lost in the crush of the crowd. During the invitation he came forward seeking the Lord. A young Chinese teacher led him to Christ, gave him a New Testament, and he went on his way rejoicing. A few weeks later Bertha received a letter from the young soldier. He had marched all the way to one of the western provinces. He was so grateful for having been led to the Lord, and said that if he had to give his life for his country, he would not fear. He knew he would be in the presence of Christ should death come. What if Bertha had not stayed in China or failed to listen to the prompting of the Holy Spirit when He bade her to go back to the ward on the third floor?

Continuing Conversions

One Sunday night Bertha noticed a fine-looking young aviator in church. He began to attend nightly, moving closer to the front each evening. On the fifth night he came forward to seek Christ and remained for the after-meeting. Bertha suggested that he come to her house the next afternoon and she would have some of the young men of the church meet him and help him in his spiritual life.

At 2:00 P.M. the next day the aviator came to Miss Bertha's house. Mr. Tai, a young Chinese preacher who had received his training at the North China Seminary and had come to preach in Tsining, was there. He had a real gift for leading people to Christ. He used the Bible and posters to help the young flyer. As Tai was seeking to lead the young pilot to Christ and into the fullness of the Christian life, Mr. Ma, superintendent of education for the county, entered the house. He had come to faith in Christ the previous July and he brought with him an unconverted friend, Mr. Yen. Mr. Yen served as an official in a county-seat town a few hours south of Tsining. Bertha had written him a letter in which she presented the gospel, urging him to come to faith in Christ. The Holy Spirit used the letter to bring Mr. Yen under conviction. The conviction grew so strong that he asked to be excused from his office for a day to visit Tsining. Bertha exclaimed, "What an opportunity!"

So there sat Mr. Yen and the aviator, looking at a poster illustrating the two roads of life and listening to what the Bible says concerning the meaning of being on the narrow way to life or on the broad way to destruction. God worked in the hearts of both men. Once they understood the truth with their minds, Bertha told them, "It is now a matter of your wills; you must decide for or against Christ."

The aviator replied, "I want to enter the narrow gate." Mr. Yen made the same decision. They fell to their knees before the Lord. Mr. Tai and Bertha prayed. Bertha then asked, "Do either of you have anything you want to say to the Lord?" Mr. Yen poured out a heartbroken confession of his sin, then of trust in Jesus for forgiveness and salvation. Then the aviator fervently prayed in like manner. By the time the evening meal was ready, they were all rejoicing in the Lord. Bertha exclaimed, "What a glorious afternoon it had been!"

Mr. Yen had to return to work, but he continued to correspond with Miss Bertha as long as the mail could get through. The young aviator, Mr. Teng, continued to attend the evening meetings and Bible class. He devoured the Word. Two days later, a Christian brother brought another young aviator to the meeting. The brother said to Miss Bertha, "Prayer brought him." This aviator also soon found faith in Jesus.

The Tragedy of War

Tragically, Mr. Tai's wife, unable to handle the pressures of war, became mentally ill and took her life, leaving behind two small children.

The mission became filled with refugees. As Christmastime drew near, the victorious Japanese armies were also drawing close. The missionaries took in several women refugees. The women would bring flour or millet and little mud cook stoves and pots. At night they rolled out their pallets all over the mission yard; each had an assigned place. The church basement was reserved for the men of the church. The city soon fell under siege. As the Japanese armies approached, the roar of the cannons became louder and louder. The people, panic-stricken, began fleeing to the west to escape the encroachment of the armies. Shops were closed most of the day and air raids were a regular occurrence.

Upon returning from the hospital one afternoon, Miss Bertha discovered that a Japanese bomb had exploded just across the street from the mission grounds. Even the Christians were in panic. Bertha kept quoting to them, "God is our refuge and strength. . . . Therefore will not we fear, though the earth be removed" (Ps. 46:1–2). Bertha said, "My own favorite verse was John 14:20: 'I am in my Father, and ye in me, and I in you.' How safe! Anything touching me would have to pass by God the Father, then it would have to get by Jesus Christ the Son, before it could reach me; and if it did, there would be the Lord inside of me. There would be no problem."

Bertha readily confessed that what the Chinese friends called courage and boldness was really Christ Himself living His life through her. She said, "Now you may be sure that I had my sins forgiven up-to-date at such a time! I was not only keeping clean enough inside for Him to dwell, but I was choosing His will in advance, daily and moment by moment."[12] Therefore, she lived a victorious life, even in the midst of tragedy.

Bertha, filled with the Spirit during those hectic times, made each day count. She never thought of personal danger or what might happen. She said, "I was completely possessed with the desire to do all that I could, for all the people that I could, while I could, for the night would surely come! What kind of a night no one knew!"[13]

As Christmas Day approached, there was scarcely any money to hold the traditional holiday dinner. However, just as Miss Bertha decided not to have the dinner, God again interposed with His grace and twenty-five dollars came from the Connelys for the Christmas dinner. They had a great time. Bertha wrote, "It was thrilling to see the joy of those who were having their first Christmas and to hear the testimonies as to the change which had come to them"[14]

Disease ravaged many in those days of privation. Miss Bertha did not escape Chinese amoebic dysentery. Earlier, while in the port city of Tsingtau, she had contracted this disease, her first real illness in China. She spent ten days in a hospital built by the Germans, and upon her release was advised to have a checkup every two months. But on Christmas Eve, just before the two months were up, the dysentery returned, an unwelcome visitor.

Bertha felt it had been nothing short of a miracle that enabled her to do all she had done as a well woman, but now that she was ill what would she do? She prayed, "Lord, I am the only one you have to use here. With what is already on, and the Japanese army only a few days from the city, I cannot afford to be sick! In the Name of my Lord and Savior Jesus Christ, I command this dysentery to leave me!" She did not experience another symptom of dysentery after that prayer.

On Christmas day Miss Bertha shared in a time of celebration and singing of hymns with fellow Presbyterian missionaries who lived in one of the suburbs of Tsining. Americans often feel that different denominations on the mission field confuse the Christian message. This was not true in China. The Chinese people were very accustomed to "denominations," since Buddhism was riddled with various divisions and sects.

Sacrificial Prayer

During the church service on Christmas evening many responded to the invitation to come into a living relationship with the Lord Jesus Christ. The after-meeting was quite long. Bertha had just experienced two sleepless nights helping to care for a Chinese baby. She honestly confessed that she was so tired she wondered if she could get upstairs to her room. At the conclusion of the after-meeting, she was approached by Mr. Teng, the aviator, Mr. Wang, a teacher, and Mr. Ma. They asked her if she would pray with them through the night. They wanted to pray for the church work, their country, and for Mr. Tai. Mr. Tai was so distressed over not being able to keep his wife from committing suicide that he felt he could never preach again.

Bertha suggested that they wait until New Year's Eve when it was customary for many to spend the last night of the old year in prayer. But they feared they might receive orders to go west to evade the encroaching Japanese armies before New Year's Day. Finally, Bertha told them, "You do not need me to pray with you. You stay here where it is warm and pray as long as you like." They rejoined, "We do not know where to find the Scripture passages which we will need. When you pray, you quote the promises of God. We cannot quote them from memory nor do we know where to find them in the Bible."[15]

Miss Bertha was absolutely exhausted from lack of sleep. She begged them to give her two nights to catch up on her sleep after which she would gladly pray with them through the night. Two of them said they might have to leave the next day. As she turned to go to her room, she flashed a prayer to the Lord saying, "Shall I pray with them or shall I not?" The Lord answered from the Scriptures: "Could you not watch with me one hour?" Miss Bertha yielded and said, "Yes, Lord, through the strength which You will give, I can."

Miss Bertha laid down some conditions for the all-night prayer meeting. First, no one but the four of them should know they had prayed. She did not want to give the devil an opportunity to make them proud by what people might say. Secondly, they would not decide then to necessarily pray all night. There was no virtue in the quantity of time spent in prayer; they would pray until what had been put on their hearts by the Spirit had been brought to the Lord completely. Miss Bertha read some Bible passages, and soon the four of them were on their knees. Miss Bertha confessed that the Spirit of God so blessed her that she felt as refreshed as if she had enjoyed a good night's sleep.

Although the men were sincere Christians and genuinely converted, they had not grasped the fact that the Holy Spirit must do His sanctifying work to make Christ their Lord in every area of life. Something of a spiritual struggle ensued. As the Holy Spirit spoke, they began to realize they must follow the will of God in absolutely every detail of life. They had to learn to hand themselves over to the Lord in definite areas. They struggled until each one had totally yielded himself to Jesus Christ, to live for Him and His glory only. By this time it was 2:00 A.M. No one had yet prayed for the church, the country, or Mr. Tai. But now they were prepared to pray for others. So Miss Bertha went to bed. The providence of God was surely in it all. Three days later Mr. Teng and Mr. Ma had to leave. Mr. Ma had a two-hundred-mile walk to west Honan. He left his baggage behind, but carried his most precious possessions: his Bible, a hymnbook, and a copy of Jane Lide's book in Chinese on the New Testament church. Victory!

The Japanese Arrive

The Japanese army was now closing in fast. A large silk store located near the mission compound was bombed on the morning of January 10, 1938. The invading army was only a day march east of Tsining. Early the next morning many callers came to Miss Bertha with multiple problems. Around nine o'clock she managed to get away for her quiet time. While before the Lord in prayer she heard the roar of planes—she had failed to hear the signal warning of an air raid. Her heart began to beat more rapidly, but as she said, "I had spiritual sense enough to know that the only way to be acceptable in God's presence was by identifying myself with Christ and His death." She had no doubt that the "mighty Creator, the Sustainer of the Universe," would hear her cry. She prayed, "Lord, there come those instruments of torture flying out of the pit of hell. (I did not mean from Japan—I meant from the Devil himself!) Now, for the sake of these helpless people who have no way of escape, will you take charge of those planes? Hold the hands of the bombers and do not let those bombs fall anywhere on this city today except where you permit them to fall."[16] A sweet peace and assurance came over her. She knew the Lord had heard. She left the attacking planes with Him and went on praying for those who would be attending the daily meetings.

When praying for people, Bertha would intercede for them individually by name before the Lord. At times, if she did not know their names, she would pray for the man with "the gray scarf, the one with the red button on the black silk hat, the stooped one, or the student," as she told it. Bertha got so involved in intercession that she not only did not even hear the planes; she forgot all about them. When she finished praying, she went to her study to help her Chinese secretary finish preparing the noon Bible class. They absorbed themselves in the task. Miss Bertha said, "The message from the Lord must be just what the Lord wanted that day, for the next day we might not be living." Suddenly, their small two-story brick house began to shake. The window panes flew out. A bomb had struck. But so great was the peace of Christ in their hearts that Bertha said she did not utter one sound; she had perfect peace and did not even have "one irregular heartbeat." She knew in her heart that God had some purpose in permitting the bomb to fall. When they got to the basement where people were screaming and yelling, someone pointed out the damage. Bertha replied, "The house does not matter now. I only came to see if anyone is hurt." No one suffered any injury, so she went out into the yard.

Miss Bertha's Life Is Spared

When Bertha looked up, the whole sky was black from the brick and tile that had been blown into powder. Her little Chinese home was virtually ruined and the pastorium had been obliterated. Other buildings and trees were damaged. Mr. Tai's mother walked up to Bertha with some cuts on her face, holding one of the Tai babies in her arms. They were not seriously hurt. But poor Mr. Tai was standing by his mother with the other screaming baby and cried, "Teacher Ming (Bertha's Chinese name), do not go out now." Bertha replied that she was going out into the larger compound to see if anyone was hurt. He pleaded again for her not to go. But she replied, "A moment's delay might mean the loss of a life!" Mr. Tai begged, "For Jesus' sake I ask you not to go out there now." Stepping back, Bertha replied that it was for Jesus' sake she was going. But since he felt so deeply about it she decided not to go. A second bomb fell right then just where she would have been. She said she was glad that she was not a "hard headed old maid that did not take suggestions." When she finally got to the girls' school she found them on their knees praying. No one was hurt.

The war had cut Bertha off from the missionary administrator in Shanghai, but she did manage to get a telegram to the American Consulate in Hankow to report the bombing. She also communicated with the Presbyterian mission in the southern part of the city. Presbyterian missionaries Dr. Walter and Mr. D'Olive walked the two miles to be of assistance. The bombing of the mission compound confused the more immature Chinese Christians. They questioned why God, in whom they felt they were trusting, permitted their buildings to be bombed. Bertha replied, "We never ask 'Why' about anything that God permits. He knew that we were here and He knew that we were trusting Him. We may not understand in this life, but this is not evil. The Lord permitted this for some purpose. He, the mighty God, does not have to explain Himself to human beings—at least not now."[17] Some packed up and left the mission compound; others were invited to stay at the Presbyterian mission. It seemed wise to move out of harm's way.

Everyone remained busy moving furnishings and furniture and preparing to leave for as long as necessary. They all worked to get the place in order as best they could. Bertha herself began to pack some things and select what she would take with her on the evacuation trek she felt she would be compelled to make. But she did not know whether to look west and keep ahead of the Japanese army or to go into a port city or even perhaps to America. It was necessary for her to take plenty of warm clothing and bedding, wherever the Spirit of God might lead her. She took few American clothes, but was careful to take all important papers and the mission account books.

Though the approaching Japanese armies were extremely close now, the missionaries did not hear any artillery barrages. So Bertha, along with some others, made their way to the Presbyterian mission until they could find the mind of the Lord. The firing began just as they arrived. The artillery barrage grew louder and louder until about two o'clock in the afternoon; it was deafening. Suddenly, about five o'clock, everything grew deathly still. They knew the city had fallen into the hands of the Japanese.

The next morning, Dr. Walter and Mr. D'Olive went with Miss Bertha into the city to notify Dr. Rankin, the Southern Baptist missionary secretary in Shanghai, that she was safe. But all the wires had been cut by the Japanese. She was unable to send her message. Then she took some Japanese soldiers to her own mission compound where they looked over the damage. It was extensive. But Bertha felt she saw the reason. She said, "I thrilled over the fact that the mighty God hears our prayers. He had guided the hands of those pilots and allowed those bombs to be dropped into our mission grounds in order to scatter us all out from there, that perhaps He might save the lives of some and protect the nerves of all." Bertha was right. After their departure, the area took many bombs. By God's gracious providence, only one life, the gatekeeper, had been lost in the bombing. God controlled the whole affair and, after all, the buildings were only brick and mortar. "This was the Lord's doing, and it is marvelous in our eyes" (Mark 12:11).

The Occupation

What would the future hold? What would life be like under the conqueror? If they stayed, the Japanese occupation would not be easy for anyone; everyone knew that. Miss Bertha herself said the army had come into their city like a "wild beast." The soldiers were granted three days' leave as a reward for capturing the city. It extended into a three-month rampage.

The first night after the Japanese takeover of the city, many young women and girls spent the night at the Baptist hospital as it had escaped damage. A Japanese soldier tried to break in and molest the young women. Miss Bertha, who was in charge while the Presbyterian doctor took a dinner break, confronted the young soldier. She said, "He buckled up, took his gun, and came out, passing only two feet from me. I did not back one inch as he passed by, but gave him another scolding, to which he grunted."[18]

A few days later, Miss Bertha returned to her own mission compound. Fortunately, not all the buildings had been completely destroyed. They were thus able to prepare some forty rooms for Christian girls and women to stay in. The outside gates, still intact, were closed permanently for protection. A passageway was opened through the fences that separated one courtyard from another. The only gate into the compound that was kept open was the front gate by Miss Bertha's single room, a room she had renovated and in which she hung her American flag. The Japanese respected the American flag. The new regime tried to convince everyone this was a "holy war" they were waging against the Chinese. Consequently, they did not want to fall into disfavor with American authorities. They said the bombing of the missionary compound had been a mistake. Bertha was able to repair enough of the Connely residence to move into it but she also kept her old single room across the street. She had a reason. She said, "I kept my room across the street, in hope that the Japanese would never know where I was sleeping on any particular night."[19]

A Safe Haven

As the Japanese soldiers ravaged the city, many women hid in trunks, clothes closets, or behind false partitions in rooms. For safety and protection, the young girls dressed like boys or little old ladies. The Christian girls were delighted to be able to return to the mission compound, where they could have a measure of comfort and safety. Miss Bertha moved about town in a U.S. flag-bedecked ricksha as she sought out the girls and escorted them to the compound. Bertha had paper pasted over broken windows so they could meet together for worship on Sunday. She reported, "Such a testimony meeting we had following the message! What praise to the Lord for His protecting care! Half of the congregation had to wait until a later date to express their gratitude for deliverance."[20] The school was refurbished and made capable of housing 150 girls, young women, and older ladies. Classes opened and life took on some semblance of normalcy.

Dr. John Abernathy, who served at that time in Tsinan, arrived in a touring car about two weeks after the bombing. As soon as Dr. Abernathy had heard about the bombing, he applied for a travel permit to see about Miss Bertha and those in the compound. The authority's reaction: "Certainly not! Tsining is on the front firing lines!" When Dr. Abernathy told the official that the mission building had been bombed and one female missionary was there alone, the official, greatly surprised, said, "I will go and take you. I must investigate the bombing of American property." Hence the touring car. The money for the needed repairs was supplied by the official for the confessed error in the bombing.

The families of the students at the mission school were responsible for their meals. Each day at noon they arrived with food for three meals. After eating together in the courtyard, they would be invited to attend the noon service. Mr. Tai delivered the biblical messages. Miss Bertha said she "saw more people born into the kingdom during that year and a half, than during my previous twenty-two years in China." It made one think of Pentecost repeated.

Little niceties occurred even in such difficult circumstance. Miss Bertha was normally able to have ice during the summer, at least until May. The ice was cut from the Grand Canal and stored in straw in little mud huts. But because of a cool summer and few now wanting ice, she was able to have ice all summer to cool her boiled drinking water and to make a daily freezer of ice cream or sherbet. At such times little things mean a lot.

Soon after the Japanese takeover, a small girl in the children's ward of the hospital died of diphtheria. Miss Bertha dressed the child for burial. Before she could be buried her infant sister also died. This potential outbreak of the dread disease forced Christians to their knees seeking protection. God answered their prayers. No serious outbreak occurred.

Japanese soldiers visited the mission compound almost daily on the pretext of observing the school. The preacher or one of the male teachers would detain them outside until the girls could be evacuated to the church basement. Then the teacher or preacher would take the soldiers through the church building, explaining to them its purpose and how they worshiped. He would even let the soldiers try their hand at playing the little pump organ. In the meantime, the girls would sneak back to the dormitory and from there through the back gate and yard into the basement of the Connely's residence where Bertha lived. With this clever arrangement, the soldiers never saw a girl.

The Japanese soldiers constantly went after the poor, vulnerable women. Even the older married women were as frightened of the Japanese as were the young girls. After the girls' school was opened, during a class before they could hide the girls, someone would often run in to tell Miss Bertha that Japanese soldiers, "the foreigners" as they called them, had climbed to the top of the houses to get a look at the girls. They would often enter the compound demanding girls. Then Bertha would have to leave class to get them down and run them out. Bertha said she must by faith stay "in Christ" to face all the new demands placed upon her.

By the middle of March, three months after the fall of Tsining, as soon as it was safe for boys to be on the streets, Bertha reopened the boys' school. She opened the school in haste before the Japanese had time to fully organize. She worked by the philosophy that it is easier to receive forgiveness than permission. Mr. Wang, principal of the former government school, gathered several young male teachers who were willing to teach for only their food. A young female church member agreed to teach the lower grades.

The soldiers would walk onto the school grounds paying no attention to the protesting gatekeeper. On one occasion a soldier climbed up on the roof of the school and upon seeing the female teacher, for an hour and a half demanded "the woman with the glasses." Finally, Bertha was able to get her over to her house in safety. Unfortunately, that ended her teaching. She would not come back. One day a group of seven soldiers came to the gate of the compound demanding women. Bertha had about all she could take. She reported them and it did not happen again.

The soldiers would often stand on the kitchen roof just to harass the people. Miss Bertha decided to tear down the kitchen and then build up the surrounding wall so high that the soldiers could not get over it. Mud bricks were brought in and masons were employed. Then the Japanese would try to impede the work. The workers would send for Miss Bertha. She would climb up on the roof and stand there by the hour to keep the soldiers from harassing the masons so they could build up the wall. She said, "Some of the soldiers came and talked in their 'unknown tongue' at me, but I pretended I did not see or hear them . . . I was busy as could be talking Chinese to the workmen—as if I had to tell a Chinese mason how to lay mud bricks!"[21]

Not long after Tsining fell to the Japanese, the Chinese tried to retake it. The fighting went on for an entire month. A ten-day artillery barrage and the small gunfire made it impossible for the girls to cross the grounds for classes. At night they would come to Bertha's home and sit on the floor and sing while she played the piano. That helped drown out the noise.

During the barrage, Mr. Tai and Miss Bertha worked together on preparations for teaching the Book of Revelation. She said, "We were trusting the Lord to take care of us, but I assure you that we, at the same time, were giving Him our utmost cooperation . . . It seemed that we were right in the midst of some of the horrors prophesied in the Revelation."[22]

One night during the ten-day onslaught, Bertha changed rooms five times because of the firing. Finally, she took her bedding downstairs and slept on the sofa. The roaring artillery and bursting shells and machine gun fire made restful sleep impossible. Another night, however, she fell sound asleep and did not wake until morning. She remarked to someone how wonderful it had been to have a quiet night of sleep. The person replied, "Quiet? It has been the worst night we have had! No one in the place slept a wink!"[23]

A Strange Birthday

It is understandable that under such circumstances Bertha forgot her birthday, that is, until she picked up the prayer calendar provided by the Woman's Missionary Union in America. The Baptist missionaries' names were recorded in the prayer calendar on their birthdays each year. There in black and white was her name. As the war raged all about her, people in America had been taking her before God in prayer. The Lord heard, and as Bertha said, "gave me just what I had needed: the ability to sleep like a baby." She came to know even in these circumstances what the Holy Spirit meant when He inspired Paul to write about "the peace of God, which passes all understanding!"

Pressure Eases

The trains were running again by March. Dr. Abernathy, who had also opted to stay in China, was asked to come and baptize a large number of new converts. While in the area he also helped to plan the property repairs. Even though building materials were non-existent on the open market, God provided through merchants who had buried glass in the ground and had stashed away hardware in hidden places. These items were brought out secretly as needed. From March to September the mission grounds were filled with masons, carpenters, and painters.

During the spring, as the flowers bloomed in the Connelys' backyard, Miss Bertha took her daily walk around the yard. She had figured out that twenty times around meant she had walked her regular mile. As she made her way around the yard, she continued the practice of praising the Lord, singing hymns, quoting Scripture, then thanking Him for His goodness. One of the things Bertha always expressed gratitude for was being able to continue receiving letters from home. They meant so much. When the trains failed to run, she had to wait. It disappointed her, but as she said, "This was the preparation for the time later when I would be interned and receive no mail for ten months."

In a letter written in July 1938 addressed to the Mission meeting being held in Chefoo, Miss Bertha wrote:

> I want to go to Mission Meeting and get kissed! I want to see the two year old missionaries and I want a new dress! I want to join with you in singing the grand old hymns of Zion, and hear what the Lord has done in each station since we last met together. But even more, I want to stand by my guns. No, not mine but by these that are here! Having been entrusted with Tsining's "preciousness" about one hundred and fifty young women, I can't leave now.

By September, the city once again had a fully organized government, and girls of grade school age could go out on the street safely. The buildings were repaired and the woodwork painted. Most of the debris had been removed from the area and the two schools thrived. The Connelys returned to China and were able to get to Tsining. It became a time of great rejoicing. The Connelys looked at Bertha and remarked, "You do not look tired." Bertha was not tired. Had not her Lord said, "As thy days, so shall thy strength be?" (Deut. 33:25).

Home Again

Bertha now felt free to take a one-year furlough back home in America. As she prepared to leave, the following citation was presented to her by Mr. Li Pei Chang on December 8, 1938:

> To Miss Smith returning to see her mother the third time—Teacher with virtue and righteousness; who knows the truth and God's Word, has been in China 20 years—with a character of meekness, faithfully serves the Lord, staunch in following Him. She has opened a school to teach, reach, lift students; during this war-time when trouble is all around, she has protected the women. Her love is perfect in caring for these women and girls that they may be kept in peace. She is going home to her native land the third time to see her own people, because she is filial. This makes us all approve of her. She is as a fragrant flower. May her journey be in peace.

Bertha remained in the United States from 1939 to 1940. She enjoyed a delightful year, a time of rest, refreshment, and reunion in the Lord. She saw many friends, all her close family, and spent wonderful times sharing what God had done through her in China. She reveled in telling the folk all that God had accomplished. The days brought new life to her soul. The Baptists, not only of South Carolina, but also throughout the Convention, were encouraged, inspired, and challenged by her ministry.

The question that naturally arose in Bertha's mind as the year's furlough drew to a close was: Should she return to the field under the Japanese government? But it did not take long to make a decision. As long as the Foreign Mission Board expressed a willingness to send her, she eagerly anticipated getting back to her work and her Chinese friends. The hearts of the Chinese were so open to the gospel, and so many were coming to faith in Christ, that she looked forward to getting on a boat headed for her beloved country of adoption and ministry.

Back in China

When Bertha once again set foot on China's soil, she found that Japan had imposed many new restrictions. But, after four years of Japanese occupation, the missionaries had become accustomed to accepting with gratitude what opportunity they did have to continue the work. And God continued to bless in a marvelous way. The afterglow of the Shantung Revival had not been extinguished. However, things were about to change dramatically.

Early the morning of December 8, 1941, the Japanese soldiers all but invaded the school. They told Bertha to take the Chinese teachers to the residence grounds. Instead, she rushed around the corner to get Dr. Connely to come and see what the soldiers wanted and why. When she burst into the Connelys' yard, she saw Dr. Connely standing with half a dozen Japanese soldiers around him. He said to her, "Go back and get your teachers. These soldiers have come to shut us up!"[24] Bertha later reported, "I had been in China for twenty-five years and during that time had learned, when anything new and unexpected came up, to get on my knees and turn it over to the Lord just as soon as possible. The problem then became His responsibility and I was saved from the worry of it."[25]

On her way to find a place of prayer to turn this situation over to God, the Word came: "There shall not one hair of his head fall to the ground" (1 Sam. 14:45). That was all she needed.

Still, the teachers needed comfort. They were upset over having to leave their pupils and be enclosed in the residence compound, so Bertha turned from her place of prayer, returned to the compound, and attempted to comfort the teachers. But the edict was clear: internment had come. What would it be like? Restrictions? Oppression? Persecution? Bertha knew her Lord would be with her regardless of what the Japanese would impose.

The Internment

Several days after the initial internment, the missionaries learned that Japan had gone to war with the United States. Only after their release from the compound did they learn of the bombing of Pearl Harbor which had occurred one day before the Japanese soldiers commandeered the school.

God, who knows the future, provided for them all in wonderful ways during those difficult days. The Lord performed what Miss Bertha called "a little miracle" in order that she might have funds to survive. During her second summer in China, she had bought a large building lot at Peitaiho, a summer resort town. She had hoped to be able to build a small cottage on the plot of land so she could enjoy a few weeks rest each summer. She never built but she kept the lot.

In the summer of 1941 she put the lot up for sale. The manager of the resort thought there would be no possibility of ever selling it since the Japanese had taken over the entire area. However, said Miss Bertha, "I am not to be laughed at if I have the Lord on my side. I turned the lot over to Him, asking Him to raise up someone to buy just at the time when He knew that I would need money most." God heard that prayer. A German businessman from Shanghai bought the lot. Not only that; the Connelys had inherited a sum of money from their family. With the funds the Connelys and Miss Bertha had, they were able to weather the storm during their internment by the Japanese.

"Earthy Bertha," being a practical person, dismissed her cook. She could do the cooking and cleaning herself, which she called "essential feminine pursuits." The Connelys and Miss Bertha ate lunch and their main meal together each day. Miss Bertha ate with them two days, and they ate with her the third day. These economical arrangements provided them with all the food they needed. Bertha and Mary Connely got into a friendly contest to see who could make the best casserole dish on just a half pound of meat. They really had fun, even in those stressful times.

Bertha bought a pint of milk each day from a German woman who lived in the area. From that daily pint of milk she was able to have milk for cooking and every other day drink a not-too-full glass. She even churned some to make butter. She had no churn but would save the cream for a few days, then put it in a glass fruit jar, and as she took her daily walk to praise the Lord and pray, she would shake the jar until the cream made butter. This would last for two meals if she didn't spread it too thick. She had margarine for breakfast, but no margarine or butter when there was meat at a meal. Bertha was amazed at what could be done when necessity was upon a person, and it surely was upon her.

Bertha made each moment of every day count. She prepared a daily schedule, being fearful of wasting any time. She started early; by eight o'clock she had finished her Bible study, then during the forenoon she would pray for four hours. She became much like the missionary prayer giant of India, John "Praying" Hyde. He too prayed four hours every day. Little wonder her dear friend Martha Franks said Bertha's greatest gift was prayer. Regardless of her internment, she was absolutely confident that God meant for her to be right there where she could continue to minister to the Chinese. Being confined to her own home and yard did not put her out of active service.

During internment, Bertha's active ministry revolved around bringing before the Lord by name all those she had been working with, all the other Chinese people she knew, and her fellow missionaries. She prayed for the countries of the world, her friends and acquaintances in America, the Lord's work, and whatever the Spirit of God laid upon her heart. She became a great intercessor during those days. She recognized that prayer constitutes the most vital service of all. During their observance of the Week of Prayer for Foreign Missions, the Chinese used to say, "We have prayed around the world today!" Because of her confinement, Miss Bertha was able to pray around the world every day.

On the days Miss Bertha was responsible for preparing the noon meal, she would have to begin by ten o'clock. She only got in two hours of prayer on those days. With few modern conveniences, it took her two hours to prepare a meal. On the days she ate with the Connelys, she could devote herself to prayer the entire morning. Many times she said it would seem tragic to have to come down from the very presence of God "in the heavenlies" just to care for the physical need of food. After the noon meal she would take a thirty-minute nap, then study the Chinese language for an hour and a half. After twenty-five years in China she still continued to work on the language so that she might be more communicative to the Chinese people. She would then spend forty-five minutes practicing the piano. Bertha never aspired to be a great musician but she could play well enough for the church services. Practice time proved a special delight. Since coming to China she had been too busy to practice seriously. But now she "got out my old college music and had a grand time," as she put it. Her daily walk to do the churning followed piano practice; after supper she read until bedtime. No wonder she could say, "There was not one lonely moment during the entire six months that we three were cut off. We had our own church service on Sunday, sitting in rocking chairs. And twice a week we had a party, which meant we played Chinese checkers, just three games and had 'light' refreshments."[26] The light refreshments were cocoa and cookies; and they relished them.

About three months into the internment an unusual incident occurred. The head Japanese official brought each of the interned missionaries the equivalent of twenty-five U.S. dollars. He said, "After the war is over, we will get this back. You will pay it or your mission or government will. In some way, it will be refunded."[27] God provides in most unusual ways.

The summer before the confinement began, God performed another nurturing, preparing work in the life of Miss Bertha. She was blessed by a choice servant of the Lord. Miss Aletta Jacobaz, a young Dutch teacher in Andrew Murray's Bible College in Johannesburg, South Africa, used her sabbatical year to visit various mission fields. A Presbyterian missionary friend of Miss Bertha heard Miss Jacobaz and reported what Miss Jacobaz was teaching. Miss Bertha said, "The one message that was reported to me was enough to put me to honest heart-searching." The message was similar to those delivered by Marie Monsen. Everyone needs a spiritual refresher course on occasion, Miss Bertha included. She confessed, "I am sure that the witness and power of this woman, which was passed on to me, had a share in preparing me for the six months of prayer time during internment, which may have meant more to the Lord's work than any six months in my active service."[28]

Great News

On one spring day, Bertha strolled about the yard looking over the tulip patch to see how many were poking their heads out of the ground. Suddenly Mary Connely ran out of the house with incredible news. The secretary to the head Japanese officials of the city came to ask if the Connelys and Miss Bertha would like to go to America. He said if they wished to go, he would make a way to get them there. Bertha immediately responded, "Yes, I will go home to my mother. Someone else can count these tulip bulbs!"

It was absolutely unheard of for a private citizen of an enemy country to be exchanged during the war. Bertha recognized it as the hand of God, upon even the enemies. Bertha wanted to go home and get her strength back so she could be ready to return as soon as the hostilities ended.

The Connelys, however, chose to stay. The officials said they could remain in their home and not be sent to a concentration camp. They felt they should stay to be an encouragement to the Chinese leaders. But tragically, the very day Miss Bertha left for America, the Connelys were sent to a concentration camp.

The Occupation of the Chinese

Many fascinating but tragic stories came out of the days of the Japanese occupation. When the Japanese first came into China in 1937, they killed many of the young educated men whom they assumed would oppose their regime. When the army entered Canton, the old pastors urged the younger Christian workers to leave and go west. One young pastor refused to go. An older pastor pled with him and promised to take the responsibility of being shepherd to the younger man's flock. The dedicated young man replied, "You do not know my people and their various problems and needs. At a time like this, they need their pastor and I cannot leave them." No one saw the young pastor for some weeks. The Christians thought he had surely been secretly put to death; so many others had. One day, however, he appeared at the home of missionary Dr. Eugene Hill in Canton. His face was black with dirt except for some strange clean streaks on each cheek. He told his story:

> I was taken prisoner when the Japanese discovered me. A party of other young men and I were kept in a public building with a yard surrounded by an iron railing. The men were taken out one by one, chained to the railing, and for the amusement of the Japanese soldiers, the ferocious bloodhound dogs which had not been fed were turned on them to torture them to death. No one was given any water during these days to wash their faces.
>
> When it came my turn and I was chained to the railing, I found that I had enough freedom to kneel. Then I lifted my face and started calling upon my God. The dogs came and started licking my face. The Japanese soldiers, knowing that I was a preacher, were so frightened that they said: "Surely, he has been made a god." They immediately released me!

His unwashed face was marked with the clean streaks from the licking of the dogs. His release was a miracle of Almighty God!

But now Bertha prepared to leave. What would it all mean? What did the future hold?

12

God's Good Hand upon His Own

Southern Baptist missionaries aboard the S.S. *Gripsholm* en route to the
United States after repatriation. Bertha (3rd row, far right). *Credit: FMB*

Three months after the first announcement of repatriation, the move
came. Seven hundred American citizens were herded into a country club
on the outskirts of Shanghai anxiously awaiting departure, Miss Bertha
among them. It was a miserable situation. Millions of mosquitoes
swarmed around their bodies literally sucking blood from sundown to
sunup. Even when they slept under nets, they could not keep the mosquitoes from their feast. The cots were so narrow it was impossible not to
touch the net during the night.

All Aboard

On July 15, 1942, after two weeks of misery, the Italian steamer, the
Conte Verde of the Lloyd Triestine Line, prepared to take the eager passengers aboard. Everyone was more than ready to climb on the buses for the
trip to the dock at 2:00 A.M. But they sat waiting; it was 5:00 before they
rolled through the streets of Shanghai singing, "On Christ the Solid Rock
I stand! All other ground is sinking sand!" They were extremely happy to

be leaving behind those hungry mosquitoes, not to mention the privations of internment. The *Conte Verde* sailed out of Shanghai with one happy group of Americans.

While aboard ship Miss Bertha penned a letter to Dr. Maddry at the Foreign Mission Board. Twenty-five years had passed since her appointment to China by the Board. She wrote, "A quarter of a century of success and failure and joys and sorrows! . . . I am glad that He has taught me that it is no affair of mine where my human body is. My only concern is to follow where He leads either to a definite work or away from it. . . . Being repatriated is truly the exceeding, abundant, above all I had thought or asked. Truly I praise Him, not only for what He has done in bringing me home where I will be free to witness to His power to souls in need, while I await the opening of China's door, but for the fact that He fills my soul with Himself, delivering from all anxiety, for myself as well for His work."[1] They were bound for East Africa where they would board another vessel for America.

According to a bulletin from the Foreign Mission Board on July 22, ships were lined up in Portuguese East Africa to make the exchange. The *Conte Verde* along with the *Asama Maru* were carrying about fifteen hundred Americans and other non-Axis nationals on their way home from Japan and Japanese-occupied territory. While at Portuguese East Africa waiting to board the *Gripsholm*, a Swedish exchange ship scheduled to take Bertha to America, she and other Baptist missionaries had opportunity to see the Swiss mission work in the port city of Lourenço Marques. They were also permitted to visit a Swedish Baptist couple out in the bush. On Sunday afternoon, a local African preacher met them and praised the Lord for His protection over them. He said, "You need not be surprised that the kingdoms of this world are at war. This world does not want our Christ and His gospel. Our Lord plainly told us of these coming events that we might not be taken by surprise."[2] It was an encouragement to all.

A few minor hurdles still remained before Bertha set foot on American soil. According to a news release by the *New York Times*, "There was a great deal of confusion on the *Gripsholm* today [July 25] as officers and passengers tried to straighten out matters over accommodations. As a result of the mix-up in cabin allotments many slept on decks and in lounges last night." Mary L. Dodson in her account said that the cabins and the dining rooms were not ready for the passengers. So the crew spread a picnic lunch on the decks. She said all agreed it was better than any food they had ever seen. She heard one man say, "Is there any such food as that in the world yet?" Over fifteen hundred people were fed well by the crew.

The *Gripsholm* had a large red cross inscribed on both sides of the hull. The vessel had been painted completely white so there would be no chance of being torpedoed. It sailed around the Cape of Good Hope and across the Atlantic to Rio de Janeiro, a two-week trip. Many interesting persons were on board, some fifty diplomats, including personnel from several South American countries. Dr. Theron Rankin, one of the Southern Baptist missionaries on board, cabled the Mission Board from the *Gripsholm* on July 27. It read: "FORTY MISSIONARIES GRIPSHOLM WELL—THERON RANKIN." The Department of State had listed thirty-nine missionaries for repatriation. Who was the fortieth? Mrs. Cecil S. Ward had given birth to a son, James. Later Dr. Rankin became the general secretary of the Foreign Mission Board.

When the *Gripsholm* sailed into Rio's beautiful harbor, the faithful missionaries saw the 125-foot Corcovado statue of Christ that overlooks Rio de Janeiro. Miss Bertha was not thrilled. The crucifix spoke to her of the spiritual deadness on the continent of South America at that time. They spent thirty-six hours in Rio. Thus they had time to see some of the sights. There were forty-four Baptist churches in the Brazilian city. They departed the next day at four o'clock in the afternoon. As they sailed out of the harbor, they looked back at the sun setting between the high mountain peaks, spreading its blaze of glory over the city, a never-to-be-forgotten sight.

As they traveled north toward New York, they spotted a tiny object on the horizon. When the ship drew closer, they saw the remains of a naval vessel that had just been torpedoed. The captain sailed around the sinking vessel to see if there were any living sailors on board, but he found none. The fate of the crew remained a mystery to Bertha.

On August 27, 1942, a lovely bright day, the *Gripsholm* entered New York harbor. All fifteen hundred passengers saw the Statue of Liberty gleaming in the morning sun. What a treat—what a relief!

After they docked, the inevitable paperwork began. The joy and excitement soon turned to impatience for those whose names began with letters at the end of the alphabet. It took the FBI an incredibly long time to screen each person and to telephone the references given to them. Miss Bertha said, "I assure you that I was ready to change my name and take any Aaron that could be found, before bedtime the third day when they got through with S!"[3] But the Lord gives patience. Soon they made their way to their accommodations. Bertha was greeted by the Mission Board secretary and friends when she arrived at the Prince George Hotel. She quickly scanned through her mail to see whether her eighty-year-old mother was still living. When she left her two and a half years before, she was not well. Bertha never dreamed she would see her again in this life, but the Lord provided an answer to prayer in a marvelous way. Bertha rejoiced that her mother was still alive, not well at all, but she would see her again. Mary Dodson said, "While interned in Kobe we started a prayer meeting, and continued it on the *Asama*. The people from China, on the *Conte Verde* did the same and we united on the *Gripsholm*. There were forty different denominations, representing nearly seven hundred Protestant missionaries. Not all of them attended these prayer meetings. However, among those who attended, there was such a unity of spirit and love for the Lord that it was a great inspiration to all. One great theme of the prayers was revival—revival in me, revival on the boat, revival in the lands we had left, revival in the church in America."[4]

Bertha soon arrived in Cowpens to a glorious reunion.

A New Ministry

In December Miss Bertha received a letter from Dr. Maddry asking if she would be willing to serve at Fort Bragg in Fayetteville, North Carolina. There was a need for workers with young people and children, especially young women. House-to-house visitation in the interest of evangelism stood as the primary task. By the time Bertha received the invitation, she had many engagements for Sunday services in churches. People were responding well to her messages. In this itinerant ministry, she also raised monies for the China Famine Relief Fund. In her reply to Dr. Maddry, Bertha stated she was willing to do whatever the Board thought best for her, then added: "I am not interested in doing ordinary pastor's assistant work. I want to give all my time to direct evangelistic work to the young men who must be snatched from hell at once." The Board chose to allow her to stay at home with her mother who at the time was confined to her room because of poor health and to continue her itinerant ministry in the churches.

In May 1943 Bertha corresponded with Dr. Rankin of the Mission Board. The Board was considering sending a few missionaries back to free China and Bertha was among those being considered. She said, "Believing the Lord brought me home to my aged mother as well as to give a message to the churches on Sundays, I am in no hurry to rush back into China as conditions are now, even in free China." She had enough engagements to keep her busy speaking in churches for over a year.

At Home

Bertha enjoyed happy years at home with her mother and reveled in the privilege of witnessing to the triumph of faith. She lived on in Cowpens until the war was over. On August 14, 1945, Japan surrendered. On V-J Day, Wednesday, August 15, at a thanksgiving service held in her church, she delivered a stirring message. It was an able survey of the wars of history and the futility of such engagements. She attacked the thorny issue of why God allows people to slaughter one another. The lengthy address demonstrated her grasp of history and the unfolding of God's providence. She had a very fertile mind as well as a fervent spirit. When Bertha finished her message, all the people said, "Amen." It had been a tremendous experience, historically and spiritually, to hear this woman of God.

Bertha remained on in America for three more years after the war ended. These were rather silent years for our woman of revival. As she said, she "sweated out" those years from 1942 to 1948. Her heart longed to return to China, and yet, being with her family was an unexpected and necessary blessing. Joy filled her heart when the door finally opened to return to China to work with a new Chinese government that promised complete religious liberty. The new leaders of the country, Chiang Kai-shek and Madam Chiang Kai-shek, were dedicated Christians and were determined that China would have religious liberty and freedom. Soon Bertha found herself headed back to her beloved China. The future looked bright—but not for long.

13

The Open Door Closes

Olive Lawton *Credit: FMB*

On the way back to the field in 1948 between Yokohama and China, Miss Bertha penned a letter to sisters Jennie and Ethel from the *S. S. General Gordon*: "I have been sick less than on any other trip. I was in bed only three and one-half days, and that only a day at a time. Of course, my head was never normal, but by lying down in time and taking dry soda crackers and an apple for a meal, I was not nauseated." Sailing never was Bertha's forte. While in port at Yokohama the passengers were allowed to go ashore on a tour planned by the shipping company. The tour was a twenty-mile drive from Yokohama to Tokyo; all aboard the bus were surprised by the incredible devastation on both sides of the highway. Miss Bertha exclaimed, "What a change in the attitude and atmosphere of Japan! One could not help but think of the expression, 'Babylon the mighty is fallen!'"

The New Work Begins with Uncertainty

When the missionaries of all denominations and groups finally returned to their fields in 1948, they immediately threw themselves into cleaning buildings and opening the schools and churches. Across China they inaugurated a full program of preaching and worship, developing and instructing the Chinese Christians. The Marxist specter had already reared its head, becoming entrenched in adjoining provinces to the west and north of Shantung. In some nearby sections, the political pendulum had swung back and forth between the Nationalists and Communists five times. Still, the missionaries prayed that the national army would eventually be victorious over the atheistic hoards of the Marxists. But it did not look hopeful.

The Connelys and Fern Harrington left Tsining just before Bertha's arrival in March. They headed for Shanghai on Friday, February 27. Frank had been transferred to Shanghai to serve as treasurer for the mission work in China. Fern visited friends in Yanchow, then proceeded to Shanghai to pack the things she had in storage so they could be sent back to Tsining, where she would serve with Miss Bertha. In a letter she wrote on March 2, 1948, she said, "Bertha's boat was due in today but has been delayed until tomorrow." The following day the boat arrived, at about 9:30 A.M. What a reunion! One can imagine that Bertha almost wanted to kiss the Chinese soil. She roomed across the street from Fern in Shanghai for a short period, which made it convenient for them to make enthusiastic plans for their new, resumed work. Fern left Shanghai for Tsining before Miss Bertha so she could get her things unpacked in Tsining before Bertha arrived with hers.

By the time Fern had her things unpacked and the garden planted, even before Bertha could leave Shanghai for Tsining, word came that the political situation was becoming very bleak. She and the Walters, a Presbyterian couple who had lived with the Connelys, began packing their things so, as she put it, "to be in readiness to leave if [the Communists] started pushing this way." Bertha wondered whether she should go on to Tsining since things were so uncertain. She sent word that if she did come, she would move into the Connelys' house and not open her house or ship her things. The following week, the Walters made the decision to leave. On April 17 Fern was surprised to see Miss Bertha standing at her door. She had been able to secure permission from the Consul to come for a short period. Fern said, "When she arrived she sat her suitcases down and started to work. She held evangelistic services in the morning, Bible classes in the evening, and in the afternoon had personal conferences with students who wanted to know how to be saved. I was tremendously impressed. She was doing what most missionaries feel should have top priority, but most of us get side tracked into other things."[1] Bertha felt she must make each day count; but then she always felt that way.

After a week or two, the missionaries began to sense that their days in Tsining were numbered. The Communists to the west, who had been driven back three times, had once again returned. This time they had a much larger army and were taking and holding everything they attacked. Yet, Tsining itself was rather quiet. The Chinese felt safe, at least for a few more weeks. The missionaries had confidence that there would be a way of escape if necessary.

Fern may have been a bit more apprehensive than Miss Bertha since she had been interned by the Japanese in the Philippines for about three and a half years. Her internment had been very difficult. Near the end, food became scarce and she suffered from beriberi, a vitamin B deficiency. For many days she had only corn mush made from corn infested with weevils and mold to eat. At first she would close her eyes to keep from seeing the weevils floating in her bowl; then she told herself they were added protein. Even though internment was difficult at best, the internees banded together to aid, encourage, and support to one another. They became a clear witness to those in charge of the camp.

The Walters decided they must leave, and departed on Monday, May 3. Bertha and Fern packed up their dishes. "Tuesday breakfast," said Fern, "we held our breaths to see how [the servants] would serve. Salt appeared in a vegetable bowl. . . . Sugar came in a pint fruit jar. Coffee was served in eggshell thin rice bowls without saucers. After breakfast Bertha and I went uptown to see what we could buy. We got some very attractive cups and saucers for about 25 cents apiece, vinegar bottle, some powder boxes of sugar, butter, and jam. We found some very pretty pitchers for cream and syrup and shocked the servants. They said they were used to brush teeth and gargle in the morning! No doubt they hurt to see them on our table but we still think they are pretty."[2]

Miss Bertha and Fern heard that missionary Alex Herring had evacuated his family from Honan Province. The Herrings moved down to the seaport of Shanghai, a move essential for their safety. Bertha sent for Alex to come and preach for them in Tsining until they would all have to leave. They felt it would be the last opportunity for many years for a missionary to render such a service to the Tsining church. As the situation continued to deteriorate, it looked as though they would have to leave even before Alex could come and hold the meetings. Bertha and Fern began making plans to depart. They received a letter from Alex saying he would be arriving on Saturday to begin a week of revival services. Fern said, "Bertha, he just doesn't know what's going on up here. We'll have to send him a wire and tell him not to come." Bertha said, "Not so fast, let's wait a minute. Let's pray about it first; maybe the Lord is in this." So, they went to God in earnest prayer, seeking His will and purpose.

"As we prayed," said Fern, "the Lord showed me the people in the streets of Tsining, lost, without hope, faces filled with the dread of living under the Communists." The church had not been a good witness because of petty bickering within. Tsining needed a fresh touch of revival. They did not send Alex a wire. He came.

The Last Meeting

God honored the meetings tremendously. Fern said, "I had never seen the Holy Spirit work in power as He did that week. At the invitation the whole audience it seemed would surge down the aisles. Alex would say, 'You don't understand.' And still they came, kneeling in front of the pulpit. Tears literally made puddles on the floor as they prayed for forgiveness from sin and for victory to live in the power of the Lord."[3] During the second service, Alex exaggerated a true illustration he was using to make a point. Afterwards the Holy Spirit convicted him. The next day he made an open confession to the congregation. This made such a deep impression on the congregation that the Chinese believers threw themselves into the meetings with all their hearts. They said, "This is a true man of God who has come to lead us. He is willing to lose face to straighten out his wrongs in order to keep right with God."[4] Both Christians and many non-Christians were gloriously transformed. They all agreed as Bertha expressed it, "What a tragedy if we had left as we had planned." They had prayed that the Communists would stay back until the week was over, and the Lord answered the cry of their hearts. The minute the meetings drew to a close, the Communists moved in.

The Move

Since Miss Bertha had feared she would not be in Tsining long, she had not shipped her things from Shanghai. She found packing easy, though it proved most difficult to think of leaving. She had been there such a short time. But thank God for that touch of revival. Before Alex arrived, she had already sent her piano and typewriter, and the few other pieces of furniture on a little truck over the border to Hsuchow in Kiangsu Province. These items had been stored by a friend while she was in the States. She planned to take by train her few other furnishings, as she said, "by hiring a man who understood shipping and changing trains to accompany the goods." They tried to rent trucks from the Tsining Catholic mission, but were unable to do so since they were busy moving their own things. Fern said, "We laid our problem before the Lord, and (would you believe it!) a huge truck appeared on May 17, asking if we had anything to ship to Hsuchow. The trucker was from Tsinan and was sending his trucks to Hsuchow to keep them from being confiscated by the Communists."[5] He could take the missionaries to Yenchow, their destination.

By Monday morning, May 31, Bertha and Fern were seemingly cut off from the outside world. (The Communists had cut every telephone wire and dynamited the railroads.) They thanked God for the trucks. So on board they climbed with their possessions. They made the trip on rough, rutty roads. Miss Bertha sat up front with the driver. Alex, a teacher, the cook, a boy looking after the freight, and Fern rode on top of the "stuff." Three of them sat on Fern's bed crate and put their feet on top of the cab and "were quite comfortable except for the fact that the crating gave one the sensation of having a corrugated seat,"[6] as Fern described it. When they reached Yenchow, they discovered the railway had been broken both north and south of the city. There was no room for them in the hotel situated inside the city wall. They found rooms at a small inn outside the city by the railway station and settled in for a week. Sleeping proved to be very uncomfortable, but they managed—they had so done many times before; they could make out now.

The floors of the little inn were tramped earth and the beds consisted of planks laid across low saw horses with stalks woven together for a mattress and straw matting over that to make it smooth. Miss Bertha had her own quilts to put over the straw mats which made it a little more bearable for sleep. Bertha said she longed for her Beautyrest mattress in Shanghai, the gift of a friend.

The Battles

The battle between the Nationalists and the Communists began to erupt everywhere. The skirmishes with the Reds forced the Nationalist army to move inside the walled city where Bertha, Fern, and Alex also retreated. The missionaries, as paying guests, took refuge in the Catholic Hospital operated by nuns. They were destined to be there six weeks before it was all over. The hospital, a large complex in the northwest corner of the city, was separated from the city wall by its truck gardens. The Catholic mission compound had formerly been an estate owned by a rich Chinese man. It had several buildings, a park with all sorts of beautiful old trees, a rockery, lake, and about two or three thousand acres of land.

The Catholic mission stood in the line of fire, a dangerous position. The Nationalist general had closed the boys' boarding school and established his headquarters there. He liked the luxury of the bishop's home. Most of the firing occurred at night, and occasionally bullets whizzed "through our room just where we had been, but never where we were,"

Bertha said. All lights were turned off at night for fear of Communist attack. The Nationalists were doing all they could to hold the city. But at night the air was filled with the sound of artillery bursts, small arms fire, machine guns sputtering away, and trench mortars exploding. Many hand grenades were thrown. It had been ten years since Miss Bertha had experienced the Japanese siege at Tsining, and here she was thrust into the same scenario.

The faithful missionaries kept busy nonetheless. Fern worked on the Chinese language daily with her teacher. Alex spent his time studying the more than forty thousand Chinese characters and gave himself to sermon preparation. Bertha delved into Bible study in both English and Chinese. They all had ample time to pray and seek the Lord.

It seemed there would be no end as the war thundered on. Night after night, as soon as dusk fell, Bertha and her small party took their seats on the cement floor below the window sill. They were trusting the Lord to take care of them, but she said, "We were giving Him our best cooperation."[7] During those long, dreary, yet exciting hours, they would sing the great old hymns they knew from memory. When they would finally decide to go to bed, they often felt more comfortable sleeping under the beds than on them. It was a stressful, nerve-wracking time. Only God's peace could sustain them.

At last they received a reply to a radio message Alex had been able to send to mission headquarters in Shanghai; a Lutheran airplane would come to pick them up on June 18. They arrived at the airport by nine o'clock. They took little baggage in order to allow as many as possible, including the Catholic missionaries, to go with them. They sat in the hot June sun all day. No plane arrived. Miss Bertha said, "How tired, hot, thirsty, and disappointed we were at the close of the day, when every plane speck viewed on the horizon had proved to be a buzzard."[8] At noon, a Catholic sister came to them by ricksha and brought some hard-boiled eggs, sour bread, and a pig lard sandwich—a very high cholesterol diet by today's standards; but it was all they had. Fern said, "The idea of lard sandwiches didn't appeal to me much, but I was hungry and they weren't too bad."

That morning Bertha had left the Catholic mission station heavy-hearted. Ming Kuang (meaning "Bright Light"), the nineteen-year-old young man she had hired to handle the baggage, had professed to receive Christ. Yet, he showed no true signs of having "passed from death to life." She knew that when the Communists took the city, he would be forced to join the army. She was willing to stay a few more days in order to see him gain the full assurance of his salvation. She could not bear the thought that he could lose his life in the civil war without having been truly saved.

When the airplane failed to arrive, they all returned to the mission station. The very next day Ming Kuang did become indeed "Bright Light." Bertha led him into full repentance and faith in the Lord Jesus Christ. His life was radically transformed. Now whatever happened, he would be safe and secure in Jesus Christ. Miss Bertha rejoiced. The missionaries had been conducting Sunday morning worship along with Sunday school and a service on Wednesday. These services were held in the barnyard. At the close of the Sunday service after "Bright Light" came to faith, he stood, with his face aglow, and thanked God for his salvation and his acceptance into the family of God.

The Impact of the Testimony

The director of the Catholic mission, a German priest about thirty-five years of age, spoke good English and had a winsome personality. He would often visit with the Baptist missionaries. He came to visit soon after hearing Ming Kuang's ringing testimony, so Bertha shared with him "Bright Light's" experience. She told it with all the delight she would have related to a Baptist preacher. The priest began to ask one question after another. Alex answered all his questions. The priest especially enjoyed talking to Alex. A German family of five, all of whom were professing Protestant believers, and their Chinese language teacher and her daughter were at the mission also. All were aware of "Bright Light's" conversion. Ming Kuang's testimony touched many. They thanked God that the Lutheran airplane did not keep its schedule.

As the situation grew more tense, the airport closed. Fern said, "We can't send out wires or letters but are thankful our communications with God still hold and thus we are not without contact with the outside world!"[9] They sensed it would be some time before they could get out, so they set up some semblance of a normal life. For example, the only place they had to walk for exercise and diversion was in the barnyard. But they kept a regular exercise routine. Because of her previous internment, Fern had become adept at making do with what was on hand. She found knitting needles and yarn in her trunk and taught Alex to knit. He would laugh at himself as he began to learn, but kept at it until he finished a light blue sweater with a white border for his baby back in Shanghai. Alex made a chessboard on the side of his suitcase and carved chess men from cheap Chinese laundry soap. Fern, a talented artist, had her paints with her so she painted half the chess men black. Bertha said that the hand-crafted chess set looked like the real thing. Alex taught Fern to play chess but Bertha confessed, "I tried once but was too dumb to learn in the time I was willing to give to it."[10] Bertha, anything but dumb, just could not sit for hours on end playing chess.

Bertha facetiously said that she and Fern had an outing once a week when they went to the "beauty parlor." Their beauty parlor consisted of the cook's big cooking pot in the barnyard that they filled with hot water for a good shampoo. It was a far cry from the real thing, but as Bertha said, "It made them beautiful enough." While in the barnyard on these weekly outings, they could see the Nationalists' planes fly in and drop parcels by parachute that contained money, rice, and vegetables for the army. Sometimes there would be several drops a day. The whole situation remained tense, despite the missionaries' attempt to have some sort of normalcy.

On the Fourth of July, they had a surprise visit from an American priest who resided at the Catholic mission. He had grown up in a German community in Minnesota. Bertha confessed he was more German than American, however. Nevertheless, they enjoyed having one with them who knew of American Independence Day. He had lunch with his fellow Americans, which meant a better-than-usual meal with a special treat, a can of Del Monte peaches for dessert. What a treat these peaches were! The normal fare at the mission fell far short of good food. Bertha said she had never seen good ingredients so ruined in a kitchen. She observed, "From the abundant gardens the only vegetable that came to us was cabbage, which had been boiled for three hours into a reddish pulp." The rice was sweetened, and Bertha said, "We would have not eaten those awful starched puddings had we not been so hungry." But Fern added, "They had plenty of fireworks for the Fourth!"—compliments of the Communist artillery.

Miss Bertha lost fifteen pounds in six weeks. But she said, "What grieved us was that this fare was the year-in-and-year-out diet of the sisters." Alex got sick and asked for rice gruel only. The gruel tasted so good that they all asked for it daily at supper time. Once the cook accidentally served the starch made for the bibs and head gear of the Catholic sisters.

The head priest, fearing for the Baptists' safety, suggested that when the city fell to the Communists, Bertha and Fern don a nun's habit so they might be taken for Germans. They thanked him with a smile but graciously refused.[11] They continued trusting the Lord. They had been born in America, and were willing to suffer whatever ignominy might come their way. They were confident the Lord could well care for them as Americans just as easily as if they were Germans.

As the days of July slowly passed, it became too hot for Alex to be comfortable in the winter clothes he had brought with him. The sewing machine from the girls' school had been put in the hospital hallway outside Fern and Bertha's room. Fern took a piece of khaki from her trunk and made Alex two pairs of shorts. She had learned to cut out garments without a pattern while interned during the previous war with Japan. This forced training served them well. Alex was comfortable and pleased with his shorts.

On the afternoon of July 12, Fern and the cook went to the barnyard where their trunks were stored to exchange a few items. Right then the Communists let loose an artillery barrage against their corner of the city. Fern and her helper made a mad dash to the haystack in the big barn where they stayed until after sundown. Bertha and Alex were at the hospital praying for a lull so Fern and the cook could get back. As it began to grow dark, Fern grew fearful that Alex would come to see if they were safe. Fern said, "Shells were falling like hail." She prayed, "Lord, I cannot let Alex Herring, who has a wife and four children to live for, run any risk in coming over here to see about me. I have just got to go back. You know where I am going to be!"[12] She started to run. But running proved unnecessary since, as she recounted the story, "God stopped those shells the minute I took the first step." It was as though someone had turned off a running faucet. They walked back to the hospital, the equivalent of two blocks. The moment they entered the hospital grounds, the shelling commenced again. Alex was just about to go for her when she burst in. God cared.

The Fall of the City

The shelling and firing continued all night. Bertha and Fern moved their beds into a small room across the hall, a bit farther away from the guns. Bertha said, "I do not know why we were so optimistic as to think we would need beds!" Since there would be no sleeping and Alex's room was more exposed, they invited him to join them. The three of them began to sing hymns. Fern said, "Bertha knows more hymns from memory than any person I know, not just the first verse, but all the verses." While singing "How Firm a Foundation," suddenly a deafening roar, a flash of light, and a blast of hot air filled with shrapnel blew the door in. They rolled under the bed and in a few minutes Bertha's clear voice came through singing the last verse: "I'll never no never no never forsake." Bertha had anything but a solo voice, but she learned to sing from the heart, and that held her in good faith under such circumstances. She said,

> Seven verses of it had seen me through three or four wars before. I finished the first six verses, reminding ourselves that no other promises than those which we had were needed, and no matter what our condition, the water could not drown us and the fire could not burn us; and

even when human strength was gone, we would have no cause for worry, for the Lord Himself would do for us all that we could need.[13]

It was into the night when the shell burst broke in on them. They were exhausted and tired. But Bertha said she was not tired anymore; she got a good shock treatment that really woke her up. Shell fragments had peppered the room. Bertha said there was not one spot as big as her hand anywhere on the wall that was not pock-marked by shrapnel. Not only that, when Alex moved from where he had been sitting, leaning against the wall, he left a perfectly clean silhouette of his body on the peppered wall. Not one of the three had one scratch. Miracle!

They moved to the basement at the insistence of one of the sisters. There they had to stand for hours. Finally, Bertha sat down on a canvas stool opposite a glass door, a dangerous place to be. Suddenly another shell burst shattered the full-length door all over her. She said, "Had my face been scarred, I would have lost no beauty, but had my spectacles been broken, I would have been ruined." Miss Bertha was born farsighted. But she neither lost her spectacles nor was scarred. She would say, "Miracle!"

Fern explained, "After the glass shattered, a man who had been scalped came running down the hall. He was being chased by the Reds. [The Communists had invaded the mission compound.] They were shooting everywhere. Pandemonium broke loose. The Chinese in the hallway said, 'We are civilians; have mercy.' They fell to the floor. I wanted to too. But I looked at Bertha and there she was standing straight and as proud as if she were waiting to receive an honorary degree. I remained standing too. The soldier stopped and said, 'We'll treat you good.'"[14] They wanted the Americans to tell the government back home they were not as bad as most Americans thought. Bertha had to admit, however, the first time she saw the place full of Communists, fear so possessed her for a second that she ran back into her room. She confessed, "How ashamed I was of so dishonoring my Lord who had been my protector and my peace for thirty-one years through every ill-wind that had blown!" But she quickly refocused her attention to the command and promise in Philippians 4:6–7: "Be careful for nothing; but in every thing by prayer and supplication with thanksgiving let your requests be made known unto God. And the peace of God, which passeth all understanding, shall keep your hearts and minds through Christ Jesus." Fern said, "The greatest miracle of all was the peace He gave us when in the greatest danger."

When things quieted down, they went back upstairs to their rooms, exhausted and starved. They had not eaten for thirty hours. Bertha and Fern went down to the kitchen for some food. Dead and wounded Chinese were everywhere. It was a horrible sight. The heat was oppressive. All they found was coffee and cold sour bread made into lard sandwiches. To make things worse, the sandwiches were covered with a cloth red with human blood. A few cookies they discovered helped somewhat. But they made out. The three of them then took turns taking a nap on Alex's bed. While Bertha slept, Alex and Fern played chess.

When the battle finally ended, the soldiers looted the city. Bertha said, "The mission had been turned into a wreck. With broken windows and doors, the hospital began to swarm with flies. Garden walls and pigpens were knocked down, and hogs devastated the vegetables. The air was foul with the stench of the unburied dead."[15] All of the lovely stained glass windows in the cathedral had been ripped out by the strafing. One of the bombs fell through the roof of the sisters' dormitory and plunged through three stories to the basement without exploding. That afternoon Fern was looking at the sky and said, "Bertha, look at the sky. There's not a shell hole in it." Bertha replied, "Well, there would have been if they could have reached it." In fact, the lovely blue sky with patches of fleecy clouds was all that did appear the same. Bertha declared, "We rejoice that it was above the reach of sinful man's destructive powers."[16] But now that they were in the hands of the Communist army, what would they do?

The Last Journey

Alex suggested they begin walking to the nearest undamaged railhead many miles away. The Communists had blown up the rail line for miles in all directions from Yenchow. Some of the Catholics had already slipped out of the city through a hole in the wall. But Bertha prayed that the new officials would give them a travel permit. After three days the Communists set up a local government office. Alex called upon the officials while Miss Bertha and Fern continued to pray. God heard and they were given travel permits to leave the following Saturday. The two women then prayed that the Lord would give them transportation. Fern asked for a cart with rubber tires and Miss Bertha asked for two. God graciously heard. The Catholics gave them two carts with rubber tires for twenty silver dollars. One of them even had springs. As they rolled out of the city, a Chinese teacher, Mr. Kao, exclaimed, "I knew that the Lord was wonderful, but I never dreamed that he could be this wonderful!"[17]

They were allowed to take only a small amount of baggage. Miss Bertha said, "What decisions for two women to make!" But off they went. They made only twenty miles the first day. At the end of the day the group was welcomed by Baptists in a county-seat town. Soon after their arrival the pastor disappeared on his bicycle. In what seemed like only a few minutes he returned with a basket of eggs, eggplant, and ten pounds of noodles.

Everyone pitched in to help prepare the meal. Bertha recounted that in a little while they were all "seated in the yard in the moonlight enjoying a good supper and feeling that we were in the suburbs of heaven!"

The group traveled on, and late in the afternoon of the third day they reached a city still in the hands of the Nationalists. They were warmly received. The Nationalists helped them catch a freight train taking ammunition and refugees the twenty-five miles to Hsuchow. The train took no rest stops. They reached the city at about seven o'clock in the evening and quickly bought tickets to Shanghai by the next train, scheduled to leave at nine o'clock the next morning. However, the Communists tore up fifty miles of railroad track that night. So they stayed with Presbyterian missionary friends in Hsuchow and, as Bertha wrote in a letter, "What a joy to again have American food and the comforts of a home! I almost forgot my blistered arms and sore lips from the parching heat."[18] Alex secured a flight on a Chinese military plane to Shanghai, and then arranged transportation for Fern, Miss Bertha, and the Catholics who had also reached Hsuchow. The following morning Fern and Miss Bertha were off by cargo plane to Tsingtau for the annual Mission Meeting. Bertha had the privilege of speaking to a Young People's Conference twice and was excited that Dr. Culpepper was to be one of the speakers for the Mission Meeting. The meeting became a season of great refreshment. Upon its conclusion they enjoyed a time of rest in Tsingtau, then left for Shanghai on the long-promised Lutheran airplane.

Bertha and Fern were "spoiled" while in Tsingtau. They slept late. The breakfast bell rang at 7:30 A.M. and, as Bertha said, "We took that for a rising bell to go down in housecoats." After the noon meal they rested. She said, "We are making up for all lost time up here where we have peaches every morning at breakfast and ice cream two or three times a week, and all the fresh vegetables we need and meat too."[19] They had supper on the beach several evenings. Bertha regretted she had no bathing suit, for she would have loved to plunge into the sea for a good swim.

For Miss Bertha, the door of service to her beloved Chinese on the mainland of China was rapidly closing, with no immediate hope of reopening. With a sad heart Miss Bertha turned her eyes toward the future. She rested in the knowledge that her trust in the Lord would enable Him to make her pathway straight. And God met that need in His grace. A new and exciting ministry opened.

Part IV
Formosa
Opens Its Doors

Bertha Smith, Leon Hwa and two students from the Taiwan Baptist Theological Seminary in prayer before embarking on missionary activities. *Credit: FMB*

14

A New Challenge

Bertha relaxing at home in 1954. *Credit: FMB*

When Bertha and Fern arrived in Shanghai, Baker James Cauthen, secretary of the Foreign Mission Board for the Orient, asked Bertha if she would visit Kanchow in South China. This field needed seasoned missionary leadership. Before responding, she went to her knees in prayer and then said, "I knew at once that I was not to go there. I did not have to see the work." The Mission treasury was saved the expense and she the weariness of travel.

A New Open Door

Two Southern Baptist missionaries, Roberta Pearle Johnson and Lila Watson, who were serving in Shanghai, had recently returned from a brief visit to Formosa, now known as Taiwan. The island, about 240 miles long and 90 miles wide, was discovered by fishermen who called it Taiwan, which in Chinese dialect means "platform in the bay." That has always been its Chinese name. When Portuguese travelers got their first view of the large island, they called it "Formosa Ilha," in Portuguese "beautiful isle."

Both Lila and Pearl became convinced by their visit that a door for gospel work in Formosa stood wide open. They urged Bertha to move there and take up the challenge even though the Southern Baptists had no work in Formosa at the time. Bertha was especially suited for this sort of task because she spoke Mandarin, the official language of Formosa. The possibilities did seem limitless; even the politics favored it.

The island had been returned to China by Japan at the end of World War II. Political leadership in Formosa was dominated by Chinese Nationalists from the mainland. The island had been restored by treaty to Nationalist China after the 1943 Cairo meeting of Prime Minister Winston Churchill, President Franklin D. Roosevelt, and President Chiang Kai-shek. As the Nationalist and Communist war raged on China's mainland, Chinese streamed to the "beautiful isle" by the thousands. When mainland China fell to the Communists, Chiang Kai-shek moved to Formosa and set up a Nationalist government. Perhaps strangely, Mao Tse-tung and his Communist hordes did not follow. Formosa became a nation of Chinese Nationalists. This opened the door for Christian missions.

Bertha continued praying that the Lord would lead her to her next field of service, and soon full assurance came that she should set up new Baptist work in Formosa. However, the Foreign Mission Board had adopted the policy: "No new work." She waited on the Lord. In the thirty-one years she had been a missionary, the Spirit of God had never directed her to do anything contrary to Board policy. She was confident that God would open the doors if He wanted her in Formosa. She waited, and God acted.

The Executive Committee of the Baptist work in Shanghai heard of Bertha's desire to go to Formosa. They said they would be willing to extend the home mission work of their Convention into Formosa and have Miss Bertha go as their missionary, provided the Foreign Mission Board would support the idea and "lend" her to them. The Board granted this request and continued Bertha's support, though she now worked under the agency of the Shanghai Baptists. She was off to her new work, this time as a pioneer missionary to an unreached field for Southern Baptists.

As the plane circled Taipei, the capital city of Formosa, on October 19, 1948, Bertha surveyed the beautiful isle. The Holy Spirit whispered in her heart what He had said to Paul in Corinth: "I have much people in this city." She said, "I knew He wanted me to find them and bring them to know Him."

Settling In

Only one place in the city provided Bertha with a private room, the Taipei Guest House near the Tam Shui River. Most inns were Japanese-style with large rooms where many persons could sleep on straw mats, which often covered the floor from wall to wall. The guest house, owned by the China travel agency, was only for transients, and guests could stay there only a limited number of days. When Bertha's allotted time expired, God met her need. The manager, a Christian, assigned her a small room ordinarily used by Chinese folk traveling with their own bedding. The room had a little narrow bed without springs or mattress, only woven cane. But Bertha was well accustomed to that sort of sleeping accommodation, even though it was hardly her favorite. A small wardrobe, a chair, and a table sat beside the bed. This meager furniture filled the room. Bertha remarked, "There was just enough space left near the foot of the bed for me to get on my knees."[1] As a veteran soldier of the cross, she knew how to make sacrifices for the sake of leading people to Jesus Christ.

Things had drastically changed from the first time Bertha sailed to China many years earlier. At that time she was met by missionaries, housed by missionaries, had someone to provide her meals and guide her activities. When she arrived in Formosa, she had nothing—no place to live, no provision for food, no fellow missionaries, nothing! But she still had God's promises: His love, His care, His presence, and His leadership. That was enough for Bertha. And Pastor Yang Mei Tsai of Chefoo was temporarily stationed there with the All-China Baptist Convention. So she settled in, ready to go to work for her Lord.

Transportation in Taipei was very difficult. The place had been inundated with refugees from the mainland to the point that the transportation system had virtually broken down. Some dilapidated buses would travel up and down the main street and across the river. Yet, no schedule could be relied upon. Not only that, when the buses passed over the river and then returned to the city, they were literally packed, standing room only, if any of that could be found. Taxies in Taipei were few—one old station wagon and two five-passenger touring cars. These could be hired, but no assurance guaranteed that they would ever make it to their destination. Pedi-cabs only came halfway to the guest house. Consequently, Bertha had to walk a mile to make a connection with one.

On her regular trek to get one of the man-pulled cabs, she would walk in the middle of the reasonably empty wide streets so she could sing without disturbing the residents on both sides. She always had a song of joy to the Lord.

Miss Bertha's first task was to locate a meeting place and to find permanent housing. For three solid days, Bertha and Pastor Yang Me Tsai walked in search of a meeting place and housing. Bertha was exhausted. She must secure property as soon as possible. Tens of thousands of wealthy Chinese were arriving from the mainland and real estate prices were skyrocketing. To cap it off, Bertha was not getting proper food and one of the two quilts she had was too thick for cover and too thin for mattress and springs. She frankly confessed, "I needed a new touch from the Lord, so down to the river I went."

New Strength

The Japanese have great love for beauty, especially in regard to water and gardens. During their earlier occupation of Formosa, they had walled up the banks of the river and made a beautiful little garden along a narrow strip between the river and the road that paralleled it. An artistic concrete bridge spanned the river. On the other side of the river a half-dozen oriental junks sat motionless. On the horizon a beautiful hill covered with evergreen shrubs and bamboo waved gracefully in the breeze. Miss Bertha found the lovely spot and there she found an ideal place of rest and meditation. Still, she felt somewhat alone.

Miss Bertha was two days' travel by steamer or a thirty-dollar plane ticket away from her nearest American friends. She felt like a stranger in a strange land. But then she realized, "I am my Father's daughter, out on His plantation where I have a right to be!" Right at that moment of realization, as Bertha put it, "He threw upon the blue screen facing me, the most beautiful rainbow that I have ever seen—such width of stripes and gorgeous colors and tints!"[2] She remembered God's promise to Noah and asked herself, "What promise would the Lord keep to me?" Then Philippians 4:19 flashed into her mind: "But my God shall supply all your need according to his riches in glory by Christ Jesus." Bertha felt she needed a great deal: a comfortable place to live, proper food, and more than that, a place where people could assemble to hear the Word of God. But God's promise gave her absolute confidence that in His faithfulness He would meet every one of those needs. And it would all redound to His honor and glory.

As Bertha pondered God's promises, she noticed two fishermen pulling in their nets. She got up to see what kind of catch they had when she caught a glimpse of gleaming color on the horizon. She trudged up a small hill to get a better look at the glorious sunset. It filled her soul. She wondered, "When the 'Son of Righteousness' comes, could His 'beams' be more glorious?" In the meantime she would trust God for everything. The heavens do "declare the glory of God."

The next day, Bertha made contact with several real estate agents. While looking for housing, she heard of a fair in progress in a large five-story government building. She took a break from her housing search, and in her usual fashion took her bag of tracts and went to see the exhibits. As the providence of God would have it, school was out and all the students and teachers in town were at the fair. She took her stand in a prominent place to hand out gospel tracts. Rarely were the tracts refused. Bertha said, "When the Word has been put into the hand and mind, the soul can be prayed for."[3] Moreover, she said, "I became exhibit number one!" [4]

Many students from the provinces had never seen an American woman, and when they kept coming for tracts, Bertha said to them, "Mei yiu la." In Chinese that literally means "no more." One young man who overheard her reply asked where she learned to say "no more" in Chinese. They fell into conversation, exchanged cards, and began chatting away. He was a professor at Taiwan University. Bertha, of course, inevitably asked him whether he was a Christian. He replied, "I have been wanting to become one, but did not know how." She said, "All I could do then was set my prayers upon him." The ice was beginning to break.

One day, while taking care of business at the Bureau of Foreign Affairs, Bertha asked the head official whether he was a Christian. He replied, "Not yet, but I want to go to your home and talk with you."[5] A secretary in the Government Land Office and graduate of the University of Tokyo laughed and said, "I am a Chinese-Formosan-Japanese." He was wearing old U.S. Army clothes and struggling to speak English. Bertha, wanting him to become a believer, asked why he was not a Christian. He replied, "I very hope. For you come to my house, pray! I very welcome."[6] She was beginning to establish a ministry and discovering that many hearts were open to hear the Good News of Christ.

Mandarin is spoken in nine-tenths of China. Therefore, Bertha was conversant with thousands of the uprooted Chinese who had fled to Formosa. They were adrift without God. Torn away from families, cut off from their homeland, they were without hope, family, friends, and thus open to the gospel. The circumstances provided an incredible opportunity to witness. Many educated people of China had turned from idolatry but had nothing to replace it with. The field was "ripe unto harvest."

Miss Bertha described the city of Taipei as being "laid out like a wagon wheel with bus terminal, railway station, and post office and other government buildings at the hub. Streets ran out in every direction."[7] She would go to the bus terminal, take out a tract printed in Chinese and start reading it. Waiting passengers would look at her amazed and finally one would get up enough courage to ask, "Do you know what you are reading?" She would answer, "Yes, would you like to know?" The person would then reach for a tract; then the whole line of waiting passengers would take one. When that bus was loaded, she would move on to the next one. Many times she would be able to converse enough with an individual to get a card or address. This way she began to build a "prospect" list. Moreover, she was getting the gospel, even if only in tract form, to a multitude of people.

A New Friend

Bertha, quite naturally, had to register with the American Consulate in Taipei. The wife of a United States Vice-Consul, Dr. Scott George, learned about her presence. The next day Mrs. Scott and her five-year-old daughter, Lois, took Bertha for a ride around Taipei. At last she had an American friend. Mrs. George begged Bertha to conduct a worship service in English. She had tears in her eyes when she said she had lived in Taipei for a whole year and had only heard one sermon. The secretary for the Canadian Presbyterian Mission Board had come and preached.

Bertha spent several days fasting and praying that God would open the door for an adequate meeting place. Then at nine o'clock on the morning of her birthday, she went to see the mayor of the city to ask him about rentals. He was a native Formosan, a professing Christian, and a most gracious person. He had been educated on the mainland and was exceedingly pleased that Bertha could speak Mandarin so well. He told her that all business houses vacated by the Japanese had already been assigned to merchants from the mainland. However, he deeded her a lot on Amoy Street on which a church could be built. But the Foreign Mission Board felt the future work on Formosa was rather uncertain, too uncertain to put money into buildings. Furthermore, unaware of the scarcity of rental property on Formosa, the Board upheld its decision just to rent property, not buy.[8]

At about ten thirty, when Bertha returned to the guest house where she was staying, she was so cold that she filled her hot water bottle and crawled into bed to get warm. In a warm bed she opened her birthday packages from relatives and friends; Bertha enjoyed her birthdays, even when alone. Fern Harrington had given her a present before she had left Shanghai in October. The box had intrigued her. She did not open it until her birthday, and then opened it last because of the mystery it held. She said, "It was too big to be a pin or anything to wear and too small for anything for the house, so I couldn't imagine what it could be. Imagine my joy when I opened it and saw a brass door knocker with 'Bertha Smith' at the top and my Chinese name at the bottom!"[9]

On Thanksgiving evening she wrote to sisters Jennie and Ethel saying, "Thanksgiving has been no different from any other day until just a few minutes ago when a telegram came from Wesley Lawton saying that my freight sailed today from Shanghai. I'm now having a real Thanksgiving!"[10] She also told them about visiting two afternoons that week and while outdoors seeing huge poinsettia bushes in bloom. She wrote, "When I get a yard I want one."

At Last a Home

Miss Bertha finally secured a house, one that provided enough space for gatherings. When the building was renovated, she began to conduct a worship service in English every Sunday afternoon. Miss Bertha was frank to admit that she not only ministered to people's needs, but they ministered to her as well, especially the Georges. Dr. and Mrs. George took the place of fellow missionaries as long as they lived in Taipei. The house Bertha secured was an old Japanese residence in need of much repair. It took two years of rent money to renovate the house. She said the old building "appeared to be the first one the Japanese built after arriving there in 1895." The contract called for the house to be ready by December 20, and she had promised to give up her room at the guest house by that date. When she moved into her new home, the only room with a floor was her eight-by-ten bedroom. She had to step from beam to beam to get to it. Can you imagine a sixty-year-old missionary doing a balancing act to get to her room? Miss Bertha was able!

Bertha's household supplies, which she had left in Shanghai, arrived on a steamer, accompanied by Joseph Chang. Joseph, a former coteacher in the Mission School in North China, had conversed with Miss Bertha on several occasions about "future work." Dr. Connely made the arrangements for Joseph to travel to Taiwan to assist Miss Bertha in that "future work" on Formosa. He served as her secretary and general helper. Joseph had a prophetic dream a few months before his arrival in Taipai. He had been reading from the New Testament for several months and in the dream he was told to read Isaiah 66:19: "I will send those that escape . . . to the isles afar off." He had dated the verse; it fit his situation perfectly.

A few days before Joseph's city fell to the Communists, he had received word from a village eight miles away that his wife had given birth to their second son. But Joseph was cut off, unable to bid his wife, children, and parents farewell before escaping. He had to flee the Communists. Many families were split up because of the war. Now God had sent His "escapee" to the "isle far off." God does prepare His servants for all eventualities.

Along with Joseph, Dr. Connely sent a cook for Miss Bertha. Most missionaries have cooks because so much of their time is occupied in the work, and if they have to take the time to cook, the mission work suffers.

As one missionary put it, "One cannot telephone the grocery order and have it delivered. There must be the daily trip to all the markets: the vegetable market, the meat market, the fish market, the fruit market, daily time-consuming activities."[11]

The cook, whose name in English means "Strong and Valiant," was named for an uncle who majored in ancient calisthenics. "The cook," Bertha said, "had suffered so at the hands of the Communists that when I returned from America in the spring of 1948, he looked as if he were getting over a siege of typhoid fever."[12] The cook's family had suffered much at the hands of the Japanese as well as the Communists. He had to leave his wife and children back on the mainland of China, hoping to bring them to Formosa soon. When in Taipei his cooking was certainly tested for the next three months when he had to cook in the backyard on three bricks. Bertha said, "I still had better food than I had been living on during my first two months in Formosa."

The First Christmas

Miss Bertha wanted to get the house ready for a party during Christmas week and for two worship services on Christmas Day, which fell on Sunday. She hired two men to begin work at five o'clock each afternoon and work until midnight. On faith she sent out invitations. She said, "Had not the Lord still been holding on my nerves, I could have been buried under the proverbial tombstone on which is engraved, 'Here lies the fool who tried to rush the East!'"[13]

The Chinese contractor doing the work did not speak or understand Mandarin. The only word he really knew was "boo," which means "know or not." And he used it for every suggestion Miss Bertha made. She said, "You may be sure that I got tired of being Boo-ed by that man."[14] When she tried to tell the head man through the interpreter that the roof leaked, the interpreter argued with her that the sky cannot be seen. She said, "When we go in and show him he says, 'of course, there are holes, there are holes in all tile roofs before the ceiling is put in so they can't be seen.'"[15] The hole in the floor for the commode was cut so big that the commode could not be screwed down. The city permit to build was delayed and a policeman, as Bertha said, "came in three times to see why we are doing building with no permit posted!"

Miss Bertha persevered to fulfill her heart's desire to have the Christmas program. She could easily get fifty people in the house because all the doors were removable paper doors. She had contracted to get fifty wooden folding chairs from the carpenter's shop. But the windows were not in, and fearing rain, which would mean it would be cold, the party and English

Christmas service had to be postponed a week. Before Bertha sent out the postponement announcement, she went to visit Mrs. George, who had suffered an attack of appendicitis that forced her to call off her Christmas dinner, to which Bertha had been invited. Dr. George asked if she could use a Christmas tree. He had been given two. Bertha gladly accepted.

Bertha, Joseph, and the cook trimmed the tree after midnight. Christmas decorations as found in America could not be purchased in Formosa. So Bertha cut little strips of red paper and Joseph hung them on the tree. The cook found cotton, pulled it into little dabs, and put it on the branches. The climate made no difference to him; he felt every Christmas tree needed snow. The next morning Joseph and the cook were thrilled to find gifts of toilet articles for themselves under the tree. Friends from America had given them to Miss Bertha and she passed them on to her helpers and friends. The cook decided to save his mild, fragrant soap for his baby when the child grew a bit older. Bertha said, "He did not realize that the little fellow would be tough enough to use a bar of Octagon soap before he would get in touch with him again."[16] It was actually some time before the cook's family could be reunited in Taiwan.

Bertha had persuaded the contractor to take his work crew elsewhere to work on Christmas Day. That rainy morning when she sat down by the fire with her Bible she was too exhausted, as she said, "for the faintest Christmas thrill. The stack of Christmas cards from friends, which I had saved to open to help make a Christmas atmosphere, did their best for me, but in my exhaustion I was saying, 'A place to live is just not worth this much expenditure of physical, mental, and heart energy!' The Lord came to me again, however, and assured me that I was preparing a house in which people might be saved, whether they came to it or the missionary lived comfortably enough to keep well and go out after them. That message gave me so much courage that I did not mind eating a Christmas dinner of canned peas heated on three bricks in the yard."[17]

Miraculous Things

As the work continued, now that it had a reasonably good beginning, God began to do miraculous things. A few days after Christmas, as Miss Bertha and Joseph were leaving the house to conduct a Bible study, a young Formosan met them at the front door. Clearly he was in an agitated state. Miss Bertha could not speak Formosan or Japanese. All she could do was smile at him and urge him in English to come again. Joseph Chang had learned a few sentences in Formosan and tried to help the man understand why they had to leave.

A few days later, Bertha received a letter from the young man written in English. He had studied under a Japanese who had hung up a shingle that read, "English taught here from 'A' to 'K.'" In other words, he did not know English well at all. With patience and persistence, however, Bertha was able to discover that the young man had been a dentist in Taipei and had lost his arm in 1945 during a U.S. bombing raid. He had a wife and parents to support. His circumstances thrust him into such a state of despair that he had contemplated suicide. The warm greeting and smile he found at Bertha's home gave him courage to ask, "Can Jesus Christ do anything for me?"

Bertha immediately sent a letter inviting him to come to her home at a certain time. Between her English, the bit he knew, gospel posters, and the small vocabulary of Mr. Chang's Formosan, they spent an evening trying to help him. Bertha explained, "Because Jesus had settled our sin problem on His cross, He could say to every person, 'Come unto me all you that labor and are heavy laden and I will give you rest'" (Matt. 11:28). After several hours the young Formosan fell on his knees and began calling upon the name of the Lord.

As incredible as it may seem in the West, he came two or three evenings a week for four months to imbibe all he could of the truth about the Lord Jesus Christ. He would listen to Joseph Chang's struggle with the Formosan language and glean what he could from Miss Bertha's English as they went through a chapter in Mark's Gospel. He lived ten miles away and finally had to stop coming because he had no money for the bus fare. One evening the following summer he appeared at the Bible class with an expression on his face that thrilled everyone. It was obvious to all who looked at him that he had become a new creature in Christ.

In February, after Miss Bertha had been on the beautiful isle for four months, Pastor Yang Mei Tsai came to Formosa with his family, representing the All-China Baptist Convention.

Professor Ma, a professor at the university, had moved to Formosa when it was returned to China in 1945. He had seen three classes of students graduate and go to various cities to accept positions. He was a dedicated Christian. Pastor Yang took a mission survey trip to the eleven cities on the railway running along the west coast of Formosa and Professor Ma accompanied him. The smallest city had a population of one hundred thousand. Bertha pointed out, "With a former student in the government land office of each city it was easy for them to get the promise of a lot formerly belonging to Japanese or a building without key money or rent, which we could purchase later at a very low price."[18] Taipei was the only city that was overly crowded. In ten of the cities visited there were no Mandarin-speaking missionaries or Chinese pastors. Pastor Yang immediately saw the opportunity for church planting and began praying for people to come and open the work.

After Pastor Yang's arrival in February, Bertha secured an old Buddhist temple that the Japanese had vacated when they left the island. The temple sat on Jen Ai Road in Taipei, and at the time, Formosan soldiers were living there. They paid them to move out and it became the church building they had prayed for so long.

By the end of March, the work on Bertha's house was finally finished and the remainder of her boxes from Shanghai were opened. She said in a letter to friends, "I am now in a position to take care of the Lord's servant! When the cooking stove was put up and I unpacked all that shower of canned goods from you, I just wanted to cook and cook. While I can't see a peach tree in bloom, I can take my choice of the fruit either canned or dried from the shelf. When I sat down on that comfortable chair, I never wanted to get up; and when I went to bed on that Beautyrest mattress, I wanted to sleep a week and dream that I was with all you dear church friends who so bountifully provided for me."[19] All of the trials, even the "booings," were forgotten.

Miss Bertha continued to get her house in order while the old Buddhist temple was being readied for Christian services. When her piano arrived, she needed to find a place for it. The first renovators of her little house had been unable to remove a weight-bearing pole located in the living room just where the piano needed to be. She at last found a builder who knew how to do it, and by the end of March, when she wrote her weekly letter to her sisters, the piano had a proper place and could be used, even though it badly needed tuning.

Bertha had designed a way to have hot running water, and two of her friends, Mrs. George and Mrs. Keihn, a Nazarene friend, had made appointments to come for hot baths and shampoos. Mrs. George had especially become a dear friend. Bertha wrote, "I gave Mrs. George a cup of blackberry jam from our Hymalia berries a few minutes ago when she came by." She loved to share.

Someone had given Bertha a piece of strawberry-print material that she had used to cover four dining room chairs and make drapes for the windows. Bertha invited Mrs. Twinem, an independent Presbyterian missionary from China, to live with her. She occupied the extra bedroom. Mrs. Twinem said of the little house, "Each room is a little gem." Bertha knew color combinations and made do with very little. The previous week she had entertained the guest house manager and his wife. Bertha said they were "going to have their dinner and company on Saturday and then eat scraps on Sunday."[20]

When the house was completed, Bertha joyously said that a "bathroom had been added, and lo! it contained a built-in tub. It was made by one brick being laid upon another, over which was spread cement terrazzo. Two women had then come in and rubbed with pumice stone all day until the tub was smooth and pretty. Earthy Bertha was getting satisfied.

Bertha put a sign on the bamboo fence of her newly renovated home, written both in English and Chinese: "Miss Smith's Baptist Mission." People began to come just to see the sign. Regular services were held on Sunday and a Bible class on Tuesday and Thursday evenings.

A few weeks after Bible classes began, one of the men who had been attending asked how he could be saved. He had no Christian background whatsoever, and Miss Bertha certainly did not want to "pick him green." She would never let a person make a profession of faith until genuine signs of repentance and a complete openness and understanding of the gospel surfaced. She urged him to come for personal help and recounted the fascinating story:

> The next morning at nine o'clock he was there. Handing him a Chinese Bible, I had him read passage after passage showing something of the sinfulness of his own heart in contrast to the holiness of God. After an hour or two he asked, "How can I, this terrible sinner, ever get right enough to have fellowship with such a holy God?" He was then prepared to hear what Christ had done for him. When he was ready to surrender his will to the Lord, he knelt by my sofa and started confessing his sins one by one. Before he had half finished his sin account, there was a knock at the door. I tiptoed out into the hall and said to the newcomer, "You just take this chair here. The man inside wants to be saved. When I get through with him, I will see you."
>
> He said, "I want to be saved."
>
> I answered, "Come inside and get on your knees."
>
> After a little while there was another knock and I tiptoed out again and said to another man, "The two men inside want to be saved. Please sit here until I get through with them."
>
> He replied, "I want to be saved."
>
> I answered, "Come inside and get on your knees." So three men were seeking the Lord, instead of the one who had come by appointment.
>
> That was the way God's work proved to be on the island of Formosa. There were always three opportunities to the one which I had on the mainland. And I had thought back there that I was doing the greatest work in the world![21]

172

15

The Work Expands

Bertha conversing with students from the Taiwan
Baptist Theological Seminary. *Credit: FMB*

Word of Miss Bertha's work spread rapidly all over Taipei. People
began to flock to her home. She said she did not need to even leave her
home to put in a full day's work for the Lord. Many came for counsel and
she led them to Christ right in her living room. Her sofa was literally
ruined by tears of repentance. She said, "To me it was only beautifully
brocaded." Bertha's gift of evangelism sparkled with real power. She not
only had a tremendous ministry in winning the lost to Christ, but she profoundly influenced new Christians who had not yet learned to walk in
Christ's fullness. A good many of these would come and weep as much
over their failure to demonstrate Christ to their friends and family as they
had first wept over their lost condition. She was dedicated to helping these
Christians move into a deeper walk with Christ and the victorious Spirit-
filled life.

Bertha knew that people who are uprooted and torn from all they hold
dear are often open to the gospel. They seem to sense their need for
Christ's strength for the transition and difficulties forced upon them.

One morning at about nine o'clock an attractive young lady knocked on Bertha's door. She asked, "What time do you have church service?" Bertha said, "Come in and we will have it now!" Bertha handed her a Chinese Bible and attempted, as was her custom, to help her see herself as God saw her. She wanted the young lady to realize that she had failed God miserably and that no one can attain righteousness by one's own effort.

The young woman, Miss Wang, was a teacher from Peking. She had graduated from Peking Normal College after having been reared in the capital, and never heard the name of Jesus until one day when she was on her way from Peking to Formosa, fleeing the Communist takeover. On her journey she spent one night in Nanking near a small Baptist chapel. Being tremendously disturbed and distraught about leaving home, she felt a desperate loneliness. The singing at the chapel had attracted her, so she went in. She saw the word "Baptist" on Miss Bertha's sign and said to herself, "That is the same word that is on the chapel in Nanking. I will go in and hear some more."[1]

Miss Wang had just arrived in Taipei. She had no place to live or work. She was sharing a very small room with others and the little bit of money she did have was soon gone for food. But Miss Bertha did not compromise the gospel in her compassion for the needy girl. She made it very plain that if Miss Wang desired to receive Christ, she must utterly die to herself. Bertha sensed that Miss Wang was not quite there, so she quite frankly said, "It is not the Lord you want. You just want His blessings . . . a job so that you can have your own money and a place to live." That shocked the young lady, but cut her to the heart. After a long, thoughtful pause she looked up at Miss Bertha and said, "I must have the Lord at any cost." That was all Miss Bertha needed to hear. They fell on their knees by the sofa and her tear stains joined the others. She truly repented and gave herself completely to Christ, the true cost of discipleship—the lesson in evangelism that many in the West need to hear. When they rose from their knees, Miss Wang was filled with "joy unspeakable and full of glory." She had now come into the family of God, linked to the great God of creation Himself. What joy!

Miss Bertha always recorded the date and name of all she had the privilege of leading to Christ. When she recorded Miss Wang's conversion, she remarked that was the day Columbus discovered America. Miss Wang said, "I have made a bigger discovery than Columbus! He only found a continent. I have discovered the kingdom of heaven!"[2] Miss Wang often came to Miss Bertha's little mission for Bible study and prayer. Bertha found her prayers wonderfully refreshing. She did not know the typical language of Zion or the so-called orthodox prayer language. She just talked to the Lord Jesus freely about everything that concerned her. She always closed her prayer with, "Lord, I am just delighted to talk to you!"

Conversions Abound

The old Buddhist temple was soon cleaned up and ready for the opening dedication service to be held on Sunday, April 10, 1949. Bertha said, "The building would not seat all that came on that day."[3] Brother Wu Yung was one of the speakers, and his choir rendered special music. He and his group met in the YMCA building on Sunday mornings and Miss Bertha met with them regularly.

April is the height of the rainy season; they had not seen the sun for twenty-four days. Clouds and rain during the winter and early spring were miserable. It also meant that everything capable of rusting, mildewing, or molding did. Miss Bertha said, "The leather shoes began growing beards. Alas! the dreary days kept on until the human anatomy felt that it would do all three—mildew, rust, and mold!"[4] As Miss Bertha was traveling to church in her pedicab for the first service in their new quarters, the sun suddenly broke through the clouds. Bertha felt as if the Lord were saying, "I am for you!" He was! The building would seat about one hundred people on backless benches, but two hundred people crammed into the building. Those standing were happy to have even standing room.

The Chinese services were moved from Bertha's house to the new building. A woman's group began to meet on Thursday afternoons. On Tuesday and Thursday evenings, Bible classes were held. Young people met on Saturday evenings and Sunbeams (children's work) met on Sunday afternoons, led by the young people of the church. Joseph Chang led the choir. In May, Miss P'eng Hsiu Lien, a graduate of North China Seminary, arrived as a full-time worker. They formally organized in September as the Jen Ai Baptist Church. Thirty-six members from the mainland composed the charter membership. The following Sunday, seventeen were baptized in a baptistry built in the yard that was surrounded by beautiful tropical trees. Miss Bertha's dream had been fulfilled. The church now had its building and Pastor Yang filled the pulpit. From this small beginning, by 1965, when Miss Bertha wrote her well-known book, *Go Home and Tell*, the church increased in membership to nine hundred, sponsored three missions, and supported a pastor, assistant pastor, and three Bible women. What victories God had given from such a small beginning.

Moving Out to Wider Fields

On Wednesday afternoon, April 27, 1949, Miss Bertha began a Bible class with the female students of the China Defense Medical Center. One of the purposes of the class was to help the students with their English. She taught in English, then interpreted herself in Chinese. Because there was no room at the center for the girls, they were forced to meet about twenty or thirty miles from the city up on a mountainside in a former Japanese hospital. It demanded a long, hard bus ride. Miss Bertha said, "The bus went over the rockiest road that I have ever ridden over. I felt that I would have my liver shaken into pudding."[5] It took her two and a half hours to get there, but it was worth every minute.

Opportunities to share Christ opened at every turn. A thousand people from Shantung Province were living in cramped quarters in a Japanese crematory two blocks from Bertha's house. She said, "Of course, . . . I could not let all those distressed people from our own Province be left without the gospel, for now they had time to listen." Thus a "wee house," as Bertha described it, was purchased for one hundred U.S. dollars to be used as a meeting house. Bertha engaged young people from the church to assist in the project. She said, "I insisted that little boys could not come in unless they had on clothes, at least pants. One day when I sent a little fellow in his birthday suit home for clothes, he gleefully came running back with his little last year's shirt which reached an inch or two below his arms."[6] But God honored the work. One of the first converts was a graduate of Columbia University who was staying there with his wife and children.

In May, just before the city of Shanghai finally fell to the Communists, Miss Lila Watson, enroute to Hong Kong from Shanghai, came to Formosa for seven months. During this time she served with Miss Bertha, arriving just in time to help plan the first summer conference for young people. Soon after Lila arrived, Miss Bertha, Lila, and Mrs. Twinem took a trip south to Tainan to have some time away and rest a bit. They traveled by train down one side of the island and up the other, making several stops along the way. In her letter to her sisters, Bertha told of the few churches she found along the way and how many unchurched people there were. She said, "The need for live mission work is appalling." She took along her tracts and used Christmas cards from friends in America to give to people in need of the gospel. Miss Bertha's vacations may have been restful and enjoyable, but they also proved to be unique times of sharing the gospel.

The conference that Bertha and Lila planned for the youth was held in a park in the mountains fifteen miles from the city. The Taiwan Coal Mining Company owned the park. The brother of Miss Lin, a young person attending the church, owned the company. After Miss Lin suggested the use of the park, Miss Bertha and others went up to see it. Upon viewing the property, they felt, "We just must have it; we stood under the gorgeous tropical trees and asked the Lord to give it to us, and in our hearts received assurance that He had."[7]

Bertha invited Lucy Smith to come from Hong Kong to be the featured speaker at the conference, and a Swedish Baptist missionary en route from China's mainland to Japan was asked to give a series of messages on the foundation of a Christian home. Bertha herself taught a Bible class and presented a daily message on the New Testament church. One day she gave a talk on an "Around the World Vision of Our Mission Fields." Ten young men, twenty-five girls, Miss Peng, a graduate of North China Seminary, and three missionaries were present. Two people were saved and several in the group dedicated their lives for full-time Christian service. At the close of the conference it was decided that a similar conference would be held the following year. This turned out to be just the beginning; conferences for all ages became an annual event.

In September, Bertha responded to a call from Mrs. Elsie Meng, a former worker in the Woman's Missionary Union in Shanghai. Mrs. Meng had moved to Formosa and desired help in starting a new work. It was some little distance from Bertha's church, about a two-hour train ride, but Bertha had God's peace that she should go. Pastor Yang released Miss Bertha and Joseph Chang from evening services at the church to help in this new work. Bertha said they "would rush home from church service by pedicab, eat the lunch that had been put on the table by the cook, take the package [meal] for supper, and with song books, Bibles, tracts, felt-o-graph board, easel, all that we both could manage, grab the 12:30 train."[8] Another twenty-minute pedicab ride would bring them to Mrs. Meng's home where they began an evening Sunday school. If they stayed late to counsel with anyone wanting to be saved, a four-hour trip home on a slow train would be necessary; and it was always crowded because tickets were cheap. If they had to stand up the entire trip, they would not get to eat their picnic supper until they arrived home at eleven o'clock in the evening. But, as she said, "We would sit at the table, open up our supper lunch and praise the Lord that the Gospel was getting planted in another city, and that at an army camp of tens of thousands of men who would be targets if the Communists should bomb."[9] Before long they outgrew Mrs. Meng's home and had to seek another meeting place. This developed into the second major mission on the island of Formosa. Miss Demerest and Miss Jeffers were sent in May 1951 to oversee the new work. It was officially organized in December of that year.

The Gospel Hall

Property in Formosa sold at a premium. In June 1949, after Miss Bertha had some months earlier secured land for a church building, the mayor sent an inquiry asking if the mission was going to build on it. If not, he had a buyer. Dr. Cauthen made his first visit to the island in that month and, as Bertha wrote in a letter home, "seeing the wonderful location and need for a Christian work in that section of the city I agreed to save the lot."[10] She continued, "Dr. Cauthen carefully stepped it off, inquired its distance from the University and Normal College from whence we could attract students and said, 'In order to save this lot I will advise the Board to grant money for a little chapel.' Now you may be sure that was a leap frog day for me!"[11] The Foreign Mission Board sent money to erect the little chapel, which was named the "Gospel Hall," then later Amoy Street Baptist Church. Southern Baptist work in Formosa was now officially undertaken.

Except for Sunday, Bertha went to the site every day to oversee the construction at the Gospel Hall. The daily visit was not easy. She said, "The workmen seemed to do more things wrong on that day [Sunday] than they did right the other six." They dedicated the chapel on Christmas Day 1950.

Exciting things began to happen. Two weeks after opening the new building two hundred children started attending Sunday school. In February, to observe the Chinese New Year season, they held a two-week evangelistic campaign. Bertha rejoiced as she reported that about forty boys and girls "joyfully entered into learning choruses and memorizing Scripture passages." After a week of Bible study on sin and the Savior, Miss Bertha asked those who wanted to stay for an after-meeting to come forward, and the others were asked to leave the hall so the grown-ups who were there could come forward. Instead, those who had been asked to leave the hall walked right up into the corner by the platform. Miss Bertha again said they should file out of the building. But to the surprise of all, including Bertha, someone said, "We all want to be saved." Glorious days!

Bertha provided straw mats for kneeling on the cement floor. As she grew older, she regularly used a prayer mat herself. What a beautiful sight—some thirty boys and girls ranging in age from ten to fifteen kneeling along with a number of adults. They lifted up their prayers before God in confession and thanksgiving for His grace and salvation. A few weeks later five more came forward to seek Christ. The following Wednesday one of these young men, age fourteen, drowned. His Buddhist parents came to the services the next Sunday to tell the tragic story. They asked Bertha to pray the boy out of purgatory. How grateful they were when Bertha assured them that their son was already in heaven because he had trusted the Lord Jesus Christ as his Savior.

Miss Bertha would never present the gospel in a superficial manner; repentance and faith had to be evident (Acts 20:21). When she returned to America at age seventy and began her ministry there, she decried the shallow evangelism she saw in so many of the churches. Bertha wanted to see *real* conversions. She exercised her gift of evangelism along pure biblical lines; she never sought mere "decisions" or numbers. She always emphasized that saving faith is a work of the Holy Spirit alone. Only the Spirit of God can grant it (Eph. 2:8–9). Our part, she would say, is to repent; the Spirit will give faith. She had no doubt learned that so-called Reformed Theology approach at Southern Seminary in her student days. And it brought about sincere repentance, true faith, and hence genuine conversions.

Sunday was a long traveling day for Miss Bertha and Joseph Chang. She said, "By leaving home at eight o'clock in the morning we were able to go to our Chapel on Amoy Street for a Sunday School, then get in our pedicab and rush to the church in time for the service. Sunday afternoons we had a service for Christians and on Sunday evenings an evangelistic service. We spent three hours in the pedicab. When we opened the chapel I determined I was never going to let myself get bored traveling. I never did. Either Joseph or I had the services to lead, so going we always spent the time in silent prayer and returning we talked English which he called 'Pedicab College.'"[12]

A varied program with different types of services characterized the work. In a short time people all over the area began to come to hear the gospel of Christ, and the work grew. When Miss Bertha retired in 1958, a church building that seats four hundred stood next to Gospel Hall. The church boasted a total membership of seven hundred members and had sponsored four missions in Taipei. Two of the missions were organized into churches, and one of those churches established a mission in a nearby village. The work of God multiplied and progressed in incredible fashion under the leadership and power of the Holy Spirit.

Mundane Matters

Because Miss Bertha lost some of her clothing to the Communists, she had to hire a seamstress to sew some items for her. Mrs. George gave her several garments, one of which was a black taffeta dress. The seamstress ripped it apart and managed to make a long skirt for Miss Bertha. However, two of the dresses Mrs. George gave her were not suitable. Miss Bertha remarked, "She [Mrs. George] is such a thin little thing that neither would go more than two-thirds of the way around me." Bertha had purchased what she called, "some very pretty rose embroidered georgette from a Chinese peddler at her door" to make a blouse. She also had two slips made from a nylon parachute. The cook and the seamstress got into a conversation about what type of material the garments were made of. The cook wanted to know if it was real silk.

Bertha had other mundane things to deal with also: her annual checkup, typhoid inoculation, and other booster shots. The doctor, she said, "could find nothing wrong with me. Of course, I did not mind if he couldn't." In her October letter, she requested a Lane Bryant catalogue for "stout ladies" and a dozen pairs of nylon stockings for Christmas.

Paul and Lydia

There were far more important matters than the mundane. The ramifications of Bertha's ministry of witness were amazing. After his conversion, a young university professor took the name of Paul. In the summer of that year, his fiancee came to Formosa from Szechuan Province in China. They were happily married in the city auditorium. Bertha met the new bride and mother of the groom. Now there were three, Bertha said, for whom she could pray. Not long after, the beautiful bride stained Bertha's sofa with her tears of repentance and conversion. She took as her new name, Lydia. Now Paul and Lydia were happy together in the Lord. Lydia felt very much accepted by her new family and circle of Christian friends, even though her own parents and brothers and sisters were in the far-off Szechuan Province of China. Not long after Lydia's conversion, Paul came to Miss Bertha deeply agitated and in distress. He pleaded with Miss Bertha to see Lydia. Her parents had just been put to death by the Communists simply because they were wealthy. Poor Lydia was beside herself. She sat on the very sofa where she had found Christ and sobbed, "My parents are lost! I will never see them again! They had no chance to be saved! Not one time did they hear of the Lord Jesus!" One can deeply empathize with the distress of the young wife and new Christian. Bertha shared with her the promises of the Word of God for the comfort and peace that our Lord can give in times of distress. Bertha did not try to offer her any hope for the parents, but she was confident that the peace of Christ would enable her to bear the sorrow. They shared biblical promises and prayed until Lydia gave herself into the hands of Christ. The young wife left with peace.

A Delightful Evening: A Family Won

One of Bertha's companions and dear friend, Olive Lawton, had come to Formosa by that time. They had marvelous fellowship and great times of prayer together. Lydia invited both Bertha and Olive to her home for dinner one evening. The young wife and the servants spent the entire afternoon preparing delicious Szechuan food that Chinese people love. Paul's father, who had a Ph.D. in science from a university in France, served as a professor at the teachers' training college in Taipai. Paul's mother, also a teacher, taught at the normal university. A second son, Robin, was a university student, a younger sister studied in high school, and a younger brother was in grade school. They all sat around the table and had a great time. Lydia felt so much at home with her new family, even though she had experienced a distressful time. The peace of Christ ruled in her heart, as the Bible promised it would.

No one in Paul's family, except Lydia, was a Christian. According to Chinese culture, Paul, not being the head of the house, could only bow his head with Lydia and silently thank God for the wonderful meal. Bertha and Olive did likewise, making it very short. The others were respectful and waited until everyone had finished praying before they picked up their chopsticks and began to enjoy the delicious meal. Bertha was grateful for the silent witness that Paul and Lydia bore before the family.

After the lovely dinner, they retired to the living room. Paul invited Bertha to tell the family about Jesus Christ. She did her best to present the truth of the gospel, trusting the Holy Spirit to speak to their hearts and clear away the cloud of doubt and ignorance concerning the things of Christ.

Several months passed. Then one afternoon Lydia came to Bertha with her mother-in-law who wanted to be saved. Lydia left Bertha alone with the mother-in-law. After an hour or two she was on her knees at the famous sofa, adding her tears to it. At that moment, Lydia came in and saw the blessed scene. She went tiptoeing into the dining room and around and around the table clapping her hands without a sound and whispering, "My mother-in-law is going to be saved!" With great joy the two went home happy in the Lord.

After the mother-in-law came to faith in Christ, she entered a Bible study class at the church. She learned the meaning of church membership and was soon baptized. Then the three, Paul, Lydia, and her mother-in-law, began to pray for the salvation of the rest of the family.

The young daughter soon came to faith in the Lord Jesus Christ. Then brother Robin. Now there were five to unite in prayer for the other two. All were particularly anxious over the father, so they made an appointment to bring him to Bertha's home on a Sunday afternoon to hear the gospel on a personal level. They talked for two hours and read the Word of God. However, he refused to humble himself before the Lord. He used the old excuse that Christianity did not agree with science. After the church building was constructed, which stood right near his home, he would occasionally go to please the family. Yet, he showed no real interest in a relationship with Christ.

Some years later, Bertha visited the parents in another city. They were teaching in a different university. Bertha found the father a new man with an entirely different attitude. The mother had been conducting meetings for Christian students in the home. The father had repeatedly heard the gospel and it began to touch his life. The mother's faithfulness in getting up early every morning for a time with the Lord made him understand that Christ was very real in her life. The knowledge of what Christ had done for his children also moved him. This led him to begin reading the Bible for himself.

By the time Bertha met him in the new location, he had become so hungry-hearted that he made no objection to Bertha telling him about his sins. She led him to see that he desperately needed Christ, was lost in sin, and undone before God. She asked him to write his sins on paper one by one and repeatedly pray, "Lord, show me any other sins in my heart." Bertha left promising to return in two days to tell him what he had to do next.

When Bertha returned two days later, she found the professor-father so convicted of his sin that he realized he had absolutely no hope of getting right with God except through the life, death, and resurrection of the Lord Jesus Christ. He sunk to his knees in complete surrender and put all of his sins one by one on Christ. The living Lord entered his heart, and Bertha left him an exceedingly happy man. A few weeks later, as he continued to study the Bible, he became convicted of his need to go to the church and be baptized. It was a six-mile journey, but he gladly went, gave his testimony, and received Christian baptism.

It is interesting to note what Miss Bertha said about her approach to leading people to Christ:

> My method in dealing with individuals was to have them list all known sin and sins by number. When no more could be recalled, to pray, "Lord, you are light. Shine in my heart and show me all that is in my nature which is unlike holy God." To settle the sin account, of sin-number-one ask, "Is that sin just between God and me?" If it involves no one else the sin can be put over on the Lord with thanks that He took the necessary punishment for it. That sin is then forever finished and can be marked from the list.

What about sin-number-two? That may have been against some one else. If so, after that sin has been put on Christ, confession must be made to the one sinned against before it can be marked out.

When the listed sins have been thus dealt with and marked out, the next step is to put oneself over on the Lord, accepting His death for that sinful nature which produces sin.

The next step that I advised was to choose the Lord's will in advance for the whole of life and for those related to it. Thus Christ could be enthroned in the heart and the Holy Spirit could be appropriated to fill and empower.[13]

That produced an evangelism of integrity

A Call from the Past

Miss Bertha had been in Formosa about a year when she received a message from a man who lived in the southern part of the island. He requested that she come and spend a week to teach a number of new converts who were meeting in his home. It seemed impossible for her to go because of the weight of the work in Taipei. A year later, the same man sent another message for her to come. He communicated that those converts who wanted help before had been led astray by a lay leader into some false doctrine. Now he had another little congregation that desperately needed Bible teaching. Yet, Bertha was more involved than ever in the capitol city. Again she could not go. That group, too, was led astray. In the spring of 1952, Bertha was asked to go to Tainan to help a new work. At that time, the third call came from the same man, asking her to come and teach this third group, but still she did not feel free to go. She traveled to Tainan, worked hard as always, and nine months later the believers there were ready to organize a church. They were very busy teaching classes, planning programs, and listening to and examining testimonies of those who wished to unite with the fellowship.

On one of Bertha's very busy days in Tainan, a little man with a black beard got off his bicycle at Bertha's door. He knocked on her door and seeing her he said, "You are Miss Ming of Laichowfu!" Then the stranger asked, "Do you know me?" Bertha replied that he seemed somewhat familiar to her. But what a surprise when he said, "I am Dr. Wang who worked with Dr. Gaston in the Baptist Hospital in Laichowfu." He was the man who had been after her for three years to come to his town and teach. What a thrill to see the young doctor who had reached Laichowfu just when she had arrived there as a new missionary. Bertha had prayed earnestly for him. After some three or four years, he had returned to his home in Pingtu, still unsaved, and opened a private clinic.

Dr. Wang and "Miss Ming" (Bertha's Chinese name) had lunch together and Dr. Wang told her how he had been saved during the revival in Pingtu in North China. He had seen three paralytics healed by the Lord's power in answer to prayer. One of them had been his patient and he knew her case was incurable. The startling miracle deeply touched his life and caused him to realize that Jesus Christ is alive, approachable, and could be called upon when needs arose. All of this moved Dr. Wang and brought him under conviction of sin. It led to genuine repentance and faith in Christ; the doctor came into God's glorious salvation.

After Dr. Wang's conversion, the Japanese army entered the city and the officers took over his building for their living quarters. His clinic was one of the best buildings in Pingtu. They confiscated his medical equipment and supplies, leaving him with absolutely nothing. Dr. Wang had no resources or money for supplies to begin practicing medicine again when the Japanese finally withdrew. So he came to Formosa to live with his son who was trained as a pilot in America for the Chinese Air Force.

Having heard that Miss Ming was trying to organize a church in Tainan, he came to see if his group of twenty-five from his town could be examined for baptism. Most of the members of his group were in the air corps and the only free time they had for examination was Saturday afternoon and evening. "We just had to go," Miss Bertha said. "It was something new in the Orient when three women took a bus to go examine a group for baptism, most of whom were men."[14]

Twenty-four of the twenty-five were ready. Their testimonies and examination proved they were clearly saved, and, as Bertha related, "We went back to Tainan at bedtime as if floating on air." Consequently, a fine church was planted in Dr. Wang's city and a pastor who graduated from a university and the seminary at Taipei was called to serve this church. The church established a mission where many servicemen were reached. A circle begun many years ago in Miss Bertha's life had now been completed.

16

The Growing Formosan Ministry

Bertha teaching at the Taiwan Baptist
Theological Seminary. *Credit: FMB*

The work continued to progress. Great strides had been taken in the
first days, but the ministry of Miss Bertha and her fellow workers
expanded so rapidly that Formosa became a major field for Southern Baptists. So the saga continued.

Youth Work and Education

Attendance at the summer youth conferences increased each summer.
In 1950 and 1951 extra rooms in a nearby inn had to be acquired to care
for overflow crowds. One hundred youth attended in 1951. Even a new
seminary was inaugurated. It had been a dream of Miss Bertha's. In
March 1952 Miss Martha Franks arrived in Formosa to teach and serve as
Dean of Women at the new seminary, slated to open that fall. Since she
was not loaded down with work and had a car, the conference committee
asked if she would search for a new, suitable place for the summer meetings. Martha finally located a five-acre plot of terraced rice patties, four
miles from Taipei with a bus stop at the entrance. The Foreign Mission

Board purchased it with money from their special appeal: the Lottie Moon Christmas Offering for Foreign Missions. The missionaries and others gave personal gifts to assist with the running expense that first summer. They had such a heart for the work that when any money came to them from unexpected sources, they assumed it was for the work on the field and selflessly used it for that purpose.

Several weeks before the conference, Miss Franks had hired a "snake catcher" to clear the grounds of the vipers. At twenty-five cents a snake he kept busy. He would keep the critters alive and take them to the city where, as Bertha described it, "he would sell the poison to a Chinese medicine shop, the meat to a Cantonese restaurant, and the skin to a leather shop." It worked. Miss Bertha said, "Only one service was disturbed by a snake crawling through the tent and only one was seen and killed by the boys, which, of course, added to their interest. The Lord answered prayer and kept the girls from being frightened by any." But that was not the end of the story.

After the conference had ended and everyone had gone home, the cook told Miss Franks that a twenty-foot snake had been spotted in the bamboo thicket nearby. Because of their fright, Martha knew they had seen something. A few days later some American men had to stop their jeep while a python the length of the width of the highway crawled across. That snake would have been worth more than twenty-five cents to the catcher—and probably would have ended the conference.

In 1953 the Baptist Mission Board granted ten thousand dollars for the first building on the conference grounds, and after that, five thousand dollars a year for five years. There was great rejoicing the summer the kitchen was added. By 1958 there were three buildings on the premises. They could accommodate two hundred guests, counselors, and speakers. In addition, the buildings also contained apartments for missionary families. Conferences for different age groups as well as the Chinese Convention and the Annual Mission Business Meeting were held there that year.

A Happy Birthday

On Bertha's birthday in 1952, Joseph surprised her with two gifts: first, a wall plaque with "Absolute Devotion to the Lord" engraved on it. Joseph said, "You are always speaking of how necessary it is to be absolutely devoted to the Lord! When I saw it I thought of you." The other gift was a small framed picture of the new seminary buildings and another picture of Bertha speaking at the opening of the theological seminary. Bertha said, "I had prayed and worked so long to get a seminary and that now since it was established, he wanted me to be able to look at it all day."[1]

Helen Liu, a young Bible woman, gave her a pair of satin slippers. In a house in Tainan where she had moved to begin a new work, she had to take off her shoes to protect the floors. When it came time for the birthday cake to be cut, the cook walked up the stairs with a cake "all decorated in pink English and Chinese greetings with two large red candles, the smallest he could find," said Bertha. He had baked the cake out in the backyard on a mud-flower-pot stove. The cook entered singing "Happy Birthday" in English and felt very proud of himself. It was a delightful day for all.

Miss Bertha was proud of Joseph. He had served her well as her secretary. But God had other plans for him. She said, "Joseph just outdid himself preaching. It is wonderful to see how he can take the line of teaching on sin and the Savior which he has heard from me and put fire into it and preach it so much better than I can. I think he is about the best preacher on the island. He is humble and sweet and walks with the Lord."[2] When the new seminary opened in September, Joseph enrolled along with thirty-five fine young men and women. Bertha felt "handicapped indeed."

Miss Bertha practiced waiting before God for the messages she was to deliver and for Bible study outlines for retreats and seminars. The following note, found on a scrap of paper in her files, reads:

> I was asked to be the speaker for the annual meeting of all the missionaries of Taipei. I was always filled up with my regular schedule with no time for extras, but I accepted that and began to pray for the Lord to put into my mind at the right time the message for them. On Sunday morning I was able to sleep a little later than on week days, so the Sunday before the meeting I awoke as usual, sat up in bed resting on two pillows and reached for the devotional book I was using, *My Utmost For His Highest* by Oswald Chambers. I read this question: "Am I willing for the Lord to use me to be all that Calvary makes possible?" My first question was, "What does Calvary make possible?" My reply was, "All that I have in Christ I have because of Calvary. Why, I could not even get near enough to Holy God to thank Him for my daily food had there been no Calvary!" I reached for my notebook and pen which was always in the bedside table for such occasions and began to write:
>
> - Christ's work on Calvary saves me from hell.
> - Christ's work on Calvary brings me into fellowship with Holy God.
> - Christ's work on Calvary gives to me God, the Trinity, to worship.
> - Christ's work on Calvary prepares heaven for me.
> - Christ's work on Calvary makes possible God's protection.
> - Christ's work on Calvary delivers me from my sinful self, from my environment, from the Devil and his angels.[3]

Bertha filled the role of a faithful proclaimer of the Word of God.

In January 1953, Miss Bertha and Martha Franks took a vacation trip to Bangkok, Thailand, to visit the new mission work there. Bertha described Bangkok as "the most heathen city I have ever been in. Our missionaries have made a start, but since Buddhism is a State religion which persecutes (other religions) so very bitterly, it will be . . . slow growth."[4] Nonetheless, they had a delightful time with fellow missionaries, then flew to Hong Kong where once again they were entertained by missionaries and enjoyed shopping and sightseeing.

Upon returning from vacation, Bertha continued to be a very busy woman. She worked in Taipei for a week assisting with church membership classes, but had to travel to Tainan every other morning to care for business. She said, "I get up about 4:30 A.M. to catch a fast train, attend to things until 2 P.M., then I catch the last decent train coming here. The next morning I make up the rest, as Marie brings my breakfast to the bed about eight o'clock."[5]

Home Again

In the fall of 1953, Miss Bertha traveled to the United States for a furlough. She kept busy telling the story of the abundant harvest in Formosa as she spoke in many churches "to the praise of His glory." One of her engagements required traveling to various colleges throughout Alabama with a team challenging the students. From November 30 through December 11, they spoke in thirteen places. The team consisted of: Irene Chambers, a field worker for the Baptist Home Mission Board, Reverend Marion Moorhead, missionary to Japan, and Dr. R. H. Falwell Jr., State Student Secretary of Alabama. Of Falwell she said, "He is about the choicest of all when it comes to spirituality."[6] Bertha never minded making evaluations on spirituality!

Bertha and her sisters traveled to Charleston during Easter for a holiday together. Upon returning to Formosa, she wrote the following to Jennie about the trip, and the death of her sister, Ethel, who had since gone to be with the Lord:

> There has been time to recall the happy trip to Charleston, and think over how very much (sister Ethel) enjoyed it all. I still marvel at the Lord's grace to me when she was taken [June 17, 1954]. I was filled with such gratitude for her deliverance from herself with all her nerves and aches and pains, and just so rejoiced over her being in glory with the Lord that there was just no place for weeping. Over and over during those days, during the funeral and before and after, there was going over in my mind continually the words *grace abounding*. And certainly it was

abounding grace which enabled me just to look at it altogether from her side. Of course, I miss her terribly."[7]

Her family was slowly slipping away.

Return to Formosa

When Bertha returned to Formosa after the furlough, she lived with Martha Franks "at our Little Ridgecrest," located just twelve minutes from the seminary by car on a beautiful hillside. Bertha purchased a car and exclaimed, "How wonderful it is to have a car! Not only does it enable me to live here in clean surroundings, but it will be of untold value in my evangelistic work. I praise the Lord for each of you who had a share in the purchase of the car and in the transportation and duty." She had to wait until April to find just the right chauffeur. She could not, as she said, "bear the thought of risking my life on these mountain curves and jammed city streets with a driver who did not know to trust the Lord." Driving was one skill Bertha never even attempted. She would put her hand to virtually any challenge but driving on Formosa's roads.

Bertha said of her return to the field, "When at six o'clock in the morning I hear the cook outside my door saying, 'Goo-morning,' to get me to take my breakfast tray, I know that I am back at work. When a hymn or Scripture passage is announced and I cannot find it for turning the wrong way, I know that I have been away."[8] At the time of her return the political situation in Formosa had become shaky. Mainland China was threatening. In church on her first Sunday back, Deacon Swang prayed, "Thank you that thus far we have been bombed only in the newspapers." That same week an earthquake rocked the island, prompting Bertha to write, "We had one [an earthquake] a few days ago, but not serious. Anyway, when your house begins to rock, one is grateful to be on the Firm Foundation and Solid Rock, ready to go or live on."[9]

While on furlough back in America, Bertha had injured her right hand in a minor auto accident; her fingers were stiff and she "wrote poorly." Her wrist was still twisted, but getting better. She said, "When the Japanese were here, they taught the blind Formosans to do massage. They walk the streets at night playing weird little tunes on their flutes so that anyone needing them may call them in. I have one come twice a day and hold my hand! He rubs, kneads, pats, pinches, strokes, pulls and wrings for twenty-five cents per treatment. I am counting on reaching my doctor's expectations to be using my typewriter and playing the piano by Christmas."[10]

189

Bertha believed that God heals, but she also used available medical help and thus maintained a healthy balance between faith and human instrumentality. She wrote to friends a little later, "My hand is slowly improving. By Christmas I was playing the organ for the chapel services and using the typewriter, and soon after I was able to comb my hair. I can now sew a little, but will not likely ever again make a dress on a Saturday afternoon for recreation."[11]

Bertha developed a small goiter in June that was removed by a goiter specialist who had recently arrived on the island. She thought she would be unable to talk very much after the surgery, but she confessed, "I suppose it would take more cutting than that to stop me from talking!" Miss Bertha's pet word for food that was tasteless was "punk." That's the way she described the hospital food. Martha and her cook took care of that need by supplying extra supplements to keep her in shape and her taste buds happy. Once when the doctor came in to check on her, he said that she was progressing remarkably well. Joseph Chang was in the room, and after the doctor left he prayed, "Lord, all these people here at the hospital are amazed over the rapid progress Miss Smith is making, but we know there is nothing strange about it. It is just your blessing."[12]

The first seminary class graduated fourteen students in May 1955—eleven men and three women. By this time, the seminary had a new chapel that was provided by funds from the Southern Baptist Cooperative Program. Furthermore, four churches had been planted in Taipei and thirteen on the entire island. Bertha described the Good Friday service of 1955: "The Lord came in power and melted hearts before Him. Like Isaiah, when we saw the Lord, we saw ourselves unclean. Slatted benches being knelt by were wept all over and little puddles of tears made on the floor under them."[13]

In July the churches enjoyed an excellent convention that was followed by the Mature People's Conference. At the testimony meeting after the message the last night, Bertha said people were "bobbing up all over the auditorium, two at a time to testify." Martha Franks had suggested this kind of testimony meeting and everyone received a blessing. Miss Bertha said, "You know modern Baptists know nothing about how to have a testimony meeting—they have never seen one."[14] On Friday, an overflowing crowd assembled when the Women's Missionary Society (WMS) and Brotherhood members of all the churches in Taipei gathered together at the conference. Helen Liu and Mrs. Meng, the two Bible women, gave presentations that day. The dining room would seat only 150 and over 200 gathered for dinner that evening. The menu consisted of meat and vegetables cooked together with plenty of rice. Bertha remarked that it was easy to stand and walk around, talking with folk while eating with chopsticks.

Following this conference, 185 younger girls and boys gathered for another conference, which proved to be as great a success. Missionary Katie Murray blessed everyone with her messages. Miss Bertha also spoke during the conference.

Everyday Life

Martha Franks raised calves for beef and always shared the bounty with Miss Bertha. They had a few chickens and, naturally, a vegetable garden. An American couple leaving for the States gave them the remaining contents of their refrigerator. One item was a quart of fresh milk and they relished it. While sipping on the delicious milk Bertha said to Martha, "There will be a lot of convenience in living permanently in America when one retires." Martha heartily agreed. They were both accustomed to drinking powdered milk which was not their favorite. Some visitors once came by and brought them a pound of fresh butter, two bunches of celery, some lemons, and a basket of apples. They enjoyed every morsel.

Martha Franks' truck often came in handy. For example, it enabled her to deliver two chests and a bookcase that Miss Bertha had the cabinet-makers construct for her study. She designed the shelving to fit her things. One shelf was designed to hold "curios or pretty vases if I ever get any," as she put it.

In August 1955 Miss Bertha again flew to Japan for her summer vacation and rest. Rest to Miss Bertha was, "getting completely away from my regular environment." She spent a day with the Connelys in Tokyo. Up in the mountains she attended a Spiritual Life Conference, slept late, and enjoyed long afternoon naps. After the conference, she took long walks through the groves of huge fir and cypress trees. One Saturday she and several other missionaries went on a picnic to Sunset Peak where they stood in awe of the wonderful view. They rode up the mountain but walked back. Miss Bertha said, "I had not walked so far in ten or twenty years." It was a three-mile hike. At the end of her monthlong holiday she made arrangements to return again the next summer.

In early November, Bertha had a delightful visitor who came for Sunday dinner. She was a little Chinese grandmother and longtime friend. Bertha described her as "cute and dear." The grandmother said, "I pray for Miss Franks just like I do for you! I pray for your cook and Joseph Chang, and I pray for the Culpeppers even though they have gone to America!" Then she said, "This morning when I got up it was raining, and I said, 'Heavenly Father, now just don't let it rain! I want to go to church and it will be too inconvenient to go in the rain!'" When the time arrived for her to catch the train, it had quit raining. Such experiences were common to these dedicated servants of God.

Seminary Labors

Miss Bertha taught Old Testament at the seminary upon her return from furlough in the fall of 1954. She did not always find teaching seminarians to be an easy task; at times it was laborious, but always a challenge. In December 1955 she wrote about class preparation in her weekly letter to Jennie: "I am at the most difficult portion of the whole Bible to understand, so the commentators say, in my course in Ezekiel." She had been asked by the dean to teach the Wisdom books in the spring, but "could not possibly do so. I will have twelve hours, and nine hours in Chinese language is considered a full load of teaching."[15]

On Tuesday of Christmas week 1955 Olive Lawton, Martha Franks, and Miss Bertha had the joy of being together for the entire day with no scheduled work. Miss Bertha wrote to Jennie, "Olive, Martha and I just sat by the fire and luxuriated in not having to hurry to some task. We ate dinner and supper by the fire on trays even though the dining table is in the living room, but we wanted to keep real warm. After supper we had time to pray together just as long as we liked which was also a luxury." On Wednesday Olive returned home. Miss Bertha spent the next few days writing letters. She wrote twenty-eight in two and a half days, "and even then did not get all my gifts thanked for," she said.

Billy Graham's Visit

In February 1956 Billy Graham came to Formosa to share the gospel of the Lord Jesus Christ. What a treat for the missionaries and Formosans! He spoke at a stadium that held eight thousand people; about forty thousand wanted tickets. Many who were unable to secure tickets gathered in the churches and listened to him over the radio. Miss Bertha and Martha received workers' badges because they were needed to do personal counseling. Miss Bertha said, "Billy Graham seems just as sweet and unspoiled as if he had never been invited to dine with the queen!"[16] True, Billy Graham never lost his childlike faith and humility even though he had been entertained in Buckingham Palace by England's monarch.

The week before Dr. Graham's arrival, Joe Carroll, a Baptist from Australia, spoke at the missionary retreat. He conducted a morning meeting and an evening service. Brother Carroll fasted and prayed at breakfast. He took only one light meal a day so he could give himself totally to the work of the conference. Harry Raley, a fellow missionary, made the statement,

"Maybe the reason more people are not saved in special meetings at home is because preachers eat so much!" Bertha said of Brother Carroll, "I do not believe I have ever seen such a man of God."[17]

Sister Jennie, who was most generous, often sent money to Bertha for mission purposes. Harry and Frances Raley, new missionaries, had visited with Jennie before they moved to Formosa. Jennie wanted to have a financial part in their ministry, so she sent Bertha twenty-five dollars to help in the delivery of the Raley's car to the island. Of course, the Raleys met Bertha. In a letter of thanks to Jennie, Harry Raley wrote: "One of the most interesting persons we have met since we have been on Formosa is your sister, Miss Bertha. We love to hear her talk. She has had some of the most interesting experiences we have ever heard. She never seems to run out of stories."[18]

Limitations

Miss Bertha was keenly aware of her physical limitations. When her schedule stressed her out, she would examine the situation and cut something out in order to rest and be properly prepared for the things she deemed most important. She had planned a weekend trip after Billy Graham's visit, but, as she expressed it, "was so exhausted I decided not to go." Since she had previously made arrangements to not be at the chapel, she just stayed home and rested. She strongly believed that her students at the seminary deserved to have a well-rested, well-prepared teacher facing them the next week. Martha had left on furlough; thus Bertha's teaching load at seminary was quite heavy. Not only that, she now served as acting Dean of Women and was teaching the class on Wisdom literature that she had formerly not wanted to teach. The load was heavy but she learned to cope.

Mrs. Helen Liu, who had been saved under Bertha's early ministry at the Gospel Hall, and whom Miss Bertha had previously taken to Tainan, came to Taipei to work with Miss Bertha. Bertha was only able to devote Friday evening through Sunday evening to the work in the churches because of her seminary responsibilities. When Mrs. Liu arrived, Bertha was thrilled because, as she wrote, "The work will pick up now that at least one person is working all the time. . . . Mrs. Liu, Phoebe, I named her, is a jewel. She will be invaluable in helping the women get ready to join the church, as she can go to their homes and teach them when they can't leave their little children."[19] Together, Mrs. Liu and Bertha served a little chapel and had hopes of organizing the chapel into another fully constituted church by the end of May. Helen became a close friend and valuable coworker.

The weekend before Easter, Miss Bertha had to miss all services because of an infection on her right eyelid. The doctor thought she had been bitten by a spider while asleep, and instructed her to rest, put in the drops he had given, and keep ice packs on it. She commented that she had "never seen a spider in our house, it being well screened, but mosquitoes do get in sometimes and some of them are very poisonous." The event she missed most during her time of rest and recuperation was the missionary prayer meeting held every Saturday at noon. Even though she followed all of the doctor's orders, the infection flared up again two weeks later. This time a different doctor ordered drops and hot packs. The infection was soon cured and she threw herself into the work again.

The missionary prayer meetings started by Miss Bertha involved missionaries from several denominations. Bertha believed in celebrating their unity in Christ, their mutual concern for lost souls on the island, and bending the knees together, seeking the face of God to ask for souls for His Kingdom.

On Easter Sunday Bertha delivered a felt-o-graph talk in a local park at a "Youngsters' Retreat" conducted by two seminary students. After her story the children quoted Scripture and sang songs; then one of the students brought a basket of dyed red eggs and had her hand one to each child as she said, "Christ is risen." The child bowed and replied, "He is risen indeed!" A number of onlookers gathered around to see what was happening. Among them was a navy lieutenant, as Bertha said, "looking so nice in his blue uniform with gold braid, to whom my chauffeur talked, and I talked with him a bit about the Lord and invited him to the chapel."[20] That night he came.

As the day drew near for the little chapel to be constituted into a full church, a time was set to hear the testimonies of those who would be baptized and become charter members of the new congregation. So many wanted to give testimonies that several services had to be set aside for that purpose. "One old woman, elegant old soul, never got up in public before," said Bertha. "I was sitting on the end of the front seat next to the organ where I sit when I play, which is all the time. She walked up in front of everybody but turned her face toward me and just told me all about it!"[21] The woman had worshiped idols for seventy-six years. Her son and his wife had been converted two years before and had begged her to turn to Christ. A neighbor had come to her house from time to time and talked to her about the Lord. Finally, as Bertha described it, "she saw all of the sins of the 76 years and, brought them to Christ." Victories abounded.

Miss Bertha suggested that the new church be a "Sunday morning church," because the buses were simply too crowded on Sunday evenings for people to get there, and only a few members lived within walking dis-

tance. The suggestion met with approval and the church was duly constituted on Mother's Day, May 14. Fern Harrington was there for the
service. Fern was now a teacher in the seminary at Baguio, Philippines,
and had come to Formosa for rest and a visit with Miss Bertha. She had
not been well. After the full day of festivities planned by Miss Bertha, Fern
said to her, "I would love to see you perform a wedding ceremony. They
would surely be married when you got through with them." Miss Bertha
smiled and replied, "Fern, I have never been able to do a thing by halves."
While visiting Formosa, Fern spoke of the work in the Philippines during
one of the chapel services at the seminary.

One day the young man who served as Bertha's secretary after Joseph
left to attend seminary asked if he could talk with her. He knew things
were not right in his relationship with Christ. Bertha canceled a Sunday
dinner engagement in order to counsel the young man. After much Bible
reading and discussion he knelt and "confessed his sins and appropriated
the Lord's death for cleansing." By faith he took the Lord as his Victor.
Then he chose a few hymns, and as Miss Bertha played the piano he sang
them to the Lord. Later he said, "People ought to learn the *is* of God."[22]

Keeping in Touch and Sharing Blessings

When Miss Bertha wrote to Jennie on Sunday, July 8, 1956, she closed
her letter by saying, "We are expecting the Communists to take Formosa!" Her postscript read, "All buildings had flags out this morning and
the streets lined with people awaiting the President escorting Vice President Nixon into the city." The knowledge of the political situation never
filled her mind with worry, however; nor did it slow her pace. She viewed
things with the "mind of Christ" and continued with her work.

When Bertha took her regular holiday in the mountains of Japan in
August, she heard Dr. John R. Rice, an American evangelist, speak. She
invited him to her place for a simple Sunday dinner of lightly fried boiled
ham, fried corn, fried apples, and a tomato and lettuce salad. This trip also
once again offered her the privilege of being with former China missionaries who were serving in Japan. In a letter she wrote to Jennie from Japan,
she expressed how grateful she was for the opportunity to work in Formosa, where she could continue to work in a Chinese context. She spent
the night with the Connelys on the way to the mountains and also saw
them at a mission meeting. It was the last time she would see Frank. In the
fall, she received word that he had died suddenly of a heart attack.
Through the years, Mary Connely had suffered ill health. No one, not
even Mary, thought he would go first.

During an evangelistic campaign in November, a young military officer who began attending the church services some six months before, came to the Lord. When he first started coming to the church, he would rush out after the service, saying, "Oh, I do not believe any of this! I just come to get away from my barracks environment and I like the rest of sitting here and listening to the singing." Miss Bertha said, "We kept our prayer guns turned on him." During one evening service, he was seated near the front. "When he opened his eyes after the silent prayer at the close of the service he found me sitting beside him," stated Miss Bertha. "When I expressed my desire for him to come to the Lord he said, 'Pastor Smith, as soon as these people have gone I want you to pray with me. I have been in misery for two weeks.'"[23] That very night he came to Christ.

In almost every letter written to Jennie in 1956, Miss Bertha told her about different house guests she entertained or a dinner party she hosted for missionaries passing through. At times as many as eighteen were seated for dinner. And, as she said, "I never have been able to do things by halves." Her table, often set with place cards, cut flowers, and the best dishes, shone with elegance. Always a gracious hostess, she wrote, "I have had my breakfast by the fire in my study where I slept last night as I gave my bed to Lucy Stokes and Annie Hoover of Japan."[24]

A New Year

Soon after the dawn of the new year of 1957, Miss Bertha sat at her typewriter and wrote her first letter of the year: "1917—forty years ago I came to China! Few missionaries have had the privilege of giving that much time to the mission field. It has indeed been short and wonderful."[25] That January she spent all of her spare time preparing messages to deliver in the Philippines, where she had been invited to speak at a series of meetings that concerned the possibility of organizing the Baptist Convention of Chinese churches of the Philippines, along with the constitution of individual Chinese churches. After arriving in the Philippines she wrote, "Here I am working away studying, praying, fasting, expecting the second day of the meeting." While there she visited several mission points with Fern Harrington. After one service where several people made decisions, Fern said to her, "Bertha, I never heard you speak like that before!" She replied, "It was not I." Miss Bertha always gave God all the glory, aware that the Lord had said, "My glory I will not give to another" (Isa. 42:8).

Later, in her newsletter to praying friends, Bertha wrote, "I had not had such a good time since revival days in North China as I experienced during the two weeks in the Philippines."[26] Fern regretted that there was no time for Bertha to see "beautiful Baguio," but had to agree with Bertha, "that the most refreshing sight-seeing was tears of Christians shed over their failure before the Lord."

Ten days of evangelistic meetings were held at the Formosa church in February. Joseph Chang preached several evenings. Bertha said of him, "Instead of using illustrations and working on the will to get the people to make a decision, he just preaches what God has done about sins, presents the Savior, and lets the truth make its own appeal. This is the way to preach to people who are not gospel hardened."[27]

In the spring the churches were busy planning and preparing for a simultaneous evangelistic campaign. Dr. C. E. Autrey, professor of evangelism at Southwestern Seminary in Fort Worth, Texas, spent two days with them to help the campaign get started. Bertha said, "He is surely a ball of fire for the Lord."[28] Miss Bertha, busy from then on, went from church to church leading conferences on how to do personal work. One Sunday afternoon, after a very busy week, she slept for two hours. She slept too late to attend the service down the mountain. Soon after she awakened, two young U.S. Army men knocked on her door. One was a Baptist from Mississippi, the other, a graduate of Syracuse University from New York state, with two years of seminary. They fell into conversation, and as always, Bertha got to the heart of the matter: their relationship with Christ. She immediately sensed that they knew very little about what it meant to be victorious in Christ. She said, "I had a good time with them in the sixth chapter of Romans telling them how we live victoriously." God had graciously rearranged her schedule by allowing her to oversleep in order to accomplish His purposes; part of the reward was also that extra hour or two of rest.

Overcoming Difficulties

By May the evangelistic campaign moved into full swing. The weather was "hot, hot, hot!" as Bertha described it. She wrote in a letter to Jennie, "It takes two dresses a day in hot weather." May brought its spring flowers, but also troubles for Miss Bertha as well. Her chauffeur was down for over five weeks with a kidney infection and spent time in the hospital twice, causing her to miss meetings, ride buses, or beg for rides. Then an epidemic of flu hit that took down her cook. Bertha was spared the illness, but not the inconvenience of less service. It hit the hardest during the campaign. Even so, hundreds were reached with the gospel. Two "May flowers" were: the news that Martha Franks and her sister, Allene, had boarded the steamer in New York and would be back by July 4, and twenty students graduated from seminary, ready for service. A beautiful bouquet from the "Rose of Sharon."

Political unrest continued, like the sacking of the American Embassy. Near the end of May, Americans were advised to not be out and about. So, Miss Bertha had a Saturday at home. For some time she had been concerned for the souls of the three Culpepper children; they had not yet come to Christ. The Culpeppers had joined the ranks of Baptist missionaries on Formosa. Bertha used that Saturday, as she described it, to "take the time needed with them with my pretty felt-o-graph stories on how to be saved." All three of the Culpepper children were born again that afternoon. She said, "So that was an ill will that brought good."[29] Soon afterwards, the Culpeppers flew home for furlough, and Bertha inherited their five parakeets—two were green and three were yellow. Fortunately for Miss Bertha, somebody else took their monkey.

Miss Bertha had a way with children. She prayed for God to show her how to make the gospel clear, not only to children, but also to people of all ages. She was convinced that God gave her a creative method of communicating the stories of Jesus using her felt-o-graph. In several of her letters home, she talked of using her felt-o-graph stories with the children, and most often the hearers "passed from death to life." She used the felt-o-graph throughout her days on the mission field—even in America with adults. It proved very effective indeed.

Conferences at the campgrounds in Formosa were held in July. Martha had returned from furlough, and Bertha wrote to Jennie about Martha's return, "I will be too excited to keep my mind and heart on the conference I fear." The bonds formed between missionaries are sometimes stronger than family bonds. Bertha was able to arrange her schedule so she could meet the steamer when Martha and Allene arrived. Soon after their arrival, Allene penned a note to Jennie at the bottom of one of Bertha's weekly letters. It read:

> You and I have heard much about this place but the half has never been told! . . . Jennie, you and I have the most wonderful missionary sisters in the world. They are doing a good job! No one knows the work that is involved in these conferences, only the ones who have planned one. I told Bertha and Martha that I wanted to see just as much of them as I could here on earth because they would get such a high place in heaven we wouldn't be able to see them there![30]

With all of the conferences, meetings, and guests, Allene said she would be glad when all the company and extra meetings were over and things settled down. Bertha told her, "One didn't settle down on the mission field."

Travels and Ministry

Miss Bertha had not planned a trip to Japan that summer and wondered why God had not led her to do so. The answer came late in July when she received a cable from the mission in Bangkok, inviting her to speak twice a day in August at a conference for young people. She decided to visit the mission work in Java afterwards, then holiday in Hong Kong in an air-conditioned hotel owned by a Christian. Just before leaving on the trip, she sent a letter to Jennie requesting prayer for a new secretary and chauffeur. The two now serving her were definitely going to seminary in the fall. It delighted Miss Bertha to see God lay His hand upon her helpers and commission them to preach.

Bertha had an especially exciting introduction in 1957. She met James Taylor, the grandson of Hudson Taylor, the founder of the China Inland Mission and something of the father of the faith mission movement. When Mr. Taylor met Bertha, he asked, "Does the name Ma Tang ring a bell with you?" Bertha replied that it did. She went on to say that he was a man from Honan who served as the county superintendent in Tsining, who had come to Christ in Bertha's house twenty years ago. She shared how they had experienced a great time of prayer together. Bertha wanted to know if Mr. Taylor knew him. Taylor replied, "Come to see my wife and she will fill you with his story."

Bamboo Princess

While ministering in a southern city in Formosa a few months later, Bertha received an invitation to the Taylor's home for lunch. There Mrs. Taylor told her of an incident that took place before she and her husband had to leave the mainland of China and take up work in Formosa. As the Japanese armies invaded Honan Province, the Taylors moved west and opened a Bible school in Sian, Shensi Province. They organized churches and saw many come to faith in Christ. Brother Ma Tang, as an ordained pastor, became a teacher in their Bible school. The students were refugees from Shensi and the eastern provinces who were deeply dedicated to Christ and the work. Some of the tragedies they had experienced truly tested their faith. One particular student was especially brilliant but did not even know her family name. Both her parents had perished in a sweeping cholera epidemic in Kiangsu Province. When her parents died, she and her brother went to live with an uncle whom she remembered was named Li. The uncle, being far from a Christian, was content to keep the nephew. However, he had no intention of supporting his twelve-year-old destitute niece. So he dressed her up in bright garments, put a flower in her hair, and took her on his back over the rice fields to the city and sold her as a white slave, ultimately into the prostitution business. Yet, the young girl had a deep conscience and everything in her revolted against her forced lifestyle. Finally, she could endure it no longer. She got hold of some poison and sneaked out to the Yangtze river to take it and drown herself in the waters.

When she lifted the poison up to her mouth, an audible voice suddenly startled her, "Go back! Go back." She looked around but could see no one. Again the voice said, "Go back. Go back!" Startled, yet terribly grieved over returning to the brothel, but afraid to disobey the voice, she returned. Sometime later a rich merchant from Peking went to the brothel and found her crying. She pleaded with him to take her out of that place and release her from such slavery. Touched by her story, he bought her and took her up into Honan Province where he owned a business. He was married with children, but the family lived in Peking.

Serving as a concubine was not as loathsome to her as being a prostitute, but she still felt terribly unhappy. One day her businessman rescuer asked, "How is it that nothing that I do for you makes you happy? I buy pretty clothes and jewelry for you, provide servants and good food, take you to the movies and theater, and still you are unhappy. The Christians are happy. I will send you to their church."[31] The next Sunday she went to a little church and an uneducated Chinese preacher preached that no concubine could go to heaven. She did not go to that church again.

As the Japanese armies began to invade sections of Honan, the rich man and his concubine moved into Sian to the very same inn where the Taylors were living. Realizing they were Christians, the miserable young woman asked Mrs. Taylor if it were true that a concubine could not be saved.

Mrs. Taylor began to counsel her and explain what the Bible had to say concerning her need for forgiveness and salvation. Soon she was on her knees pouring out her heart in confession. She rose praising the Lord. A short time later the husband sent for his wife and children to join him in Sian to get away from the invading Japanese armies. The businessman's wife was a well-educated and cultured woman who had been teaching in the Peking language school. The husband had been so impressed by the change in his concubine that before his wife's arrival, he went to Mrs. Taylor wanting to know how to be saved. After an hour or two of witnessing and sharing Bible promises, he, too, came to faith in Christ. Mrs. Taylor said that he poured out such a volume of sin in his confession that afterwards she felt the need for a bath. But the Lord met him, and he rose with his heart cleansed from sin and as a born-again believer.

In the meantime, the wife had heard about her husband's concubine. She purchased a revolver with the intention of shooting the concubine, then the husband, then the children one by one, and lastly, herself. But when she entered the home, the concubine was quiet and humble and remained in the background, giving the wife her rightful place. Upon witnessing the change in her husband, and hearing his testimony, and seeing the concubine such as she had never seen one before, the wife decided that she wanted to know how to be saved. After seeing Mrs. Taylor, she came to faith in Jesus Christ and arose a new creature.

The concubine, whose name was Chu-chun (which means Bamboo Princess), applied to the Bible School. Mrs. Taylor wrote a note to the husband requesting that he release her to attend school. Not only did this newly born-again Christian man release her, but he also placed a sum of money in the bank in her name. She could live on the interest while in school and use the capital for her old age. He said that Bamboo Princess was now free to live her own life and would be no more to him than any other woman. Mr. James Taylor baptized all three of them in the nearby river the following Sunday, and they became faithful members of the local church.

After some years passed, Pastor Ma Tang was off for the weekend preaching in another city during the Easter season. Early on Easter morning he went out by a river to spend time with the Lord. As he was praying and rejoicing in the resurrection of the Savior, he began to think of those to the west who did not know Christ. He became very burdened for those in the outlying provinces of China, Tibet, and even as far as Palestine. As Pastor Ma prayed earnestly, he began to feel that the Lord would lead him to form an evangelistic band that would take the gospel all the way to Jerusalem.

As the providence of God would have it, Pastor Ma was at the river praying, while other faculty members of the Bible School and students were having an early morning sunrise service in the school yard. The Taylors had drawn a map of the outlying provinces of west China and Tibet on the ground. During the service, they challenged anyone who felt led to go and stand on the map where he or she felt the Lord may be leading them. One by one the students stood on different points of the map. Some felt called to the provinces of China and Tibet. One wanted to take the gospel to Afghanistan. Another was willing to go as far as Arabia to the city of Mecca. When Pastor Ma realized what the students had done and how he had been praying to the same purpose; he was thrilled with the leading of the Holy Spirit.

The students prayed and studied the various countries and traveling conditions for months. Finally, a group of twelve, including Bamboo

Princess, went forth. They actually divided into two groups. One group went toward the northwest and the other to the south. They had their work well organized. They planned to stop at certain centers and preach the gospel until some were saved, and then organize them into a church. One of the workers would stay with the new congregation until local leaders were trained and the work could be carried on. Then the worker would travel on and attempt to repeat the same task. They were following the Pauline pattern almost perfectly. They felt that eventually a line of churches would be established all the way back to the Holy Land.

As they continued their westward ministry, they found young people who had preceded them all along the way, hoping to keep ahead of the Japanese army. Some were graduates of China's best universities. There were even some from Bible colleges who desperately wanted to serve the Lord.

The group became known as the "Back to Jerusalem Band." They traveled through city after city and led many young people to Christ. Every place they touched, young people volunteered for Christian work. Pastor Ma Tang himself went to the city of Chengtu to enlist the interest and support of the churches in the new venture. There a great number of college students were saved, many of whom felt the call to preach. Their need for Bible training led Pastor Ma to establish a seminary on the border of Tibet. By that time, two of the mission workers were already in Tibet. Although they were experiencing severe trials, at times having to hide in tall grass by the hour, God was giving them great success. Many were won to Christ. How did it all begin? What launched such a tremendous far-flung movement? It all began many years before in an all-night prayer meeting at Bertha's house when Pastor Ma gave himself completely to the Savior for whatever service God called him. What a victory for Miss Bertha's ministry, not to mention Pastor Ma, Bamboo Princess, and many like her.

The Last Year on the Field

Despite all the victories, sadly, Miss Bertha's days in China were drawing to a close. Early in January 1958, which was to be Bertha's last year on the field, she made an important decision. She wrote to Jennie saying, "I have asked to be relieved from the seminary this spring so that I could go to as many churches and chapels as possible during the year."[32] Her seventieth birthday was approaching and she must retire. Soon after making this decision, she received more than twenty calls issuing invitations. It seemed that God was beginning to prepare her for the sort of ministry she would soon exercise in America.

In March Miss Bertha traveled to Kaohisung for eight days where she led the daily morning prayer meetings, delivered messages in the evening, spoke at the Woman's Meeting, and, as she said, "On Sunday I spoke twice." Her house in Kaohisung was cold. Despite the cement floors, she "did not suffer since I had my electric pad and do all of my preparations in bed."[33] In writing to Jennie about her trip she wrote, "I would put a fireplace in [the house in Kaohisung], and if I did not have the money I would pray some down from heaven by way of somebody who does have it."[34] She was still "earthy Bertha."

"Six Turtles," a community in a valley between high mountains where Bertha had spent ten days six years before, invited Bertha back to minister. Katie Murray accompanied her on the trip. The congregation was made up primarily of Formosans, with a few mainlanders who were teachers, post office clerks, or telegraph operators. A woman from a mountain tribe who was eager to attend the meetings, traveled ten miles down the mountain. She rode on a bicycle with a two-year-old child in a little chair attached to the front, her bag of clothes lashed to the rear, and a tiny baby tied on her back. The route she took had many suspension bridges with foot boards missing. Miss Bertha said, "I hope she got enough spiritual refreshment to compensate for the even harder journey back up [the mountain] to an unsaved husband."

In May, while trying to lead Christians into a life of victory and joy at a meeting for mainlanders, Bertha asked one old woman if she had any unconfessed sins in her life. The woman said she didn't know. Then Miss Bertha asked, "Do you get angry?" The old woman replied, "Do you think I could have a daughter-in-law and not get angry?" Miss Bertha then told her that anger is often a sin. The following evening when Miss Bertha looked at her she could see that "her faced showed the sin still in her heart." Again she was urged to confess her wrongdoing and bad attitude. That night the mother-in-law went home a miserable woman. She could not sleep. On Sunday morning she arose "with tears streaming and confessed her sin to the daughter-in-law, who also began crying and claiming the fault to be hers. The son mingled his tears with theirs and took all the blame upon himself, and after breakfast went out and bought the old mother a present."[35] By the end of May, Bertha had led thirteen different meetings. Her energy seemed inexhaustible.

Back in America, Mr. Tisdale, a dear friend of Miss Bertha, had for nine years been sending out her annual newsletter. In 1958 he changed jobs and could no longer keep up this labor of love. But soon it would no longer be needed because before long Bertha would return home to Cowpens in retirement. Nonetheless, she gave herself tirelessly in her remaining time among the Chinese.

Continuing Travels

In June and July Miss Bertha traveled to the Philippines, Korea, and Japan. She reported that she went without a hat, spoke forty-three times, directed prayer meetings and personal interviews—and she gained five pounds! She took advantage of passing through Japan to lead eight meetings for missionary Elizabeth Watkins. She also visited with Mary Culpepper Walker, and spoke three times while with her.

The General Convention of Formosa met in late July. Joseph Chang was elected to serve as president. At the time he was serving as pastor of the Jen Ai Church. Miss Bertha was asked to sit on the platform with Joseph during the last evening session. Alex Herring, who had been on the island for approximately a year and had served with Bertha in China, gave the closing message. Miss Bertha was asked to stand while Joseph made a few remarks concerning her forty-one years as a missionary. In his remarks he asked "if it would not have been worthwhile if the only results of the work had been Joseph."[36] (She had known him since he was twelve.) After his comments he asked Alex to pray for Miss Bertha.

Another spiritual treat came in Bertha's last year in Taiwan. She, along with the other missionaries, was blessed beyond measure when Miss Corie Ten Boom led a "little retreat for us for about two hours beginning at ten o'clock." These times of fellowship and challenge provided food for the soul.

Bertha wrote to Jennie, "Old people surely get spoiled. Let's you and I help each other and keep ourselves from getting old." When Bertha first went to China, she thought that her fellow missionaries in their early forties were old. Now near age seventy herself, she did not like to talk about "getting old." Always young at heart, she nonetheless realized she was "becoming of age!"

A Painful Prospect

Bertha found it very painful to think of leaving the Chinese. She was still working fifteen hours a day and was never too tired to get up the next morning. And God continued to honor her labors. Just a short time before her last leave of Formosa, she planted a new church in the heart of Taipei, the capital city. "Imagine my delight," she said. "I went to visit the building which had been secured for the new mission to find it just a half block from a little lot that I had considered for a church site soon after my arrival in Taipei. In six years' time we saw that the question had not been whether the Lord wanted the church in the center of the city or in a residential section where we had gone first, He had planned for one in each location."[37]

A strong church was established in a short time with the help of seminary students as coworkers. This church asked her to give a full week to special meetings during her last week on the island. She was still going strong. However, according to her mission board's policy, all missionaries were retired on the first day of the month following the month of their seventieth birthday. November 30 that year came on Sunday. It was her last official day of work as a regular missionary. What a wrench it was to think of leaving the Chinese people. Bertha confessed:

> Becoming of age! What pain! I never dreamed that anything in this life could ever hurt like giving up work with the Chinese and returning home. . . . I felt that I was just then qualified from experience for missionary work. The forty-one and a half years had been very short, interesting indeed, at times thrilling, and always rewarding. Every trial along the way had been forgotten as soon as the next person was saved.[38]

On Miss Bertha's last Sunday in China, everyone had such a glorious time that she wondered why November could not have had thirty-one days. Bertha felt, as she said, that she was just beginning to qualify for real missionary effectiveness. She had spent forty-one and a half years ministering to the Chinese, and the years seemed so very short. But how fascinating, interesting, thrilling, and rewarding they were! Bertha said every trial she had encountered on the way was forgotten in the blessings of God.

Bertha had been appointed before the Foreign Mission Board adopted a retirement policy. Yet she did not disagree with the Mission Board's retirement policy even though she said, "I signed up for life, and I thought I should be permitted to go on for life."[39] She felt that would be at least 100. She had a great-grandfather and uncle who lived to be 100 and 103 respectively; Bertha knew she had good genes. But the Board had supported and undergirded her, and the policy, after all, was by and large wise. She left it to their discretion. As her dear friend Martha Franks said, "Bertha always worked well under authority and respected places of leadership—and that to her credit. But had it been up to her, she would have never retired." Bertha wrapped it all up by saying, "The dear Lord was so wonderful to me that during the last ten days, He moved the hearts of seven people for whom I had been praying for some time (one of them for nine years) to turn to Him. They came one by one asking for personal help. What joy in my sorrow to see them at the airport when I left. Praise the Lord for the gift of eternal life. What contrast in my emotions when I flew away from Taipei to those I had when I docked in Shanghai nearly forty-two years before!"[40]

Miss Bertha, our "Woman of Revival," had to "go home and tell." She was convinced God had called her to do so. And go home and tell she did. Incredible as it may seem, a new saga of service that spanned almost thirty more years was about to begin.

17

On the Wings of a Dove

Taiwan Baptist Theological Seminary faculty members
including Bertha and Martha Franks. *Credit: FMB*

Bertha left the Far East with a heavy heart. Twenty years later she would still say, "It almost killed me to leave China." For over forty glorious years she had labored among the Chinese, first on the mainland, then on the island of Taiwan. God had cut a swath of revival through the largest nation on earth, and in many respects Bertha stood at the cutting edge of the movement. What a legacy she left: the first Baptist missionary on Formosa, six churches on the island that God used her to help plant, not to mention untold blessings in Shantung.

The Huai Ning Church in Taipei had requested that Bertha stay on after retirement. Her Chinese friends had as much difficulty with the change taking place in Miss Bertha's life as she. In a letter to the Board, however, she wrote, "Having cooperated with our marvelous Board for nearly forty two years, I am not about to ask to do otherwise now. However, I do feel it necessary to ask for your prayers that I may have the strength of the Lord to do so. Only when one has given his or herself to the Chinese for this long a period can they know what pulling away is like. But I thoroughly approve of the policy of the Board and am grieved at the way some are taking it." So, it was home to America. She knew God was sending her home—and sending her with a message.

But what would America be like? Would they respond to her message? While home on furloughs and during World War II she had enjoyed good experiences of ministry, but how would she be received now? The Holy Spirit had given her the commission of Isaiah 58:1, "Cry loudly, do not hold back; Raise your voice like a trumpet, And declare to my people their transgression, And to the house of Jacob their sins" (NASB). Still, she had to ask those questions.

It soon became evident that the American years were to be glorious years. Miss Bertha was far from retired. An important ministry unfolded for her even before she returned to America. It became something of a launching pad God would use to fling her into full-time ministry in the United States.

Bertha had received about three thousand dollars from a deceased relative. With this money, a small savings account, and several gifts from friends, she financed a world-wide visit to various mission stations. On this tour she visited thirty-four countries. She ministered as she visited, and her tour became a revival pathway around the world.

Because of Bertha's deep commitment to the principles of fellowship with the Holy God, confession of sins, absolute committal to Jesus Christ, the crucified life, the fullness of the Holy Spirit, and evangelism, she was destined to be used by the Spirit of God to precipitate genuine renewal wherever she went. She was so energized with the power of the Holy Spirit that fallow ground broke up, barriers tumbled down, churches were deeply moved, and many souls came to Christ. Her world-wide tour is a fascinating story in revivalism.

A New Beginning

In May 1958, prior to retirement in December, Bertha traveled and ministered for seven weeks in the Philippines, Korea, and Japan. She spoke over forty times besides directing prayer meetings and giving personal interviews. After her seventieth birthday, she was invited back to the Philippines to serve for two months. She sought permission from the Foreign Mission Board to fill this engagement after retirement and to visit mission points in Europe, Nigeria, and Ghana on her way home to the States.

Bertha was relieved about the political situation in Formosa, the land she so loved. The Chinese Communists from the mainland, who had been committed to capturing the island, began to shell two small off-shore islands occupied by the Nationalist Armies—Quimoy and Matsu. In a message delivered to the world, President Eisenhower pledged to keep the integrity of the Nationalist government in Taiwan and to the two nearby islands. Bertha said, "When we heard it we rejoiced!" To Jennie she wrote, "Of course, all are waiting with baited breath, as it were, to see what the Communists are going to do about the shelling." Eisenhower's strong stand kept the integrity of the islands and they remain a free sovereign state to this day. She could now leave with confidence and a peaceful heart. The work would go on.

Before Bertha left Taipei, she had witnessed the ordination of five young men to the ministry. And now the moment drew near when she must prepare for her actual departure. On December 13, 1958, she typed a letter to Jennie: "Last Wednesday night at the farewell meeting of Amoy St. Church which used to be the Gospel Center, which I opened in 1950, they had a lovely Farewell service and presented me with a pin, carved coral which is a beauty. Then a few individuals wanted to give something themselves so two or three gave things that will take space."[1]

As Christmas approached, Bertha made her final preparations for the round-the-world trip. She had dresses made by a tailor from material Olive Lawton had brought from the States when she returned from furlough (Olive had been assigned to Taipei and would live with Martha). She also tried on hat forms until she found one that fit, then purchased navy silk in the city to cover it. She said, "I wanted a silk hat so I could wear it with thin dresses in the tropics and then with a suit in northern Europe." She worked hard to keep the weight of her two medium bags within the limit of forty-four pounds.

Because there was no meeting scheduled on the Friday night before Christmas, Martha Franks got out the projector and they viewed slides Olive had brought from home. Some were scenes of home that brought a little homesickness. Others were pictures of Norway that included a slide of Marie Monsen. Bertha, Olive, and Martha were thrilled as they remembered the impact she had exercised on so many lives. Bertha's upcoming trip would include stops in Norway and Sweden, where she hoped to visit Marie. She also wanted to see the land of the midnight sun and visit the mission field of the Southern Baptists in Spain.

Around the World

On January 13, 1959, Bertha left on the first leg of her trip for a ministry in the Philippines. Missionary Britt Towery of Formosa wrote, "It will be a long time before we in Taiwan get used to the fact that Bertha Smith is really gone." She planned to stay in the Philippines until February 16. From there her travels would take her to Singapore.

Bertha had wanted Jennie to meet her in Europe. She had been trying to persuade Jennie to come to Taiwan for several years, but Jennie said, "Such a trip would swallow all of my savings in one gulp." Bertha offered to take the money she made from the sale of her possessions to cover Jennie's expenses. She wanted Jennie to meet her in Taiwan, stay with her for a month, then go home by way of Europe. Returning through Europe would cost no more than a direct return from Taiwan. But Jennie chose not to leave the old homestead. So Bertha went on her own. What a fascinating itinerary God arranged for her trip of January 13 to September 15, 1959:

January 13–February 19: The Philippines
February 10–March 6: Indonesia
March 6-16–Australia
March 16-24–Malaya-Singapore
March 24-30–Saigon, Vietnam, and Bangkok, Thailand
April 1-4–Rangoon, Burma
April 4-6–Ramna, Dacca
April 6-13–Calcutta and Benares, India
April 13-23–New Delhi, and Ludhianan, India
April 23-24–Iran
April 27-30–Cairo, Egypt
May 1- 4–Lebanon and Jordan
May 15-20–Israel
May 21-25–Istanbul, Turkey, and Athens, Greece
May 28-30–Rome, Italy
June 1-8–Ghana, West Africa
June 8-July14–Nigeria, West Africa
July 15-20–Italy, Switzerland, Germany, Denmark, Sweden, Norway, Netherlands, Belgium
August 15-September 7: British Isles
September 7-15: Visiting nieces and nephews around New York City
September 15: Spartanburg and Cowpens, South Carolina

The Philippines

Needless to say, Bertha kept on the move—and she spread blessings everywhere she went. While in the Philippines she spoke several times during Religious Emphasis at the Baptist University. She said, "I am having about 600 students attend my evening services and have marvelous attention." She also spoke to the nurses at the hospital. The Northern

Baptists (now American Baptist Churches) invited her to speak at their mission meeting during the closing session.

On February 19, Bertha wrote sister Jennie about her trip to the south end of the island of Mindanao. To get there she drove eighty miles over rough Philippine roads through beautiful coconut plantations, banana and coffee farms. The coffee plants were in bloom with fine white small lacy blooms. The bushes were only three or four feet high and very fragrant. Bertha said, "They did not smell at all like coffee." There were few churches in that section of the Philippines. The work had only begun a few years prior to her visit, but, as Bertha said, "It is marvelous what has been accomplished."[2]

Indonesia

On February 20 Bertha flew to Indonesia, arriving in Djakarta at five-thirty. Then on the twenty-sixth, she flew to Mt. City on a small plane where she stayed with Grace Wells. She wrote, "I went to church in a cute little pedicab down near the ground. The peddlers bicycle part being in the back instead of the front. It does not matter if he spits on a windy day!"[3] On Sunday afternoon she flew to Kediri where the Baptist hospital and seminary are located. While in Kediri, Bertha stayed with Catherine Walker. Dr. McCall, formerly of China, was president of the seminary where six women and twenty men were students. Bertha spoke daily at the seminary for a week. Blessings abounded throughout this "retired" missionary's visit. Several students asked for personal conferences. Miss Bertha talked with one student about his sins that he had to make right. Afterwards he went to others and apologized for his wrongs against them. By the time he got to Mrs. Walker's home, as Bertha described the scene, "He sat with his head on the desk and sobbed like a baby." He requested time the next day to apologize to the entire student body. He had rebelled against school regulations and against other students because they would not join him in his rebellion. After he opened his whole heart, he just sat down on the front row and wept. Many praised the Lord for the radical change they saw in him. One evening all the missionaries of the station assembled at the home of Dr. Kathleen Jones and Ruth Ford for ice cream and cake. Dr. Jones announced that Dr. Crawley of the Foreign Mission Board had written them to make the most of Bertha's visit, that she was one whom the Lord truly used. The group asked her to bring a message and she spoke from one of her favorite passages, Romans 6:11–14. After a tour of the hospital the following morning, she went to Saraboja on the east coast of Java. She had a first-class air conditioned car. She said, "I can tell you that it was appreciated for it is H-O-T!" A businessman from the hospital traveled with her. After a full weekend of speaking in Java, she flew to Djakarta, then on to Australia.

Australia

Bertha kept up her faithful correspondence with Jennie in all the fascinating places she visited. Jennie had written and asked if she planned to see Billy Graham in Australia. Bertha, who deeply admired Dr. Graham, replied:

> I have seen him and heard him five times. He and I were first on the same program at Ben Lippen when he was only 22. I thought him a wonder then. I heard him for a week at Winona Lake in 1946. In 1953, the first time he came to Formosa, he took meals with me and the last time he came, I was the one who hauled him around in my car to see the Baptist work and to the airport. He is now on the Foreign Mission Board, and at last October's meeting, when I was retired by the Board, he made a little speech in my behalf and Dr. Crawley took the trouble to write and tell me about it.[4]

Bertha attended the Billy Graham Crusade in Melbourne. When he heard she was there, he had her sit on the platform one evening and give her testimony. He then invited her to stay at the hotel as his guest. She said, "After the introduction I was invited out by so many for meals that he will not have to pay much for food!"

A Good Plan

Bertha discovered a way to maintain a high level of energy during these months of travel. She planned a full day of rest once a week. She also found her side trips and rides into the countryside very refreshing as she beheld the beauty of God's creation in the different countries. Good planning! Then off to her next engagement.

Burma

From Burma Bertha wrote, "The idolatry in this twentieth century is appalling. I've seen more people bowing before idols than all my life up to that time. Of the 200,000 Baptists in Burma only 8,000 are of Buddhist background. Others are the tribes' people who were animist. They have 1,800 churches and 1,500 pastors, but I fear the spiritual state is rather low. There is no prayer meeting tonight, which tells a good deal."[5] And to think, this is the land the legendary missionary Adoniran Judson opened

On the Wings of a Dove

up with the gospel. Miss Bertha came away from this part of her tour with
a heavy burden for the lost.

India

Bertha exclaimed, "What a great day I had yesterday in Calcutta." Saturday evening she had tea with the British Baptist missionary who served
as pastor of Carey Baptist Church. He took her on a tour of the church,
then on Sunday morning sent for her to attend the English service. She
was served the Lord's Supper in Carey's church. At three o'clock she
attended the Chinese Baptist service in Carey's old church. She witnessed
the baptism of seven Chinese in the same pool where Judson and Luther
Rice were baptized. Bertha spoke, reveling in the fact that she stood
behind William Carey's pulpit and declared the gospel to a church full of
Chinese. In spite of the joys experienced, she said, "I have surely gotten an
eye full of heathen worship in Calcutta!"[6]

The Holy Land

Miss Bertha's tour of Jerusalem proved to be a real delight. She wrote,

I spent most of the afternoon, after a little rest, in Gethsemane. Sunday
morning after early breakfast I went to resurrection Garden with my
Bible and stayed till noon. Sunday afternoon I took a taxi down to the
traditional place of The Last Supper. It was too late to get in . . . I sat on
a bench outside and read John 12–14. When Jesus said, "arise and let us
go hence," I got up and slowly walked along outside the wall reading
chapters 15 and 16. I even got up on Mt. Calvary . . . I went over a good
bit of the hill top so as to be sure to be on the right place. I was up there
alone so I knelt and prayed in two places, feeling that I was not far from
the place of the crucifixion. From there I walked around to the Garden
Tomb again, even though I had to go two or three blocks."[7]

Lebanon

While Bertha was in Lebanon, one of the missionaries took her to see
the cedars of Lebanon. She spoke to young women at a picnic there and to
the women's meetings of the churches, then to students at the school.
While in Ajloun she led morning worship for the hospital staff at 7:15
A.M., for the school at 8:00 A.M., then visited the primary school, about an
hour's drive from Ajloun where there was also a clinic.

213

A Preview of the American Ministry

While Bertha was traveling, she received a letter from Miss Edwina Robinson, executive secretary of the Woman's Missionary Union of Mississippi, inviting her to be with them for three weeks in 1960 to speak at various associational meetings. Miss Robinson expressed how much it would mean to the work in Mississippi to have Bertha with them, bringing a first-hand report from the mission field.[8] It was a preview of what lay ahead. Miss Bertha had known Edwina for a long time and had received her warmly when she visited Formosa in July, 1956. But now Bertha was off to Africa.

While in the northernmost station of Ghana, Bertha spoke several times. Many of the engagements were far apart and it proved difficult for the drivers to get her where she needed to be. In one place she spoke to the chief of the tribal people. She said, "I took the opportunity to tell the chief about the Lord. He listened most courteously and thanked me, but that was all. I do not like speaking through interpreters but, of course, that is the best that I can do."

Miss Bertha had a "jungle experience" in Nigeria. The traveling party took a short ride down river by boat, then loaded into a jeep with all their camping gear. The trip was delayed three hours by a stalled truck stuck in the one-lane road. They reached camp quite late at night but were able to set up cots and mosquito nets and prepare dinner by moonlight. It was ten-thirty by the time they finished eating. Still, a crowd had gathered. Men and women of all ages and children in their birthday clothes came to hear. Missionary Dale Moore asked Bertha if she would tell them about the Lord. She replied, "I thought I was too tired to talk, but started in with a preacher to interpret for me and forgot all about being tired—how they listened!"[9]

The next morning women came walking in from other villages, bringing their babies on their hips. The mud church where they were to meet had two openings for doors and eight or ten openings for windows. When the bell rang, the local people started coming, bringing the chapel benches out of every house! Bertha liked the idea of the people using the church pews when there was no meeting in the church.

Bertha had many speaking engagements in the schools and churches while in Nigeria. She also traveled to the many different mission stations and observed the work. At one station she stayed with her friend Doris Knight on the school grounds. They shared breakfast on the upstairs porch every morning and enjoyed the grounds and beautiful view of the palms and all sorts of tropical trees and flowers. She commented, "The work is surely interesting." One evening they had to call off the meeting because of "rain on a tin roof."[10] Europe was next on the agenda. Bertha especially looked forward to her visit with Marie Monsen.

Norway

Bertha felt anything but disappointment in her visit with Marie Monsen in Norway. She said, "Miss Monsen though 82, is quite remarkable yet, and it is wonderful to see her again. She is quite stooped but can walk long distances, and her mind seems as keen as ever. She wears nice clothes and keeps herself properly looked after."[11] It would have been a treat to hear those two "Women of Revival" fellowship over the great things God had done in and through their lives.

In every letter that Bertha wrote to Jennie she mentioned her anticipation of receiving the next letter from home. Sometimes she would get two to four at a time. Regardless of Bertha's agenda, those letters took first place. From Britain she wrote, "Everywhere I have turned in Scotland I have longed for you, as the historical places would have so much meaning to you. The most interesting place to me since leaving Rome was the birthplace and home of David Livingston."[12] Now America loomed on the horizon.

Home at Last

After seven months of travel—speaking, teaching, sightseeing, and visiting mission stations and friends—she was home. Her plane landed at Memorial Airport in Spartanburg, South Carolina, at about four in the afternoon on Sunday, September 13, 1959. As she deplaned she waved to the large group of well-wishers, then immediately focused her camera and photographed the crowd. She quickly found her sister Jennie, with whom she would live as long as Jennie lived. They hugged each other tightly, then kissed each other on the cheek. Bertha had come home to retire, but as her relatives said, it would be a busy retirement with lectures to mission groups scheduled all over the country. God had already opened many doors in the States. Before arriving home, Bertha received an invitation from the church in Cowpens to attend a welcome meeting the night of her arrival, but she wrote, "I could not attend church that night. I always give the first few days to my family."[13]

Now a new challenge arose before her. The time had come to begin planning her American ministry, which would prove in many respects to be as significant as that in China. Who would have thought God would give her almost thirty years of fruitful ministry among the churches in her native land?

Part V
Ministry
in America

The Peniel Prayer Center under construction. *Credit: Melten*

18

Lift Your Voice Like a Trumpet

Miss Bertha's childhood home in which her sister Jennie never left and Bertha returned to after her return from Taiwan. *Credit: Melten*

Bertha received a grand welcome from family members when she arrived home. She went back to Battleground Road, Cowpens, South Carolina, to the lovely old home her father had built so many years earlier. Bertha always had deep love and respect for her family. Martha Franks said that is probably the reason she went back to Cowpens. Bertha prayed for all her close family by name every day. Bertha's commitment to her family is also reflected in the fact that she hosted an annual family reunion after returning to Cowpens.

Bertha was proud of little Cowpens. Not only did it hold many memories of happy childhood days; it boasted of a famous Revolutionary War battle. Seventeen years after her return at the age of eighty-seven, Bertha authored a small booklet entitled, *The Life and Times of Cowpens Battleground Community*. Even though the small town had a smaller population than in Bertha's childhood days, it was still good to be home. She took up residence with her sister Jennie who had lived in the family home all her life. Jennie, who had never married and had bouts of loneliness, eagerly awaited her return. What a time of reunion, remembrance, and reminiscing they had!

Moreover, Bertha always kept the door of her lovely Cowpens home open to people in need, even strangers. On one occasion, during a terrible snow storm, a Christian couple from Fernando Beach, Florida, were all but stranded in Cowpens. They had crossed paths with Miss Bertha in a conference but really did not know her. They went to her home, told her of their plight, and she immediately said, "Please come in, you are welcome here." They described their time with Bertha as "a glorious 18 hours." They shared in the things of Christ until the storm passed. That was Miss Bertha's spirit, and Jennie shared that attitude.

Bertha had not been home long when invitations to conduct mission conferences began to come in increasing numbers. She was invited to conduct spiritual life meetings, to tell about the revival in Shantung, and to share her multifaceted missionary ministry, in addition to receiving a host of other invitations. She wanted a recuperation period after her round-the-world mission trip, but the call came clearly; and she knew she must respond.

The New Work Begins

As the waning months of 1959 drew to a close, Bertha began to accept engagements. By 1960 invitations were coming from all over the country. She spoke repeatedly at World Missions conferences and events promoting missions' awareness and commitment among Southern Baptists.

From January 31 to February 7, Bertha spoke at the National Baptist Church in Washington, D.C. during a missionary conference. Many Baptist missionary leaders were on the program; Bertha was the featured speaker on Tuesday and Thursday. She was busy all through February and March. In April she began a speaking tour for Woman's Missionary Union (WMU) in Mississippi with Edwina Robinson. She spoke on seven occasions between April 4 and April 8 in a different county each time. Between April 12 and April 21 she spoke eight times. She soon discovered that traveling on tour for the WMU was strenuous work, even in America, but she found it exuberating. On the long hard tour, she met with the Baptist Young Women for an associational conference in Jackson. Because of her love for youth, this meeting had special meaning for her.

Helen S. Liu carried on considerable correspondence with Miss Bertha during those days. Helen was a close acquaintance and coworker from Taiwan who was saved at the very first meeting held at Gospel Hall in Taipei. She and her husband Lawrence became the proud parents of three children. Bertha wrote a letter to Jennie while still in Formosa that reads: "The biggest event to report and the biggest thing that has happened in Taipei recently is that Helen's husband was saved last night and that gloriously! (They had prayed for him for five years.) She is the splendid Bible woman at our church, who was assigned as a seminary student to work there when we opened the chapel and has been there ever since . . ."[1]

Helen was known throughout Taiwan as a most effective Bible woman and prayer retreat leader. Once during an evangelistic campaign everyone went door to door inviting people to the meetings. The street assigned to Helen was made up of apartment houses with dark, dirty, rickety stairs. People who escaped from the mainland were packed in like sardines and Helen spoke to many of them. Miss Bertha admired Helen because of her concern for the Chinese.[2] The Women's Department of the Baptist World Alliance appreciated Helen's work so much that they paid her way to the Baptist World Alliance when it met in Brazil in 1960.

Helen was able to come to the States as an extension of the trip to the meeting in Brazil. She visited several places of interest, enjoyed a speaking tour arranged by Marie Mathis and Mildred McMuray of Woman's Missionary Union, SBC, then attended one semester of study at Southwestern Baptist Theological Seminary in Fort Worth, Texas. Martha Franks had arranged that with Dr. Robert Naylor, the president. Miss Josephine Norwood, executive secretary of Woman's Missionary Union of Maryland, arranged for her to speak to the Sunbeam (young boys and girls) group at Camp Wo-Me-To. Her letters indicate that she also visited with Miss Bertha and a friend in New York City, where she worshiped at the well-known Calvary Baptist Church. Helen said that Miss Bertha was the spiritual mother of her Christian life. In a letter to Bertha, written prior to her return to Taiwan, she said, "Oh! May God give a spiritual revival to American churches and seminaries, for the pastors and professors to have power of God and preach more on God's Word. (Less jokes and analysis, but more Bible verses and Bible truths!) Sometimes I cry with bitter tears to see the flocks of God are so hungry, have not spiritual food to eat. It's unbearable to be hungry physically; it must be more painful to be hungry spiritually."[3] Bertha resonated with that.

Continued Travels

Miss Bertha continued to travel widely to share the Word of God and her personal testimony of what she had seen God do in revival. On November 16 she spoke at Providence Baptist Church in Gaffnee, South Carolina; on Sunday morning, November 20, she spoke at Mt. Lebanon Baptist Church in Greer, South Carolina; and, on November 23 she was at First Baptist Church in Knoxville, Tennessee. Miss Bertha's notoriety was beginning to spread as the larger churches began to get their eyes on her.

Nineteen-sixty was a most fruitful year as her ministry was developing and expanding across the South.

In 1961 Bertha once again received a significant invitation from the executive secretary of Woman's Missionary Union of the Mississippi Baptist Convention. She invited Bertha to be with them for two full weeks in April. It would involve a hectic schedule, and even though she was now over seventy, she was well prepared for it. The tour began in North Carrollton Baptist Church where she spoke in the morning, afternoon, and evening sessions for the Associational WMU meeting. She shared sacrificially for the next two weeks.

A New Book

By this time, Miss Bertha had made the decision to write *Go Home and Tell*. On September 26, 1961, Bertha wrote to William Fallis of Broadman Press, "My motive is to relate some of the things which the Lord did during my years in China. I tried to omit all purely human interest experiences. It is all fact told as simply as possible." Baker James Cauthen, chief executive of the Foreign Mission Board, agreed to write a foreword. Bertha explained, "He will vouch for my truthfulness! He was in China when some of the miracles reported took place. When telling him something of what I was writing I remarked that I did not tell of any of the demon possession which we missionaries encountered lest it be too much for the average reader to accept. He urged me to tell of it in order that Americans be enabled to understand the Hitlers, the Khrushchevs, and others. Therefore upon his suggestion I added a short chapter on that subject." Broadman published *Go Home and Tell* in 1965 and republished it in 1995 as a volume in the Library of Baptist Classics.

Personal Results

As 1961 neared its close, Miss Bertha continued to teach, preach, write, and lead others to Jesus. Her schedule was beginning to be as full as it had been in China and Taiwan. Many opportunities for speaking came through Woman's Missionary Union. In September she was with the women of Alabama for an Institute for Associational and District Leadership held at Shocco Springs assembly grounds under the leadership of Miss Mary Essie Stephens, director of women's work in Alabama. The meeting ran from Tuesday through Friday, September 11–13. On Tuesday, to launch the meeting, Bertha conducted a prayer retreat that lasted four hours. On Friday evening she led another retreat that began at seven o'clock. She delivered four missionary messages. It was a busy but productive four days.

Martha Leathers, a young women's leader, wrote saying, "We were thrilled to have you with us last week for our institutes. Your messages were such a challenge. I am especially grateful for the prayer retreats which were such an inspiration to my own heart."

Bertha's Potent Message

Some Christian leaders, it seems, do not grasp God's truth about spiritual awakenings. Miss Bertha had a very relevant message for them.

A mission conference was held in San Francisco for missionaries home on furlough. Several of the veteran missionaries, Charlie Culpepper, Jane Lide, and Miss Bertha stood and declared, "You need to be filled with the Holy Spirit." Southern Baptists were hearing, many for the first time, the message of real revival. The missionaries said at the close of the meeting, "It was a good meeting . . . hearts were hungry." In December 1962, thirty-five furloughing missionaries gathered at Camp Lebanon near Dallas. They were not making much spiritual progress on their own, so they telephoned Miss Bertha and asked if she could come and speak to them again. Tommy Halsell, a leader and missionary to South America, said, "She told me to let her check and see when she could get a flight. She called me back soon, had booked a flight within the hour and was in Dallas by early afternoon. When I met her at the plane she had a worn out Bible and a prayer mat. She had been drinking at the fountain. I hadn't."[4] That experience changed Tommy Halsell's life and ministry. He went away filled as did several others.

As previously noted, Miss Bertha always warned pastors to be prepared for the crowds to decrease each night during a revival. Most churches like to see the crowds increase service by service, but Miss Bertha promised that it would be the opposite. In most instances, she was right. On occasion, church membership would even decrease following a revival. Pastor B. Conrad Prikle of B. H. Carroll Baptist Church in Ft. Worth, Texas, wrote Miss Bertha on December 4, 1962. He made the point:

> As to the spiritual climate of the church, the Lord has continued to prune and purge the church. The church members who were saved during the revival have a glorious testimony for our Lord. We have a new converts class for them and the Holy Spirit is working mightily instructing and establishing them in the faith. Our numbers have decreased somewhat since the revival, but this is due to the purging of the church. . . . I feel led of the Holy Spirit to try to get you and dear Mrs. [Rosalee Mills] Appleby to pray with me and others while there for this much needed revival.[5]

A Mission Trip

A special ministry treat came Miss Bertha's way in 1963. She spent six months with Otis and Martha Brady in British Guyana, South America, to help start new work. Otis said, "From the time I was a child Miss Bertha had a big impact on my life. She was related to my father and I recall the impact upon our family with her great commission heart and message. Sin and the Savior was the theme of her life."[6] In Guyana Miss Bertha was known as Aunt Bertha, a token of respect. But she would say, "I am just a plain woman plus the Lord Jesus Christ." She taught Bible lessons each week at Central Baptist Church, the first church started by the Bradys. Otis said, "I typed her lessons. I wondered how she could get much out of these outlines which usually were just listing of verses of Scripture. But when she stood to teach, believe me, she was a great inspiration."

On May 31, 1963, Bertha wrote a letter from British Guyana to Martha Franks. She began by saying, "Tomorrow is June, the month in which I will leave here if the strike is over!" Because of a transportation strike, she had received no mail for seven weeks and had no street car service or gas for a private car. Consequently, food was in short supply. They had little bread and no flour, but rice and potatoes were available if one could afford them. She said, "What grieves us is the hunger of our group—to see them getting thinner and thinner as they come to church is a trial indeed. Some families are able to give their children only one half of a banana a day."[7] Water was also in short supply because of limited chemicals to treat it. It came on only three times daily for an hour or two. But victories in Christ were being won. She was excited about Campbell, a young preacher from Nicaragua whose parents and grandparents had been won to the Lord by English Baptist missionaries. Bertha said, "Campbell had godly grandparents who brought him up right and he was genuinely saved and called to preach. He finished at the Bahamas Bible Institute while the Bradys were teaching there and was ordained."[8]

When Miss Bertha first arrived in Guyana the Bradys and Brother Campbell asked about her call and work on the mission field. As she shared, they became hungry for the fullness of the Holy Spirit. She said, "We had a prayer retreat on Good Friday following a week of night meetings on sin and the Saviour. For the first time the three fasted and prayed and each got a blessing from it, and their hunger was deepened."[9] Miss Bertha could not conceive of having a prayer retreat without prayer mats to kneel upon, so she asked for some. Martha stitched them up and Otis and Brother Campbell helped Bertha stuff them.

Each day at one o'clock they spent an hour praying for the work. One day a caller stopped by so the prayer time was put off until evening. Miss

Bertha said, "The Lord sent the interruption." As they prayed that night, Brother Campbell began to pour out his heart to the Lord. With his limited English, he cried, "Lord mash me up!" Miss Bertha said, "Before midnight the Lord did just about that!" They all prayed until 12:30 A.M. By that time they were all filled with "joy and peace from the dying and cleansing."

About two weeks later, several of the brethren were discussing their spiritual state. They called for Bertha and she went to them, taking L. L. Legter's little book, *The Simplicity of Being Filled with the Holy Spirit* with her. Mrs. Otis Brady took the book to her room and two hours later, Bertha recounted, "came rushing into my room with the light of heaven on her face, exclaiming, 'I have been filled with the Holy Spirit!'" Brother Campbell took the book next and by lunchtime he was bubbling over with the joy of the Lord. Then Otis Brady found "fullness." He confessed, "I struggled. I wrote letters asking for forgiveness. I prayed. I dreaded going to the evening meal with nothing to share. I relaxed in our recliner and prayed. Then suddenly the Lord revealed to me how by faith to appropriate the infilling of the Holy Spirit. Jesus Christ became the Lord of my life. The Bible became alive. Prayer became a blessed privilege rather than a duty. Service became ministry. My joy radiated from Jesus, not people or circumstances. I came to realize that Jesus wanted to work in me before working through me. I was relieved from the necessity for results. It became clear to me that my responsibility was to be obedient, and it was the responsibility of the Lord to get results. I learned it was far more important to know what God is doing rather than what others are doing for him. Power was in the name and blood of Jesus." Bertha said that Brady was so filled with joy that his seven-year-old son John asked, "Daddy, have you taken a laughing pill!" He laughed into the night with his head buried in his pillow to keep from disturbing the others. Bertha said, "He need not have been careful about disturbing me, for I was so thrilled and filled with laughter myself that I did not go to sleep until after midnight."[10]

A seven-week course on the biblical doctrine of the Holy Spirit had been set up. After dinner that evening at Bible study, Brady shared his testimony with the group and told them he had been hungering for the fullness of the Holy Spirit for years. On two other evenings, Mrs. Brady and Brother Campbell gave their testimonies. These three testimonies created a hunger in the hearts of those attending the Bible study for the Holy Spirit. By the time the course ended, five others wanted to be filled. Bertha recounted, "Two were gloriously filled that night, one had to go make some confessions, and the other two were just not quite ready to go all the way to 'death.'"

Of course, Bertha said she must keep herself in the place of death to self and filled with the Spirit. So she would go and sit on the velvety grass of a park just three blocks away—a quiet place amidst the beauty of palms, ferns, blooming shrubbery and flowers. She described her experience: "I had no more than told the Lord why I had gone there, when a wave of heaven's joy started anew in my soul—not since the first year that I went to Formosa had I had such an experience with the dear Lord. It was good that I had chosen a place where there was no ear to hear except the one to whom my praise was intended!"[11] Personal revival is not a momentary experience alone; it continues and deepens in the yielded life. Bertha beautifully personified that basic principle.

The middle of June still found Miss Bertha in Guyana. The transportation strike had not yet ended, but the Foreign Mission Board had arranged to send relief funds so the children could receive at least one meal a day at the Christian Relief Center. Reverend Arnoldo Campbell, who later became a pastor in Brooklyn, New York, said, "We all shared the same home for about six months, which gave me opportunity to observe Miss Bertha up close, on a daily basis. I saw the different facets of her life, and it was all genuine . . . Miss Bertha was a woman who truly loved the Lord, and sought to become all that God intended her to be in this life. She spent hours in daily Bible study and prayer. She practiced meeting with God before meeting with men. Her life in the home was consistent with what she portrayed publicly."[12] When Arnoldo encountered Miss Bertha in ensuing years, she would always ask, with a twinkle in her eye, "Brother Arnoldo, are you still being filled with the Holy Spirit?" "The last time I was with her," he said, "which was a few years before her promotion to Glory, I asked her for what I considered a last word of counsel to me. The word was: 'keep a short sin account.'" He stated, "My life, spiritually, has not been the same since meeting Miss Bertha. I look forward to the time when we will be together again, to part no more."[13]

A fascinating note from two friends in Guyana, Theo and Lucy Cheea Toro, summed up the ministry of Miss Bertha. They simply said, "Thank you for making us know the Lord as our personal friend." This "thank you" gave Miss Bertha satisfaction. After all, this was the purpose and goal of her ministry: to introduce people to Christ in such a way that He became a close companion and friend.

Back in America

Bertha always sought opportunities to help Chinese friends in America. Wang Ming-Kang, a Chinese student, wrote, "At first let me tell you again I enjoyed very much to meet you again at your home. I was sorry to bother you and your sister too much. I have a good beginning in West Virginia University and fortunately accepted a scholarship as the Research Assistant here. I hope I can save some money for my poor country."[14]

By 1964 Marie Mathis had begun to call Miss Bertha "Our International Missionary." And it was a proper designation. Various nations around the world sought her. A fascinating trip to several mission fields under the auspices and support of the Baptist World Alliance developed. She had an extensive trip south of the Rio Grande clear down to Rio de Janeiro, Brazil, and back to her beloved Far East. There she led prayer retreats for missionaries and their coworkers and held other meetings in schools and churches. The world seemed open to this "Woman of Revival."

Zimbabwe

Bertha had an eventful and fruitful ministry in Southern Rhodesia, now Zimbabwe. It is interesting how it unfolded. In a letter written to Jennie, she poured out her heart:

> I called one of the missionaries in South Rhodesia after talking with you this morning and when I told him that I was canceling my visit there he was just smitten. When he asked if I could go two weeks later I told him "no," without a moment to think or pray. The moment that I hung up the receiver I felt as if a dagger had been thrust into my heart. I knew that I had done wrong. I walked the floor and cried to the Lord to know what to do and then felt that He wanted me to go two weeks later than originally planned. I thus sent a cable (cheaper than telephone) that I would arrive May 13th which will be two weeks later than I had originally planned to go.[15]

Jennie had not been well and was having some difficulty coping with Bertha's "globe trotting." Earlier in April, missionary Virginia Cannata of Rhodesia wrote to Jennie saying, "I want to give you a great big 'thank you.' If I were there I would give you a great big hug to go with it. . . . We thank you so very much for being so willing to share Miss Bertha with us for a while."[16]

People would write not only to Miss Bertha but also to Jennie. Although her health was always poor and she did not travel as did Miss Bertha, she was a companion when Bertha was at home. She supported her traveling sister with prayer and real commitment. She was loved by all those who knew her.

Reverend Bob Beaty, a close friend of this author, was a missionary in Rhodesia at the time of Miss Bertha's visit. He had a fascinating encounter with Miss Bertha. Bob was a very energetic man and she tried to slow him down a bit, but they were two of a kind. He was a great man of God and found the message Miss Bertha proclaimed much to his liking. Together, they had a fruitful ministry. He wrote:

> As she was speaking to different groups in Rhodesia in about 1965, the Shona interpreter who was the hospital chaplain became under conviction. When he was a student at the Baptist Seminary (1961–64), he had committed fornication with some African girl. Then this time later, he "broke" and confessed all the sin.

Many wrote letters of confession of "speaking evil, one of another. . . ." They were learning and practicing restitution.[17]

The trip to Rhodesia proved to be a real touch of revival for many.

Back Home Once Again—in Texas

During a stay in Fort Worth, Texas, Bertha met a young deacon and his wife who wanted to be filled with the Holy Spirit. The wife was president of the local Woman's Missionary Union. Bertha said, "It was a glorious experience, to see them die to themselves and be filled with the joy of the Lord." While in Fort Worth, Miss Bertha conducted a week of meetings at Richland Hills Baptist Church. Pastor James E. Bass said to her, "We know that the blessings came from Him, but we know also that you were the yielded vessel that bore them." The students at Southwestern Seminary in Fort Worth profited greatly when she spoke to them in chapel services. They flocked around her afterwards. Many were deeply moved by her ministry. Dr. Cal Guy, Professor of Missions, required his students to read her book, *Go Home and Tell*. He also required associational missionaries who were on campus for training to read it. A student wrote, "O that people could get a taste of what the Lord is really like when one walks with Him."

Jim Elliff, who was with Christian Communicators Worldwide and had been a student at Southwestern, said, "I had a number of encounters with that straight-backed lady. . . . I traveled and preached itinerantly during the whole of seminary days, and God was bringing confession and quite a stirring through a number of students and professors"[18]

The Book and Letters

Bertha's book, *Go Home and Tell*, became the suggested mission study book for the year, and thus gained increasing notoriety. A woman from

Bessemer, Alabama, who heard Bertha at Shocco Springs assembly ground, said that she did not believe she had ever read a book that had helped her in her prayer life as much as that one. In June, Bertha received a letter from Major Daniel A. Janison of Albuquerque, New Mexico. He wrote to acknowledge that she had been responsible, under God, to change his life. Miss Bertha often asked, "How are you getting on with the Lord?" This was somewhat reminiscent of the question Marie Monsen often asked of the Chinese during the Shantung Revival. God used it in the major's life as He did in many others.

Other letters arrived in Miss Bertha's mail box. A letter from Joseph Chang contains statements similar to those of the apostle Paul:

> I am moving deeply in my heart when I read your letter. You have planned and prepared everything for me. How can I show my thanks to you in my heart! I praise the Lord, even though I can not enjoy what you have prepared for me now. It seems that I have already received your blessings. I am keeping my morning watch daily in the church at the altar, and one of the hymns which I sing every morning is: "I know not why God's wondrous grace to me he hath made known, Nor why, unworthy, Christ in love redeemed me for His own." It is really true. . . .

Bertha continued to hear from Helen Lui from time to time. In a letter dated April 14, 1965, Helen requested a copy of *Go Home and Tell:* "Please send one to me, and I find one man who is a very good translator and he might like to translate the book. . . ." In August they exchanged further correspondence regarding the translation of the book into Chinese. The process was slow but finally accomplished. Bertha's legacy lived on in China, this time by writing.

Southern Baptists were hearing, many for the first time, the message of real revival.

At a Woman's Missionary Union meeting in November, a member was given Miss Bertha's name as someone to pray for. After the meeting a friend suggested she read *Go Home and Tell*. Upon reading it she wrote to Miss Bertha: "The further I read the more inspired I became." While reading the book, a young woman from West Texas discovered that she really did not know the Lord. She soon came to Christ. An eighty-year-old diabetic and retired rural postman wrote to Bertha telling her how much he enjoyed reading the book. He asked, "Oh how can the hearts of some people be filled to overflowing and some not so?" One woman wrote that she had gone through *Go Home and Tell* for the third time. The book was obviously a great success, a classic, a best-seller. In fact, it was Broadman's best seller from its publication in 1965 through 1974.

Frankness

Miss Bertha, obviously a spiritual woman, was nevertheless quite frank in expressing her feelings about things that were not to her liking, especially if there was any form of ungodliness involved. In April 1966 she visited Clemson University and had an experience that moved her to write to the president, Dr. Robert Edwards. She wrote:

> I am a retired missionary after 41 years of service in China and Formosa. Last week when speaking at Liberty, SC, I spent a few days at The Clemson House and on Thursday afternoon I walked over to see the university campus. Three of my brothers studied at Clemson years ago. The last time I visited Clemson was at commencement in 1933 when my brother's son graduated. Of course, I wanted to see some of the new buildings and get up to date on the grounds.
>
> To my amazement, because it was Senior Day, I found drunk students, some in cars, some on foot acting like wild men. As I walked on the sidewalk drunk students in a car yelled at me in a most rude manner. On other driveways they were yelling at other people. I entered a building and did not see the campus or modern buildings. When I asked one connected with the university why such conduct could not be controlled the reply was, "When someone gets killed it will be stopped." What have we come to that young men graduating from our beloved Clemson are permitted to act in such a manner! If students have not learned in four years college training to behave any better is there no power invested in the university to control them? If not, it is time for the citizens of South Carolina to speak. I feel that I would be sinning against the future young men of our state who will be studying at Clemson if I do not call your attention to such conduct." [20]

She sent copies of this letter to the governor, superintendent of education, chairman of the board of trustees of Clemson, two congressmen, and the president of Clemson Alumni Association. Miss Bertha put her convictions into action. She did not put off until tomorrow what she felt should be done today.

Lorraine Sugg of Jackson, Mississippi, told of her eighty-four-year-old father having a lengthy theological discussion over "religious quacks" with Bertha. Miss Bertha made some negative remarks about a faith healer she knew about. The old man said one should be sure of what one says about people, especially if we do not know them. Miss Bertha insisted, however, that this man was not the great healer people believed him to be. Then the gentleman replied, "Miss Smith, you seem very sure of the fact that this man is not what he claims to be—a healer. Do you have any proof that he is not?" Miss Bertha replied, "If you mean did I ever go to his healing service, I did not. I know enough about him to know that he doesn't have the gift of healing, though." The father asked, "Do you know of someone he said he healed and the person was not healed?" Miss Bertha seemed thoughtful when she answered, "No, . . . but I just don't believe he can heal. Many people claim to be able to heal, but they cannot." He said, "There is a man who lives just up the highway from here and he used to be an alcoholic. I worked with him in AA [Alcoholics Anonymous] for a time, and he tried hard to stop drinking but he was never able to conquer his habit. He heard about this faith healer and went all the way to Texas where he was speaking. He attended the service and he went to the front during the invitation. The man prayed for him and he has been sober ever since that time. He continues to attend AA but he has not had a drink in over a year." Miss Bertha became very silent for a moment and then confessed, "I ask you to forgive me . . ., and I ask God to forgive me, too, for talking about something I don't know personally. It was wrong of me." Then Bertha recounted the time in China when Mrs. Culpepper was healed and the time in Taiwan when she met a Japanese man who had a genuine gift of healing. She also said, "Yes, I believe God does heal and He uses certain people to do His work. I realize now that I was wrong to accuse someone of not being God's workman and I will never do that again."[21]

When Bertha's frankness carried her too far, she knew how to confess and mend fences. Furthermore, Miss Bertha never became so critical that she could not see her faults.

Bertha was also very frank in dealing with individuals, even in their prayer life. For example, Dorothy Antley, who lived in North Miami Beach, received a call from a pastor friend in northern Mississippi to invite her to attend a prayer retreat for a week with Miss Bertha. He said, "It is a must that you come." She was able to make all the arrangements and went. The sessions began on Sunday. On Monday morning of the conference, Dorothy received a phone call from Miss Bertha inviting (or commanding) her to come to her place each morning for Bible study and prayer. Miss Bertha said, "If you have driven a thousand miles to be with me, you must need some special help." Dorothy said, "Praise the Lord for her! I would not take anything for those precious hours we spent together studying and praying."

One morning during their prayer time Dorothy was praying. Suddenly, Miss Bertha's hand came down on her Bible at Dorothy's bowed head and she said, "No, no, Dotty, don't pray that way; don't beg God. We don't have to beg God for strength because He is our strength." Miss Bertha also taught Dotty to pray, "Lord, send your searchlight into my soul to reveal to me the things that are displeasing to you so the Holy Spirit will not be grieved."

Globe-trotting Again

Bertha wrote a letter to Dr. Frank Means, of the Foreign Mission, Board accepting an invitation to go to Argentina starting in January. She looked forward to a great trip, and it was. God blessed it wonderfully. When Miss Bertha returned home from three months in South America, she wrote to Dr. Means: "I spent two and a half weeks in Chile, six weeks in Argentina, four of which were spent at the Baptist Camp, two for mission meeting and two for the Summer Bible Conference of the WMU nation-wide."[22] She spent nearly a week in Uruguay where the Lord worked powerfully, especially in the hearts of some of the missionaries. Dr. Culpepper had visited there the previous summer and had prepared their lives for Bertha's message. She took a side trip to Paraguay at the request of the committee of the mission where she spent five days in meetings with the missionaries and attended two church meetings.[23]

She also traveled to Brazil for two weeks where she conducted meetings in São Paulo for the Chinese. She wrote, "There are 10,000 Chinese, many of whom are Christians who were eager to hear the Bible in their own language. Some of our Baptist church members who were saved in Formosa are there." As can be imagined, that was a thrill for Miss Bertha. She also conducted a one-day prayer retreat for the Southern Baptist missionaries, then held meetings in Brazilian churches.

Miss Bertha enjoyed two wonderful weeks in Guyana and was, as she expressed it, "thrilled to see the growth of the work since I was there in 1963. The whole trip was, as is usual when visiting mission fields, one hundred days of 'joy and heartache.'"[24] She felt that the greatest spiritual blessings came at the Woman's Bible Conference in Argentina, and to the church members in Guyana. Her heartache was that some of the missionaries, it seemed, really did not know how much the Lord wanted to bless and use them.

Back in Harness

Back home Miss Bertha threw herself into her usual itinerant ministry. Her travels were far and wide. A message delivered in Memphis, Tennessee, made a tremendous impact on the congregation. The pastor said, "Your ministry at Seventh Avenue Baptist will be felt until Jesus comes." In the fall she worked with the pastor of the First Baptist Church of Atlanta. They enjoyed a delightful time in the Lord. Her ministry in 1966 was filled with abounding goodness from the Lord. She shared some of that goodness with a student at the University of South Carolina by sending him a monetary contribution. She was always generous with her money as with her time. When this author and his wife moved to London, England, to fill a professorship in evangelism at Spurgeon's Theological College, Miss Bertha paid for the installation of a heating system in our home.

By 1968 Miss Bertha had become well-known across America as a conference leader. She even led four Christian Life Conferences in Alaska. One happy attender wrote, "My name is Sybil and I met you here at Muldoon Road Baptist Church here in Anchorage, Alaska. I was saved while you were here and you had dinner in my home. You remember I asked you to pray for my husband. He was gloriously saved three weeks ago and the Lord has begun to bless our lives together."[25] What a blessing to Bertha to hear such a report.

After Bertha spent a month in Alaska, Reverend Chron wrote: "Thank you for being God's woman. We are seeing great things happen since your visit. The Holy Spirit is working! Many, many have been saved this week also." Another wrote: "Someone is being saved every day. There were eleven the first Sunday. . . . Then one or two every day are being saved in the homes. The prayer groups have continued. They are every day at 10:30, the young people's at 4:30." Bertha's gift of evangelism still functioned well.

Bertha traveled back to Texas in 1969 to minister to the Calvary Baptist Church in Dallas. A significant part of her ministry in local churches centered on aiding and deepening the prayer life of the church staff. At Calvary, the pastor said, "We appreciate your great leadership here with us, as you led many to dethrone self and place Christ upon the throne of their lives. . . . The daily prayer life of our church staff has been deepened as we gather together each morning."[26]

Miss Bertha loved and was devoted to the Southern Baptist Convention. Each year the SBC Foreign Mission Board would bring retired missionaries to the annual Convention meeting. Bertha never missed; it was one of the highlights of her year. And she always proved a blessing to someone. She also spoke regularly at the Ridgecrest Baptist Assembly, a retreat center for Southern Baptists near Asheville, North Carolina. What a treat to hear her in that setting. One of the attendees told the following story:

> On Saturday night we saw Bertha seated near the front row. We made a bee line for her afterwards in that host of women. Upon asking to meet

and talk with her on prayer, she suggested that we come to her cabin on the mountain side early Sunday morning.

We found her having her breakfast of beef broth, which she finished as we chatted. Miss Bertha asked if we had a perfect attendance record at Sunday School. We admitted that we didn't and she replied, "Good, we'll stay here and pray!" As we began to get seated in the living room, she said, "Throw those pillows down for your knees as we pray." When Miss Bertha spoke, obedience was the immediate result! She prayed, Golda prayed, and then it was my turn. Much to my surprise and chagrin, she stopped me in the middle of my prayer saying, "Pray your own prayer, not one you've formed from hearing others."

Being the sensitive person I am, I could have really been hurt by such stern discipline, but I realized that I was indeed praying in a stereotype fashion, saying what I thought would please Miss Bertha, rather than God. It was a lesson to me that I will never forget and I praise Him for her perception and her boldness in teaching me. It was indeed a day to remember.[27]

Continuing Conference Results

Bertha, never remiss in her circulatory letters, always expressed her gratitude for the blessings of ministry. She said in one letter, "Some of you very close friends who pray for me daily and have especially upheld me during the pastor's prayer retreat held out in the hills thirty miles from Phoenix will be interested in the results." At the conference, she had talked about hindrances to prayer and sin in preachers' hearts and lives. Then, as usual, she urged them to be alone for a while and make their sin list. In all her conference messages, the subject was "Dethroning this Big I." By the end of the conference, as she said, "They were ready to really do it and what a joy to hear them tell the Lord so. They then could appropriate the Holy Spirit to take over and make the dethroning of self and enthroning of Christ real."

As a result of the Phoenix conference, on Sunday morning several pastors went before their congregations for confession and testimony. One pastor challenged his congregation, "All who want to be filled with the Holy Spirit meet me here at the church today at 2:30." Ten came. When they had finished their sin list, laid on the cross all that did not involve others, and faced the fact that they must make confession to those they had sinned against, six left saying "that it was too great a price to pay." Four remained and let the Holy Spirit take over and fill them. The results were not always great in numbers, but they were great in spiritual depth.

It was in the 1960s that this author had his first real encounter with Miss Bertha, though her name had been familiar for some time. She came for a week to Ninth and O Baptist Church in Louisville, Kentucky, where I served as pastor. I shall never forget that week. She gave me the traditional warning that the crowds would probably decrease each night. They did. Some just could not quite cope with the full demands of the Spirit-filled life. So they stayed away. Night after night she set forth the truths of what it is to walk in the Spirit and see the Christ-life transplanting the self-life. It was a wonderful week indeed.

Never shall the church forget the night Miss Bertha spoke on the heinousness of sin and the absolute necessity of cleansing. She made her traditional appeal to "make out your sin list." All were deeply touched, including this pastor. I would never ask my people to do anything I would not be willing to do, so after the service I went back to my study to make out my "sin list." I did not think I would have a terribly long list because God had done a great work of cleansing and filling in my life in the early fifties during my second year in seminary. I had attempted to live by those principles ever since. But as God spoke to my heart, I found that my sin list was longer than I had ever anticipated and many things had to be put right with God and others as well. It was a deep, rich, liberating experience for us all. This was typical of how God used Miss Bertha in the first decade of her American ministry. Her bold message was being heard far and wide, not only among Southern Baptists, but in other circles as well.

19

Filling Hungry Hearts

Bertha autographing copies of her book *How the Spirit Filled My Life.*
Credit: Melten

"You will never know how wonderful it was to be with you. The Lord uses you to 'full capacity.' He creates such a longing within me for Him. I have never known how He works through people until I knew you, but O how blessed it is and I thank Him and praise Him for you and of course because of Him I love you fully."[1] Thus wrote a Christian friend from Memphis, Tennessee. Bertha's continual ministry of filling spiritually hungry hearts opened many new avenues of service and blessing during the 1970s.

Travels

In April Bertha traveled to Georgia to meet with the women of the Chattahoochee Baptist Association. They met at Toccoa, the Georgia Baptist Assembly grounds. One hundred and seventy-five women from eleven different associations in northeast Georgia attended the WMU Prayer Retreat. That same month she spent a fascinating time at the Baptist church in Flowery Branch, Georgia, leading an associational Christian Life Conference.

While in Flowery Branch, Miss Bertha was the guest of friends who took her fishing. They said, "Miss Bertha caught eighty fish. Of course, we were baiting the hooks and removing the fish she caught." The rope holding the submerged cage containing the fish broke. One of the companions took an unexpected plunge into the water to retrieve the fish. She came up wet, but with all of the catch. Bertha probably thought she should stick to being a "fisher of men."

More and more, Bertha's services were taking on the flavor of Christian life conferences, although she was still much in demand for missionary conferences. Miss Bertha did not accept invitations lightly. She first asked God if it were His will for her to meet with the group or church that invited her. For example, in a letter to a church in Kansas City she wrote, "In spite of family friendship and my personal interest in your church, formerly when you wrote I felt no leading to go. It must have been that the time had not come."[2] But now she felt the Holy Spirit was leading her to go in the fall. She carefully explained to the church the two types of meetings she felt God would have her conduct:

Christian Life Conference—held from Sunday morning through Friday evening with Training Union on Sunday from about seven years through adults—this is because young people have to study on week day evenings.

Prayer Retreat—two or two and a half days, all day. Two 45 minute periods in the morning and afternoon or an hour with a 30 minute break. A covered dish or finger lunch. Two 40 or 45 minute periods in the evenings.[3]

Southern Baptist Convention—Denver, 1970

The Southern Baptist Convention Annual Meeting was held in Denver in 1970. Miss Bertha attended and, as usual, shared her room with a Chinese friend. June Andrews had experienced the fullness of the Holy Spirit in 1967 under her leadership, as stated in the Prologue of this biography. But June was still having some problems each time she was asked to share her testimony. She saw Miss Bertha the first day at the Convention and asked if she could speak with her. At the time Miss Bertha was having lunch in a fellowship hall. She said, "Honey, I'm having lunch right now with these friends, but if it's important we can talk." June asked for an appointment. Miss Bertha said, "If you have faith to believe God can put us together again I will meet with you at that time." June had faith. They met in the Brown Palace Hotel at a small table at 3:00 P.M. Before any sharing took place Miss Bertha prayed. She commanded the devil in Jesus' name not to interfere and then asked God to be in charge of the conversation and to oversee their meeting place. When June shared her problem, Miss Bertha exclaimed, "It ain't nothing but the devil!" That was not the best of English, but it was true. Bertha then prayed with June and gave her some sound advice. They shared a taxi as they returned to the convention center. On the way, Miss Bertha reached into her purse, pulled out two tracts, handed them to June and said, "These will help you if you will read them and act upon their message." June's anxieties bothered her no more.

Carrying On

In the early seventies, sister Jennie broke her shoulder and afterwards suffered from arthritis. Bertha referred to her as a semi-invalid after the mishap. But Bertha carried on. Nineteen-seventy-one saw her holding a special series of revival preparation services at Alberta Baptist Church in Tuscaloosa, Alabama. Dr. Thomas E. Halsell, the former missionary she had met in Dallas and inspired to the Spirit's fullness, served as pastor. In his column announcing the coming of Miss Bertha he wrote, "We often say to a speaker, 'enjoyed your message!' This word 'enjoy' will not fit in the case of Miss Bertha. However, there will be real, deep, abundant joy that will result, if we obey her message. If you sit at her feet and study her Bible lesson, your life will not be the same afterwards . . . one way or another." Such became the testimony of many pastors.

At that time, Miss Bertha wrote to members of the Christian Life Commission, an agency of the Southern Baptist Convention. Again, her forthrightness, if not brashness, surfaced. She radically disagreed with some of the decisions of the Commission. She said in her letter to the head of the Commission, "Had I had a chance to see you at the Southern Baptist Convention last year, I would have told you in advance that I was going to move that the Convention call for your resignation. However, after I felt that to be the best way to remove one serious cause of disagreement in the Convention there was not time to even locate you by telephone."[4] Obviously, Bertha was never reticent to let her feelings be known.

How the Spirit Filled My Life

Miss Bertha toured Central America leading prayer retreats for missionaries in July 1972. When she returned home, she found a letter from Ras Robinson, an editor of Broadman Press, asking if she would write a book on how the Holy Spirit had filled her life. It was September before she was able to answer all of her correspondence. She wrote to Mr. Robinson, saying she could not possibly have the book ready by November 1, 1972, the suggested date. From November through early March her calendar was filled with engagements, and she hoped that by March the new Peniel Prayer Center she was creating at Cowpens would be completed. Moreover, she went on to say, her autumn engagements simply could not be canceled. On September 18 she was to lead a prayer retreat for pastors at a Baptist camp in North Carolina, then the last week in September, she would be at Southwestern Seminary again. Regardless of her heavy schedule, she agreed to write, and promised that she would try to get the manuscript to Robinson by May 1, 1973. Ras Robinson asked Jack Taylor, a friend and preacher, to write the Foreword. Miss Bertha had sincere appreciation for Jack and had served with him on many occasions. Thus a new book stood in the offing. She did finally complete her manuscript, and God had another tool to bless lives. Selections from *How the Spirit Filled My Life* are included in the 1995 edition of *Go Home and Tell*.

The Peniel Prayer Center

A Prayer Center, a place where people "with hungry hearts could come, see the face of the Lord, and get on higher prayer ground" became a dream of Miss Bertha. She was convinced that lay people would profit by gathering in small groups as did ministers. She could not accept all invitations. Friends suggested she prepare a place where she could offer prayer retreats to anyone who wished to participate. It would also mean she would be able to be home more where she could look after Miss Jennie. In 1971 she was able to purchase a house for fifty-five hundred dollars on approximately one acre of ground located across the street from her own home.

Her pastor, Bobby McFalls, a native of Spartanburg County and former student of Cowpens High School, said, "Miss Bertha came by the church and talked with me about her feelings of the Lord's leading in her life to begin a prayer retreat. Never was any person more committed to prayer. She told to me one day that she believed it should be named Peniel, [the "Face of God"] what that meant, and so it was named. Miss Bertha had been a missionary in China for many years and knew little of the details in organizing, incorporating, and qualifying as a 501(C 3) ministry and asked for my assistance. Several times we would work and rework the Articles of Incorporation before it was done. She rejoiced when this step was behind her." They gathered a small group of trustees and the work began.

Early the same spring, Bertha met Pastor Bob Dollar. He was a bi-vocational pastor and vice-president of Franchise Sales for Days Inns of America. Cecil Day, the original founder of Days Inns, was a great Christian. Dollar was a very astute businessman, and Miss Bertha tapped into his expertise for Peniel. Dollar gave Bertha five hundred dollars at the first meeting, and along with the seven thousand dollars she previously raised, the dream of Peniel began to be realized. But such a small sum could hardly launch such a project. Then God intervened and spoke to Bob Dollar. It is such a fascinating story, let him tell it:

"When are you going to start?" I asked. "When we get the money," she [Bertha] responded. "We already have $7,000 for the property. And the lot has an old house that can be fixed up."

Knowing something about real estate, I pressed for details. She continued, "The house is large enough for 15 to 30 guests depending on how we go about it." "Well, go for thirty," I suggested. "The cost won't be that much more, and it would be awful to need the space and not have it." "The cost for thirty will be $65,000," she observed.

After a little while we were on our knees praying about these plans. Following the "Amen" I asked if she had a "board" of some sort that was helping her with this project. Upon learning that she had a newly selected group of trustees I made a proposal.

While praying, I explained, the Lord gave me a "nudge." And, if you will call a meeting of the trustees, I will come over and recommend to them that they proceed immediately, and I will go with the chairman to a local bank and request a loan for $65,000 for Peniel. The chairman can sign for Peniel, and I will endorse the note. "You did get a nudge from the Lord," was her response.

My net worth really was not all that impressive, but there was no mistaking the "nudge." And, I thought that if it got going, and people got blessed, the money would come in.

A week later a call came from Miss Bertha. "Brother Robert," she enthused . . . "the trustees want to meet with you tomorrow." "That's fine, I'll be right there," I confirmed. Actually, by now I had cooled off. I had a slight touch of "pledgers remorse." But, I had given my word.

Interestingly, as I departed the Day Building on that Thursday morning to go to Cowpens I was met by two men who wanted to see me. I knew that they sold commercial washing machines, and assumed it was about that. I apologized for not being able to stop for them, but would meet with them at nine o'clock the next morning. Hurrying on I departed for South Carolina.

There was a remarkable conclusion to the financial part of the venture. After the Cowpens trip, I returned to my office on Friday. The two men from the day before were back, and with three others. We all took our places around the conference room table, and they announced the purpose of their trip. They wanted to buy some franchises in the Southeast. Eight franchises! They handed me some documentation that included financial statements that revealed a combined net worth of $100,000,000. In other words, they qualified! Sometime later, with the business matters over I walked them to their car. I could hardly wait to get back to the calculator to see what my commission would be on those eight franchises. Would you believe . . . $65,000. Amazing!

I remembered Luke 6:38: "Give and it shall be given to you, good measure, pressed down, shaken together, and running over shall men give unto your bosom."[5]

That would certainly not pay for all that was ultimately needed, but it got the project launched in good style.

So the work began. Dollar served as trustee and faithful supporter for many years. He described a typical trusting meeting:

A Trustee Meeting was always a colorful experience, frequently preceded by a delightful lunch at her home. It appeared that the luncheon routine was designed not only to please the taste, but to inspire, and to teach patience. First, a loaf of "Daily Bread" scriptures would be passed around the table and each of the six or eight members present would pick out a "verse" and read it aloud. A prayer of "Blessing" followed. Then, the lesson in "patience" as Miss Bertha asked for our plates to be passed to her, so that she could meticulously serve each plate from the tasty choices that were arrayed before her at the head of the table. It took a while, but one surely enjoyed what was to come.

Afterward, we would walk across the street to the Prayer Center for the "meeting." It was an experience to be cherished. We were in the presence of a spiritual giant. She was the Matriarch. We were not intimidated. Her love precluded that. But, we gave her the respect that she deserved. Frankly, I was always in an extended state of awe. For example, at the meeting after her ninetieth birthday she reported on her recent six week "teaching mission" to Taiwan, and announced her plans to lead a tour of the Holy Land the following spring. Surely, she must have been tired at times, but I never heard it mentioned. She gave new meaning to the expression, "boundless energy."

The necessary business would be concluded and all would agree it was a great meeting business wise and spiritually, and the work did progress well.[6]

In a progress report mailed to friends in September 1972 Bertha reported, "When we had paid for the house and lot, including a year's tax, insurance, recording deed, and other incidentals, we had about seven thousand dollars left. With that and what has come in week by week, we have been able to continue the work started in July. We praise the Lord for having brought us this far. . . . When completed there will be eight bedrooms upstairs, and six rooms and chapel on the first floor plus an enclosed porch." The building was planned so that each bedroom slept four and the chapel would seat thirty-five or forty. Other rooms downstairs included a lounge and book room combined, two offices, and the kitchen and dining room.

The work was going well, even though slower than hoped. In her February 1973 newsletter, Bertha spoke of the outstanding debt and funds needed for furnishings for Peniel: "This is a very special call for prayer help! Recently a trustee remarked, 'The ox is in the ditch and he is too heavy for us to pull out.' Another replied, 'No! The cattle are on the hillside, all belonging to the owner who began the center and hath brought us thus far.'" In her June 1972 letter she reported that only ten thousand dollars was needed to complete the building. Many had sent gifts of money; others had sent items needed to furnish the Center. In a letter to a friend written on August 20 she reported, "You should see Peniel Prayer Center now. After having stopped work in February and awaiting more funds, we are starting up tonight working at night only; it will take about a month to finish up. We only lack $5,500 having enough money to finish it."[7] For one who knew intimately the One who owns the "cattle on a thousand hills," fifty-five hundred dollars was certainly not impossible to obtain. By August of 1973, Bertha was negotiating for the furnishings for the Peniel Center. They had decided to double the original capacity for the Center.[8] When the unfinished furniture arrived, two couples from Memphis spent one week of vacation time finishing eighty-three pieces of unfinished furniture. They had wanted to come for the dedication and for a retreat, but decided the best thing they could do was help with the work itself.

The Completion

By October Peniel Prayer Center was completed. The dedication service was held on October 28, 1973, at First Baptist Church of Cowpens, just up the street from the Center. The congregation exceeded the capacity of the church, even though there was a downpour of rain. Jack Taylor suggested that the Lord had sent the rain to save the embarrassment of not being able to accommodate the entire crowd. An offering of $5,016 was received. On the top of Miss Bertha's program she penned the words: "all program in The Spirit, praise to God for dedication."

Reverend Manley Beasley, evangelist and Bible Conference speaker from San Antonio, Texas, led the prayer. Reverend Jack Taylor brought a most inspiring message. The well-known preacher, Dr. Stephen Olford, recognized Bertha with these words, "God does not make duplicates; there will never be another Bertha Smith." When the service ended, a parade of folks under colorful umbrellas walked from the church to the Center for an open house.

"The Lord was especially near," stated Bertha, "as speakers and trustees at the close of the day knelt from room to room personally committing all those who would use that room in future years to the Lord for His blessings. When we reached 'The Upper Room' on the third story for a time of real intercession, heaven came down."

Even before Peniel was complete, Mrs. Curtis McCarley had come to work with Miss Bertha. She was a pastor's widow. Her first assignment was typing the manuscript for *How the Spirit Filled My Life*. She proved to be a most valuable person while Peniel was under construction and more so when it was completed. She did general secretarial work, banking, and served as hostess as the folk arrived for retreats. Furthermore, she took care of registrations and enjoyed counseling and praying with those who came for help. Miss Bertha said, "Mrs. McCarley has taken a great burden of responsibility off my shoulders. Praise the Lord evermore!" Dorothy King served as a part-time secretary, mainly doing dictation. She once said, "At times I have come under conviction as Bertha dictates." Greg Ellison, a young man, served as a helper.

Retreats at the Center were scheduled for March, April, May, September, October, and November each year with special conferences in the summer. Groups of thirty-six people met for two and a half days with sessions lasting all day long. Bertha had a special ministry to furloughing missionaries. The only breaks were for private prayer, rest, and meals. Participants were expected to remain the entire time except in extreme emergencies. Registration fee, including insurance, was only five dollars and the fee for rooms and meals was only twenty-five dollars for the entire conference.

Those who came to the retreat heard the morning bell ring at 6 A.M. Participants were to have their personal devotions before the breakfast at 8:00 A.M. Chapel services began at 9:00 A.M., and participants divided their time between the chapel and the prayer garden until noon. After lunch, they rested or walked until activities in the chapel resumed at 2 P.M. Bible studies occupied the afternoon and participants continued their spiritual feast until lights went out at 11 P.M.

On Sunday, October 28, 1973, the Spartanburg *Herald Journal* published a fine article about Miss Bertha and the Prayer Center. Excerpts from the article read:

> Ordinarily, one might say that the completion of such an undertaking was the culmination of a person's life work, or the realization of a life long dream. But for Miss Smith, or Miss Bertha as she is fondly known by thousands of Christians throughout the world, it is one of many candles lit to illuminate the darkness of men's souls . . .

> She says it takes two days to get people in "praying tune" (even preachers) and so the first two days will "bring the Bible to bear on our daily lives to see how we're failing the Lord. When the Holy Spirit brings conviction and cleansing, then they're ready to pray. There are many promises in the Bible for those who unite in prayer and you can't unite when all are not in tune . . ."

> The average life one would imagine for two elderly spinsters in their eighties is a far cry from the activity at the home of the Misses Smith on Battleground Road. In addition to the two, there is a full-time secretary, a cook-maid and another helper to stay with Miss Jennie while Miss Bertha is gallivanting about the world taking care of the Lord's work.

Three retreats were held at the center in November. Ten young men from Mobile Baptist College (now University of Mobile) attended the Thanksgiving weekend holiday retreat. Eight were ministerial students. Miss Bertha said, "The only recreation they needed was someone to answer their questions on how to live the Spirit-filled Life." One young man prayed, "Lord, this is the best Thanksgiving I have ever spent in my life! —Eh—This is the first Thanksgiving I have ever had! I have never before known how to thank the Lord!"

Mrs. Lorie Oglesby worked at Peniel. At Bertha's suggestion she would pray for the person who would be sleeping in each bed that she made. Little wonder blessings abounded. One of the special blessings of going to Peniel was to visit the prayer garden, but more of that later.

After the early days, Bertha set in place a regular schedule for Peniel retreats. She would host one conference a month for nine months of the year (no winter retreats), then take two weeks out of each month for her itinerant ministry. This approach worked well for many years. One resident of Cowpens wrote:

I'll never forget attending her retreat at Peniel. Very few people from Cowpens would attend. I'm proud to be one of the few that did. Her teachings helped me to see myself as a sinner and not my husband. When she asked to list all our sins on a piece of paper that she had given us, I hesitated for a while. She peeped over my shoulder and asked, "Wilhelmenia, are you having trouble?" I said, "Yes, I am. Miss Bertha, I'll just tell you the truth. I was thinking about all the things my husband was doing wrong and I couldn't seem to think of mine."[9]

Bertha soon remedied that problem!

The New Book Published

Miss Bertha's book, *How the Spirit Filled My Life*, was released in 1973. Writing the book had not been an easy task because of her time schedule and heavy responsibility with Peniel. Two friends from Memphis flew up to care for Jennie so Miss Bertha could go away and write for three weeks. She dedicated the book to them and thanked their husbands for becoming temporary bachelors. Time and again, God made her pathway straight.

Bertha began receiving words of commendation on the new book. A director of missions in Florida had the following experience:

My wife handed me a book by Bertha Smith, *How the Spirit Filled My Life*. She said I should read it.

During the next week, I read it through three times. It helped to change my life. Discovered were things I had let slip out of my consciousness.

My positions as a pastor of a "first" church, trustee of a Baptist college, vice-president of the state Baptist convention, and more than 20 years in the ministry, including a denominational position for five years, had left me focused on the wrong goals. I was looking to self, not to God and His Holy Spirit for power.

Miss Bertha's book helped to refocus my life's goals, and my search for strength and power.[10]

China Still Receives Blessings

Amazingly, Miss Bertha regularly touched the lives of Chinese people in America. The following letter written on November 5 reads:

My name is Angela Kao and I am the Mr. & Mrs. Ching Nien Yu's cousin. Mr. Yu is working in the China Air Lines as an inspector right now. I had a chance to meet him in San Francisco last Thursday because he was inspecting the San Francisco branch of the China Air Lines. He gave me U.S. $50 cash to mail you as his share of the prayer center. But for the sake of safety, I exchange the cash with my personal check. Mr. Yu also wants to give you his best regard.[11]

The concern and love with which Miss Bertha continued to be remembered in Taiwan must have been rewarding for her. A Christian businessman of the Chang family who owned The Treasure Lacquer Paint and Printing Ink Company, Ltd., in Taiwan had promised to give her $100 for traveling expenses if she should ever come back to Taiwan. After hearing about Peniel Prayer Center, he sent a check for $125 to help with expenses. Christian love had spanned not only many thousands of miles but also many hearts. But then, Miss Bertha was hard to forget.

Abroad Again

Bertha made a ten-day trip in July of 1973 to Colombia, South America, where she held a prayer retreat for missionaries and spoke to them for a week at their annual missions meeting. She also conducted two meetings a day for the missionary children. Blessings abounded.

The missionaries in Guadalajara wanted Bertha for a retreat during the summer months preceding their mission meeting. Bertha responded. The first day of the retreat she led a Bible study. Then she sent the missionaries to their rooms to meditate and pray, using the Scriptures that had been read at the Bible study as a basis for their meditation. In her usual fashion, Miss Bertha asked the missionaries to pray specifically, asking God to bring to mind any sin they had committed, then to ask God to forgive that sin. One of the missionaries said, "When the sins had been confessed-up-to-date, we were encouraged to ask for the filling of the Holy Spirit, and fill He did!" Upon completing her devotion in the evening session, Miss Bertha asked if anyone wished to give a testimony about what God had been doing in his or her life during the prayer times. One member of the group reported that "One by one men and women, tears streaming down their faces, made things right with their fellow Christians and missionary brothers, moving from place to place all over the room, embracing and weeping as forgiveness was asked for and received. The meeting continued in this way until almost midnight."[12]

The following day Miss Bertha left. The mission meeting proceeded as scheduled, but things were very different. An attitude of cooperation and unity permeated every session. Spirit-filled missionaries made the difference.

Bertha's Continuing Commission

Bertha's commission to see that God's people were filled with the Holy Spirit and know the principle of dying to self through identification with Jesus Christ remained in the forefront of her ministry. In a letter to a friend in Columbia, South Carolina, who was seeking a new church home, Bertha highly recommended Dr. Edward Young, then pastor of First Baptist Church in Columbia. Young later became pastor of Second Baptist Church of Houston, Texas, and president of the Southern Baptist Convention. Bertha wrote, "I do know that he preaches and witnesses and does his other church work in the power of the Holy Spirit." But, she went on, "What would you think of joining the church nearest to you and being light and testimony there and praying down the power of the Lord. . . . I have known churches changed by the presence of two Spirit-filled people. . ."[13]

Bertha and Prayer

Interesting things would happen when one prayed with Miss Bertha. One close friend of this author was praying with her one day. He was on his knees pleading with the Lord to help him die to himself. He felt someone tapping him on the shoulder. He looked up, and there stood Miss Bertha. She had gotten up off her knees. She looked him straight in the eye and said, "Young man, you don't have to beg God to help you die to yourself. You just tell Him and He'll kill you." That statement revolutionized the prayers of that young man.

The author and his wife were praying with Miss Bertha soon after she returned from a marvelous prayer retreat with pastors in Arizona. As we were on our knees together, and she was praying for the Holy Spirit to continue His work in the lives of the Arizona pastors, she got one particular pastor on her heart. She began to pray for him but couldn't remember his name. So right in the middle of her prayer, she turned to my wife and asked, "Betty, what is that brother's name that I was telling you about?" After she told Bertha his name Bertha replied, "Oh, yes, that's right," and then she continued to pray for the man. She could talk with you and the Lord in the same breath just as naturally as breathing itself. Her prayer life was incredible. As one friend said, "Her tears wet the carpet as we kneeled and agonized over the needs of our people."

Intercessory prayer held a central place in the retreats at Peniel and in Bertha's various conferences. Miss Bertha continued to be deeply burdened for revival. In a conference I attended with her, someone made a plea for prayer for revival. At that very moment God convicted Bertha's heart. She had not been praying enough for spiritual awakening in America, even though she spoke on it continually. Broken hearted, she poured out her confession before the Lord asking for forgiveness and praying for the Spirit of prayer that she might intercede effectively for spiritual awakening. What a tender heart. It convicted us all.

Occasionally, Bertha would receive a prophetic word from the Lord while in prayer. A friend tells the following story: "When I was at First Baptist Church, Hendersonville, North Carolina, my pastor, Dr. Rich Liner, one of our college students, Steve Woody and myself attended one of Miss Bertha's weekend retreats. Steve had shared with me (and only me) beforehand, two major decisions he was dealing with at the time. One was a job offer he had received, and the other was concerning his girlfriend—whether to ask her hand in marriage or not. Steve did not share that with anyone else. During the Saturday evening session, Miss Bertha was leading us in a prayer meeting. She came over to Steve and began praying for him to go ahead and pursue the job opportunity and that the young lady he was dating was God's choice for him to marry. Steve was overwhelmed to say the least, even more so when he discovered I had not talked to Miss Bertha about his situation."

Bertha and Tongues

Some Baptist leaders looked to Miss Bertha for answers to the tongues movement. She was very cautious and careful with regard to emotionalism. If things began to get out of hand, she would simply stop it.

Miss Bertha did not deny the possibility of tongues, but to make it a general experience for everyone definitely rubbed against her grain, theologically and practically. Any extreme experience would cause her to question its authenticity. For example, she once related the story of a man who previously had some great emotional experience and came to her and said, "Oh, what an experience I've had." Then he elatedly related what had happened in his life. Miss Bertha got out the sword of the Spirit and said, "Are you sure that was of the Holy Spirit, or was it of the devil?" The man was taken back with a gasp. He did not say a word but turned and walked away. When Miss Bertha saw the same gentleman a year later, he came up to her and said, "Oh, Miss Bertha, I am so grateful that you said to me what you did a year ago. It put me on my knees before God, and I have come to the conclusion that my experience was not of the Holy Spirit, it was of the devil. Now my life has really gotten straight and right before God."

Miss Bertha would countenance no extremism. Nor did she countenance the physical embracing that often takes place in some emotional meetings. She was very sensitive to temptations faced by God's children. At times, if a woman was embracing a man in her religious zeal, Miss Bertha would actually rebuke her and say, "You take your hands off that man." She saved many a person from pitfalls.

Bertha and Pastors

Many preachers whom Miss Bertha touched produced long-lasting fruit. A letter from an evangelist's wife shows the power of Bertha's life:

> Miss Bertha, I am the wife of Evangelist Jack . . . I praise God for you and your work for the Lord. Jack had gone as far as anyone could go and still stand in the pulpit each service before God's Sheep trying to feed them, when he himself needed a work of grace. God was going to send him to the Southern Baptist Convention that year and reveal a new life unto him. Little did he know when he left this small town—so depressed and heart broken—that God had packed you also and you both were headed in the same direction. One was feeling rejected and away from God, and one was filled with the Spirit of God going to reach out in the name of Jesus and claim those like him who needed a deep working and filling of the Holy Spirit.
>
> One night in a prayer meeting . . . Jack confessed his sins; he thought all was well when suddenly you, Miss Bertha, took his hand and quietly said, "Lord make him tell it all!" That night he died the best he knew how to and he arose a new person in the Lord.
>
> When he got home, I had a new husband; the children had a new Dad. He hasn't preached to God's flock quite the same. Praise The Lord![14]

More Conference Work

Ben Lippen Conferences, something of an American counterpart of the Keswick Convention movement of Britain, was held each year in Asheville, North Carolina. People by the hundreds would come to rejoice in the wonderful spiritual feast provided. Able leaders like Stephen Olford and others led the services and Miss Bertha attended regularly and often spoke. These were times of spiritual enrichment and blessing.

Miss Bertha's beloved friend Martha Franks was now retired, home from Taiwan, and busily engaged in her American ministry. In a letter to the Koo family, Miss Bertha wrote of Martha:

> Martha Franks called me last night. She'd just gotten home from a prayer retreat in North Carolina at a Baptist camp. The camp holds five

hundred women. This is the second time within the last year that Miss Franks has held a prayer retreat there for women, and many who wanted to go couldn't get in.[15]

Miss Bertha often called on another missionary friend from Formosa days, Katie Murray, for prayer. Katie would pray, often write a note on the letter, then return it to Miss Bertha. Martha referred to Katie as "the praying one." How wonderful to have such friends.

Bertha's Problem

Some people had an immediate dislike for Miss Bertha when they first met her or heard her speak. One woman avoided her on every occasion until the Lord changed her heart. She wrote to Bertha: "Please forgive me for all the times I thought of you as a 'meddling old woman,' and believe that I thank the Lord daily for you and Jack Taylor and his books and how the Lord has used you as 'salt' to sting my pride. . . . May our Lord continue to bless you and your wonderful work of helping poor proud Christians to 'see themselves.'"[16]

Bertha's aggressiveness was probably the reason for some negative reactions. But it also motivated her to seize every opportunity to minister—and that means every opportunity. For example, she once received a letter from a pastor friend, telling her how much she had ministered to him on the telephone. He wrote, "Your encouragement came at a time when I needed it most." God worked in unusual ways in this lady.

When a group from the Peninsula Woman's Missionary Union in Hampton, Virginia, came to Peniel for a conference, one of the ladies at the retreat got sick. When the lady from Hampton became ill, Miss Bertha took her to the doctor. As seen before, she believed in using the means for healing that God dictated for the moment. But she certainly did believe God often heals in response to prayer alone. "We know that nothing is impossible with Him if we believe," Bertha said.

China Still in Her Heart

Although Bertha said she never wanted to return to China or Taiwan for a long period of time, she still had a special place in her heart for the Chinese. Americans who had Chinese friends or perhaps an exchange student in their home regularly called on her. A friend from Thomasville, Georgia, wrote to Bertha concerning a young Chinese student from Hong Kong who was with them for the summer. She requested that materials be sent that might help the young man spiritually. That same year a missionary friend wrote her and rejoiced over her tremendous ministry among the Chinese. She reminded Bertha that it had been fifty-seven years since her appointment and that God was still using her as significantly as when she first went to China. She received newsletters from friends in many parts of the world. Bertha truly had become a world missionary.

At Christmastime 1974 Bertha received holiday greetings from around the world. Many of the missionaries who wrote newsletters would say how they were looking forward to being with her on their next furlough at Peniel Prayer Center. Bertha had invited Martha Gilliland, a medical missionary in Ogbomosho, Nigeria, to the Center. Dr. Gilliland was unable to attend at the time, but wrote, "But, oh, how I would have loved it. Perhaps when I am on furlough I can have that privilege. I shall look forward to it."

A thrilling note was added to the bottom of a letter to Miss Bertha from a pastor's secretary:

> When I heard you say that for six years you tried to get to God without going by Jesus and the cross, the Holy Spirit convicted me that's what I had done. I had been listing my sins and repenting and to make a long happy story short, I was baptized Sunday night December 15. My husband said I had been like a person who knew the words to the song but not the music. Well, praise God, now I have the music too, and that music is Jesus. You had a big, big part in it and so I had to tell you. This will be the merriest Christmas of my life. Thank you, and I thank my Savior and my heavenly Father who kept me under conviction all these years through His Holy Spirit.[17]

1975 Arrives

Miss Bertha's 1975 schedule was already full. She seemed to get busier with age!

January	Writing Book
February	Writing Book
February 25–March 2	Conway, Ark., First Baptist Church Bible Conference with Steven Olford
March 6–9	Cowpens, S.C., Retreat at Peniel Prayer Center
March 10–14	Mobile, Ala., Cottage Hills Church Conference on Revival and Holy Spirit with Jack Taylor Group
March 17–21	Greenville, Miss., First Baptist Church, Jack Taylor Group
March 24–25	Marietta, Ga., Green Acres Church, Association Wide Conference on Evangelism, Peter Lord

March 27–28	Lightfoot, Va., Dedication of New Smith Memorial Church building, Jesse Bowman
March 31–April 3	Retreat at Peniel Prayer Center, Cowpens, S.C.
April 7–9	Franklin, N.C., Pastors' Prayer Retreat for Associations
April 14–18	Lancaster, S.C., Springdale Church, Pastor W.P. McCloud, Doug Willet, and Alex Booth
April 21–23	Decatur, Ala., Association Wide Prayer Retreat for Pastors
April 28–May 2	St. Louis, Mo., Jack Taylor Group
May 5–9	East Orange, Fla., Jack Taylor Group
May 13–16	Retreat at Peniel Prayer Center, Cowpens, S.C.
June 5–8	Titusville, Fla., First Baptist Church with Pastor Peter Lord
June 8–12	Southern Baptist Convention
June 13–14	Titusville, Fla., First Baptist Church and conference center
June 17–20	Peniel Retreat at Peniel for Baptist Students of Mobile, Ala., graduating from city high schools who choose this in preference to a trip to Washington, D.C.
June 23–27	Lebanon, Tenn., Immanuel Baptist Church, Jack Taylor Group
June 28–July 4	Ridgecrest Foreign Mission Week
July 7–11	Mobile, Ala., Youth Camp of 300
July 14–18	Blakely, Ga., First Baptist Church with Peter Lord
July 28–31	Peniel Prayer Center Retreat
August 2–3	Family Reunion at home in Cowpens
August 4–8	Homework and Retreat in August at Peniel
September 8–12	Shreveport, La., Highland Baptist Church, Jack Taylor Group
September 15–18	Peniel Prayer Retreat, Cowpens, S.C .
September 22–24	Fayetteville, N.C., South River Association Pastor Retreat, Mack Roberts
October 6–10	Atlanta, Ga., First Baptist Church, Jack Taylor Group
October 16–19	Peniel Prayer Center Retreat
October 20–24	West Texas Association Wide Pastors' Retreat, Jack Taylor Group
November 3–7	Conover, N.C., Woodlawn Baptist Church, Jack Taylor Group
November 11–12	South Carolina State Convention
November 13–16	Peniel Prayer Center Retreat
November 27–30	Peniel Prayer Center Retreat, Ministerial Students
December 6–7	Gadsden, Ala., World Mission Program, Meadowbrook Baptist Church[18]

It may appear that Bertha was really overdoing it, considering her age. But she knew how to take care of herself. On one occasion when she flew into Alabama to hold a conference, the minister of education of the church said to her on her arrival, "Miss Bertha, shall we go and pray?" Bertha replied, "No, no, no! I'm going to rest. I'm 86 years old; we'll do all things in order." Most wise! That is how she kept up her incredible energy level; she stuck to a sensible routine.

Bertha also kept up her daily walks. If it were raining, she would walk up and down the stairs of her home. Not only that, she was most diligent to keep her own spiritual life healthy and vibrant. She not only urged others to keep their "sin list" up-to-date; she also cared deeply for her own. So often she cried out to the Lord, "Show me leaven" (leaven being a Scriptural metaphor for sin). And God heard and kept her abiding in Christ. Satan cannot cope with that spiritual attitude and discipline.

Sister Jennie's Health Problem

The day after Christmas 1974 a doctor was called in for Jennie who at the time suffered from diabetes and arthritis. But there was more. The diagnosis was alarming: cancer. On January 8 she entered the hospital for breast cancer surgery. She came home on January 20 with an eleven-inch incision that "is healing too slowly," as Bertha put it. Once a week Jennie had to return to the doctor by ambulance for observation.

In February, a friend named Carlene from Mississippi called Miss Bertha and asked if she might come to Cowpens and stay for a week or so. Miss Bertha asked Carlene if she could come and help her with Miss Jennie. Carlene expressed, "I learned that she had been praying that the Lord would send her some help. She allowed me to stay in her home for two weeks doing various chores and helping some with Miss Jennie. Just to be in her presence was a delight to my heart."[19]

Miss Bertha had scheduled January and February at home to write. But as she said, "The Lord knew that it was not for writing, but to nurse Jennie." Still, the call to her work came upon her. With a sitter she had used for two years when she was away, a nurse for eight hours daily, and a nephew and his wife next door to care for Jennie, she started out on a busy schedule of Christian Life Conferences and Prayer Retreats. Bertha declared, "As long as I can go, it must be as Paul wanted to go to Rome, 'In the fullness of the blessing of the Gospel.'"

In her February 1975 newsletter Bertha thanked everyone for praying for her cataracts. She said, "I went to an eye surgeon recently expecting him to set a date for removal of cataracts. After thorough examination he said, 'Come back at this time next year for examination.'" Miss Bertha had given up night driving for the past three years, but was praying that by next year God would provide a secretary "who can do all the driving," as she put it. Although she drove very little in China, she did drive in America.

Providing for Peniel

In every newsletter Miss Bertha gave a report on the financial situation of Peniel. In 1975 an outstanding debt hung over her. Certainly twenty-five dollars per person for an entire conference could hardly keep it going. But many would send in unsolicited gifts, and God provided. Countless letters in the archive files demonstrate the love people had for Miss Bertha and the blessings they received at Peniel. These gifts kept the work alive and solvent. Miss Bertha was never anywhere close to being wealthy but God did meet all her needs.

A Baptist woman from Southside Main Baptist Church in Greenwood, South Carolina, saw that Miss Bertha was free on Monday, May 19, 1975. Since the General Meeting for Baptist Women had planned a program on Taiwan, she wondered if Miss Bertha could meet with them for a ten-thirty meeting to be followed by lunch. A vacant spot on Bertha's schedule was an invitation for someone to seek to fill it.

People would often write and request that she come and minister to them. On one occasion Bertha received a letter from someone who noticed that she had July 28–31 open for a retreat. The person immediately wrote and asked if he could get a group and come to Peniel. Bertha usually obliged. A friend said whenever she looked at Miss Bertha's schedule, she felt ashamed whenever she complained she was too busy. Cassette tapes became popular in the early seventies, and so Miss Bertha would normally have the conferences taped. These tapes expanded the ministry even more.

"Mundane" Matters

On one occasion a lady friend asked Miss Bertha, "Who will help me as I battle with this question? Is it right to wear pants suits?" Miss Bertha faced some very down-to-earth little problems as well as the bigger issues, but was always gracious and answered as best she knew the mind of the Lord. About the pants suits for women, Bertha was dead set against them.

Bertha was very strict about what women should wear and how they should look. On one occasion, my wife and I were with her at a State Evangelistic Conference. A former seminary student and his wife were there. The young wife was a new Christian, having known the Lord only a short time. She was an attractive young lady and dressed in a fashion Miss Bertha thought worldly. She sharply rebuked the young wife who broke down weeping. My wife, whom Miss Bertha deeply loved and admired and would listen to, looked at her and said, "Miss Bertha, you should not have said that. The girl is just a very young Christian and she loves and admires you so much. She did not realize that she was not dressed appropriately." Miss Bertha said, "Oh, I am so sorry. I did not realize that I had been so harsh with her." She immediately went to the young wife and apologized.

Bertha's Honesty

Though Miss Bertha was blunt and frank at times and offended people on more than one occasion, she was sensitive when she spoke or acted ungraciously. On occasion God used her frankness to glorify Himself or to enable people to see themselves. A retired pastor wrote, "Many years ago she once rebuked me on a shuttle bus at the Southern Baptist Convention. I mentioned I did not like to fly. She said, 'Where is your faith, young man?'" Once while she was praying with a very obese preacher, he prayed, "Lord, you know I have a tendency to overeat." Miss Bertha broke in: "Don't try to fool God, just tell Him you are a glutton."

In March a caravan from Calhoun County Mississippi took off to Greenville to attend a Christian Life Conference to hear Miss Bertha, Jack Taylor, and Ron Dunn. Some of the members of this group stayed in the same hotel as the speakers. During the conference they had some private time with Bertha. She gave each of them a copy of the tract "Not I But Christ," sent them off to make a list of their worst sins, confess them to God, and ask for forgiveness. One member of the group said, "This was really a time of self-examination and repentance." When a young man named Don returned to Miss Bertha's room and told her he wanted to be useful, she said, "Young man, you get yourself in a useful condition, and He will wear you out." When they were ready to pray he reached out to hold her hands. She looked at him kindly and said, "Young man, I would like to hold hands with you, but that's not the way I do it." She then went to her knees on the concrete floor to pray.

On occasion Miss Bertha would stay in the home of Dr. and Mrs. T. D. Hall. She would lay her hands on the heads of their four young children and pray for them. Their daughter, Donna, was greatly impressed. She went home and wrote out her sin list. "I think she had about sixty-three sins on there; she had confessed them all and then threw the list away," said her father. "I remember when I found it in my office all crumbled up, I got under conviction because my sin list was not that long. From that time forward (she was about 8) her walk was closer to the Lord." When

Donna finished high school, she told her mother that she would like to be able to help Miss Bertha, perhaps with her writing. No one mentioned this to Miss Bertha, but one day at a conference Miss Bertha asked Donna what she was going to do now that she had graduated from high school. She then invited her to come and live with her. That thrilled Donna. She lived with Miss Bertha for a period of time, helping around the house and doing secretarial work. What a tremendous experience for a young lady!

Bertha and Books

Miss Bertha's second book, *How the Spirit Filled My Life*, continued to be used of God. In the mid seventies, a lady wrote, "I have finished reading *How the Spirit Filled My Life*. Oh! How it brought me under conviction regarding my life and relationship to God! I want so very much to allow the Holy Spirit to fill me completely. I have been a Christian for 35 years. The past 15 years I have worked for the Lord. And now realize it's been me . . . the past month or so I have let the Lord show and reveal to me the sin in my life."[20] This woman was clearly well on the road to the Spirit-filled life. Later, Bertha wrote a third book on the needs of the world's mission fields, entitled *Our Lost World*.

Though Miss Bertha's books were in great demand, especially by people attending her conferences, she would never sell them at the conferences. In the first place, as she would point out, there were so many materials she had to carry for her own speaking that she could not carry anything extra. Yet, one feels that Miss Bertha never wanted to appear commercial. She would, of course, recommend books, and if people wrote to her she would send them. Moreover, she would promote and send the books of others that she felt would be a blessing and benefit. For example, she sent a pastor in Madison, Wisconsin, a copy of Jack Taylor's book, *Victory Over the Devil*. Miss Bertha was concerned that good Christian literature of all sorts get into the hands of God's people. She realized that the Holy Spirit greatly extended the ministry of anyone who could write and share scriptural truths. Rare indeed is the Christian who truly desires to grow in the Lord and does not read good Christian literature.

Miss Bertha did not, as seen, confine herself to Southern Baptist circles, though she was fully committed to her denomination. In the summer of 1975, she attended and spoke at the Evangelical Institute of Greenville. In August, Bertha spoke at a missionary conference held in the Cleveland Park Bible Church. The associate director of the Evangelical Alliance Mission, a former missionary to India, was also a featured speaker. Bertha's willingness to respond to these sorts of invitations revealed something of the breadth of her appreciation for the entire evangelical world.

In her December 1975 letter to friends she reported, "What a glorious year has ended! Every retreat at Peniel seemed to be richer in spiritual blessing than the one before . . ." When the participants left the retreat center, Bertha said, "They could say with Paul, 'I am crucified with Christ, nevertheless I live, yet not I, but Christ liveth in me'" (Gal. 2:20).

A glorious though exhausting year was coming to a close. By Christmas, eleven months after her surgery, Jennie was sleeping and eating well and Miss Bertha said, "She is the essence of patient sweetness. She has been sustained and kept from pain eleven months, with exception of a few days." Bertha began to realize she needed to stay at home more. She wrote, "My schedule for next year leaves me at home one week each month. Pray that I will stick to it!" God still mightily worked in and through her as she approached ninety years of age.

20

A Vessel for Noble Use

Bertha's sister, Jennie E. Smith as a young
adult. *Credit: Melten*

One day Bertha received a letter saying: "Grandfather came back a little overwhelmed—he thought you were a retired missionary. He did not
expect you to be so active in home missions. I guess he kind of expected
you to be on the front porch in a rocking chair counting the cars!"[1] When
Miss Bertha was not leading retreats or speaking at conferences, she was
busy at home opening mail and writing letters. Floods of letters continually poured in. One woman wrote, "When I tried to recount my blessings
of the last year, you and Peniel were at the top. I just want to thank you
again for showing me the way to be filled with the Holy Spirit. I just get
real excited when I think of a whole new year 'filled.'"[2] Bertha truly was a
vessel fit for noble use.

Bertha's "Patriotic" Ministry

An article featuring Miss Bertha appeared in the *Spartanburg Journal*.
She was pictured holding the last in a set of twelve plates that had
belonged to her grandmother. It had been a wedding gift, and through the

years all the other plates had been broken. The plate was about 150 years old. Misses Jennie and Bertha still used the old pots and pans that their mother had used and they had a hand-made chair in their collection that was over three hundred years old. It came from ancestors who had settled in Virginia. Bertha had a sense of history. The article went on to say, "Miss Smith, at age 87, has authored a booklet, *The Life and Times of the Cowpens Battleground Community*, which has been printed and is being sold as part of the bicentennial celebration in the area."

Bertha eyed the 1976 bicentennial celebration with much excitement. She was quoted as saying, "My main concern is that we can get this country straightened out and get some morals back into the lives of the people. I'm afraid it's too late though, about 40 years too late." She had a rather dim view of the prospects of America regaining its moral fiber without revival.

Open-Hearted People

Often these people who registered for a retreat at Peniel realized something of their spiritual condition and need before they arrived. One person wrote, "Miss Bertha, I am not the dedicated person I should be." These open-hearted people, to whom the Holy Spirit had already spoken, usually received the greatest blessings. When people came to hear Miss Bertha with an open heart, they often said, as did one, "You really exposed me to myself. To say I had a soul-searching experience is an understatement."

Portions of one of Bertha's newsletters disclosed some of the wonderful blessings of God during those days:

What wonderful news to share with you! This year our Lord has "touched" Peniel with three very special blessings. First, He has added to our Staff, Greg Ellis, whose natural and spiritual endowment has prepared him for the co-worker we need. When Mrs. McCarley (Peniel's secretary and Director of House Affairs), Greg and I kneel to pray, we are united always in one accord.

Secondly, we have been blessed with an opportunity to buy the two acre wooded lot adjoining my home in front and Peniel Prayer Garden in back. The lot will cost $12,500. From the $9000 given to us just for that lot, we have made a down payment sufficient to hold it. We lacked $3500, but praise the Lord, $240 has already been given to be applied toward the purchase of this land.

Thirdly, we are "shouting" praises and thanksgiving to the Lord for His abundant blessings on those attending prayer retreats. A Georgia chiropractor was so blessed at a retreat in the Spring that he wrote this to a former schoolmate in Michigan. "You just cannot keep on living without attending a prayer retreat at Peniel Prayer Center." In a few days the Michigan doctor called Peniel and said, "My friend, telephoned me that I cannot keep on living without attending one of your prayer retreats. I want to keep on living. Can you give me a room at your next retreat?" Praise the Lord, we had room for him.[3]

1976 had been a great year. But a sad one was in store.

Jennie Is Called Home

Bertha's sister, Jennie, four years her senior, was called home to be with the Lord at age ninety-two. Bertha and Jennie were so close. They even remained especially close while Bertha served in China by writing weekly letters to each other. The year before Bertha retired, she wrote to Jennie from Formosa saying, "You spoke of our weekly letter for forty years which would be more than two thousand. . . ."[4] Jennie's death was a real wrench in Bertha's heart, even though she rejoiced, as she said, "in the fact that Jennie no longer suffers the pain of her earthly body, but now dwells in the full presence of our Lord, Jesus Christ."[5]

God answered two special prayers for Miss Bertha concerning Jennie. She said, "I could not think it right to ask the Lord to heal her, but did regularly pray that He would spare her from long drawn out suffering, which He did. My second request was that she not be called home when I would be alone leading a conference, which would have to be stopped, thus interfering with the church program which has perhaps been planned for a year. When Jennie left us, I was in New Orleans with Jack Taylor and four other speakers, and the conference went right on without a ripple. Praise His Name!"[6] God does hear His children's cries.

A New Year

Some folk would say Miss Bertha started the new year off right. She flew to California the second week in January 1977 to spend a month at the Mar Monte Hotel, a health resort, to do something about her weight. It was not the first time she had taken control of her weight. In 1955, she and Martha Franks, who suffered from diabetes, went on a diet together in Formosa. Martha had studied diets and had learned to plan meals with proper food value and little fat. Bertha went down to 130 from 145. After losing the weight she said, "I am going to keep down to 130 the rest of my life, I hope. . . . How wonderful to be rid of so much cushion in front and the rear below the waistline!"[7]

When Bertha arrived in California for her time at the health resort, a Mrs. Winters met her at the Los Angeles airport and drove her to Santa Barbara. On the way they stopped at a Chinese restaurant and enjoyed a lovely meal. Mrs. Winter warned her that it would be the only good meal she would get for a month. She was right. Bertha remarked as she got into the program, "No wonder folks have to take a vacation to reduce! No one would have time to go through the routine any other time." They went to the dining room eight times a day—"not to eat eight meals but to eat one-eighth of a meal eight times," as she put it. Since they ate so little at each of those eight meals, they could walk immediately afterwards. In a letter to her secretary on January 11, Bertha said, "I have eaten four times today—it is now 2:30 P.M.—and walked half a mile each time afterwards. I will get in two and one half miles today." It was reminiscent of all the walking she had done in China.

The hotel was on the beach with "beautiful scenery in every direction," as Bertha expressed it. The sunshine was gorgeous, "just right to walk with a sweater." She wrote, "All here are excited over the woman who was here with the last group who had not moved her hands or fingers in years. She woke up one night and involuntarily moved her hands. At first she thought they were not hers."[8]

After being at the resort a month, going through all the examinations and rearranging of diet, the doctors told Miss Bertha she could possibly live to be 120. It seemed at times that this would be the case, but her only desire was to live to be 100. The trip and arrangement had been made by a friend who urged her to go. Bertha thought the friend was going to pay the expenses. But when she arrived, she found this was not the case. The cost of the program was tremendous. Miss Bertha did not know what to do. She simply did not have the money. But she made such an impression on the staff with her vitality at age 89 and the way God was using her life, that they refused to charge her anything. As always, God's wonderful provision came through. Such experiences were common for our Miss Bertha. If the Lord ever cared for anyone, He surely cared for this servant, as He does for all His children. Miss Bertha had learned, as she often said, "one cannot tremble and trust at the same time."

On February 14, 1977, while flying home from California, Bertha wrote to a friend, "Will you be my Valentine? I am eager to get home after five weeks away . . . when away so long I miss Sister Jennie so much more."[9]

The Prayer Garden

Besides leading retreats at Peniel and an engagement in Snyder, Texas, Miss Bertha was busy dreaming and making plans for a prayer garden she wanted to develop on the grounds of Peniel. It was soon under construction. She said to friends, "I wish you could see the change in the new section of the prayer garden." Two men from Mississippi worked for three weeks cleaning the undergrowth of sixty years. Gifts for the garden continued to come in for which she was thankful.

She planned to enclose the area with, as she expressed it, "proper fencing, plant white pines inside [the] fence, make walk ways, provide seats, and other improvements." Bertha wanted it completed by Easter so they could have an early morning Easter service in the prayer garden with guest speakers, testimonies, singing, and fellowship to celebrate the Lord's resurrection.

"Advanced Retreats," as Bertha called them, had been planned for March, August, and November. These retreats were for people who had already attended a previous retreat, but wanted to return for more fellowship and in-depth study on the Spirit-filled life.[10]

That year also witnessed a special treat for Miss Bertha. A celebration was held at Winthrop College. Bertha was honored by receiving the college's highest honor: the Mary Mildred Sullivan Award. How thrilled she was.

Another Great Celebration

Bertha's 1977 schedule soon shaped up to be as full and as busy as the previous year. A great celebration took place on August 16 at First Baptist Church in Spartanburg, South Carolina. Miss Bertha knew some sort of notice would be given to honor her sixtieth anniversary of sailing to China, but she had no idea it would be such an affair. Ollie McCarley and evangelist Jack Taylor secretly worked together to make it all it deserved to be. Everyone was invited, and those who could not attend were asked to send letters for a scrapbook. An offering was taken to endow the continuing ministry of Miss Bertha through Peniel Prayer Center. God's people responded generously. As one person expressed it, "Six gold plates were piled high with dollars—ones, fives, tens, and checks." This love offering was presented at the close of the program by Jack Taylor. The program featured the life of Miss Bertha in a presentation entitled, "Behold the Handmaiden of the Lord."

When the celebration began, Miss Bertha was escorted onto the platform by Jack Taylor who presided. She was wearing a soft blue dress with blue shoes to match and carrying a white handbag with a delicate gold chain handle.

Jack Taylor shared his story of the revival that broke out at Castle Hill Baptist Church in San Antonio, Texas, in December 1969. He was pastor at the time and declared that Bertha's visit had sparked the awakening.

Donna Hall sang, and later in the evening, when Martha Franks spoke, she said, "Once when getting ready for furlough Bertha had a blue dress made with blue shoes to match." She turned, smiled at Miss Bertha, and said, "Blue dress and blue shoes." Blue had always been Miss Bertha's favorite color. Actually, one rarely saw her in anything but blue.

James Mann, U.S. congressman from South Carolina, who attended the celebration, said of Bertha, "Of all I have met, none drinks of the cup of service more deeply."[11] When Bertha's secretary and traveling companion presented her with the scrapbook of letters, Bertha said, "I'll do this when I get old" (meaning read the letters). Her pastor then presented her with a large-print edition of the Bible from her congregation. She thanked him, then said, "I certainly appreciate this large type. When I get old enough to need it, I'll certainly appreciate it." The congregation also presented her with a lovely portrait of herself. Her humorous reaction: "What a beautiful woman." In real humility, all she could say in response to it all was, "Bless the Lord, oh my soul, and all that is within me bless the Lord, my God." Students were present from the Blacksburg and Cooley Springs schools of South Carolina where she first taught. Fern Harrington, who had stood firmly with Bertha during the Communist crisis in China, spoke words of reminiscence. Manley Beasley shared Bertha's vision of revival for America.

A resident of Cowpens, Ray Moore, who saw Bertha off when she departed on the train in 1917 (and was there to welcome her home after retirement in 1958), shared the conversation he overheard between Bertha and her father when she was departing: "It's a good work but it's mighty far from home," said her father. Martha Franks told about riding with Bertha one day. She talked so much that a bee blew in the car and stung her tongue. That slowed Bertha down a bit.

Martha also related that several of the school girls wanted Bertha to go to their weddings. On one occasion Bertha and Alda Grayson went ahead of the pastor to a town for one girl's wedding. After they arrived a heavy snow fell; the pastor couldn't get through. The Chinese never change a date for anything. There was nothing to do but for Bertha to perform the ceremony. Alda said, "I never saw Bertha nervous before. She was shaking. Her Bible was shaking so much that she tried to find something to place it on. She got them married all right."

Unfortunately Charles and Ola Culpepper were unable to attend the celebration but they sent a cassette tape. Ola said, "Bertha's constant habit to pray, to witness, and expect to win souls, impressed me." Charles said she was faithful, frank, always busy, and ran some of the preachers to death.

More Memories

One of Bertha's missionary friends said, "Bertha worked as hard at resting as she did at working. One time she went to Japan for a summer holiday and she wanted to rest properly. She got up, cooked her breakfast, put it on a tray, ran back and got in bed to have breakfast in bed."

Before Jack Taylor gave Miss Bertha an opportunity to speak, in tribute to her ministry he said, "Miss Bertha started six churches in Formosa and the last five years she taught Old Testament in the Baptist Seminary." When Bertha stood to speak, she said, "I was carrying 15 hours of work every day. I went to bed tired, woke up refreshed. I signed on before there was retirement. I signed up for life. I never dreamed anything in this life could ever hurt me, ever touch me in this world and hurt like giving up the work the Lord had called me to. But one night He said to me, 'I want you to go home and do what you can do to help bring a revival to Southern Baptist Churches so the whole world can hear of the Savior, not just this little island you're on.'" And God certainly used her for that purpose.

An official letter dated August 16, 1977, stated, "The library of Luther Rice Seminary, Jacksonville, Florida, (now in Atlanta, Georgia) was dedicated on December 7, 1972, and named the Bertha Smith Library in honor of 'Miss Bertha.' This was done in recognition of her foreign mission service and in appreciation for her continuing ministry to the minister." One can only imagine how thrilled Miss Bertha must have been to receive such encouraging words.

The following challenge to commitment to foreign missions and particularly for China was written by Miss Bertha to commemorate her anniversary:

A Challenge to Commitment

Jesus declared, "The night cometh, when no man can work!" (John 9:4)

China was wide open to the Gospel for forty years (1911–1949); from the overthrow of the empire, when Religious Liberty was written in the constitution, until the communist take over.

In our best day, Southern Baptists had only two hundred and fifty missionaries scattered from Harbin on the Trans-Siberian Railway to Canton.

We had at that time enough educated young people in our churches to have sent out ten thousand missionaries and a sufficient number to make money to support them, with a few million who should have been in tune to pray down the power of the Lord upon them.

Alas, how we failed the Lord. The night came and what a night. Eight hundred million Chinese are now in slavery. Christian leaders have died in prison. Churches have been closed, people arrested when as many as five worship in a home, and Bibles destroyed.

In the same way, other nations, where we have missionaries, are being subdued and the "too few too late" are being forced out. It is now or never to take the "Gospel of Light and Life to those who walk in darkness not knowing where they go." (John 12:35)

But we know where they go. Jesus said, "No man cometh to the Father but by Me, I am the door."

It is now or never to give the knowledge of Him to nations that are still open. Ten years from now will be too late.

To what extent are you responsible for those who are in that awful place of agony called hell, which was not made for man but for the devil and his angels? What is your part in giving saving knowledge to your generation?[12]

What a celebration it was for the great woman of God.

1978 Dawns

When the bells rang loud and clear welcoming in the new year, Miss Bertha was busy planning a trip to Israel, cosponsored by Jack Taylor. In Israel they held a spiritual life conference for missionaries.

Upon Bertha's return from the Holy Land, she had time at home to catch up with correspondence and get out a February newsletter. When one reads the words written by Miss Bertha, it is impossible to miss her enthusiasm and joy over what God was doing through her life.

What a joy to share with you the Lord's workings at Peniel another year! People, age 16 and up, from all walks of life have come. High school and college students, many public school teachers, one college president with his wife, and men and women engaged in all phases of church work, but with the same heart-hunger, have come. Some long for a life of victory for themselves, others, especially pastors, wanting the same first for themselves, that they might share the glorious Life of Joy and Power with their congregations. It seemed to the staff that each Retreat was more richly blessed than the preceding one![13]

Another Loss

Miss Bertha lost one of her helpers at Peniel. He had been a dear friend and of great assistance at the Center. Bertha lamented, "What a blow to lose Brother Greg! When he came, he told me that it would be for only a few years. I had not expected it to be this few. I am most grateful to the Lord for giving him to Peniel during my sister's illness when I needed someone to share responsibility."[14] Change and losses proved difficult for Miss Bertha, but she had a way of setting her sights on God and trusting Him for the next day, the next employee, and the next event, with a measure of peace that was comforting. She had truly learned to "be anxious for nothing," as Paul admonished. At the same time she mourned the loss of Brother Greg.

Bertha rejoiced over the fact that Peniel was "now debt free." Two of the trustees had previously borrowed money on their own to help in the completion of Peniel. They paid back the loans in three years instead of five, and rather than letting Peniel pay them, they each contributed the money as a gift to Peniel. The total sum was thirty thousand dollars. A beautiful token.

Off to Taiwan

Things did not always fall into place for Miss Bertha. She had planned a trip to Taiwan and deposited a check from a lady to help cover costs. A few days later she received a phone call from the donor asking her to delay the deposit. It was too late because she was already off to the Far East for her mission trip. She wrote the person who sent the check when she returned: "Upon my return from Formosa there it was [the check] returned for lack of funds with another fine of $7. Therefore, you owe me $114. I could have waited for what you owed if you had just asked. You need not have sent checks for money that you did not have. You need not repay the $114. I will help you that much."[15] Then Bertha invited her to come for a visit. Whether she did or not remains a mystery.

Bertha had a great time in Taiwan. She wrote about it: "Twenty years after that sad day when my seventieth birthday forced me to change fields, I arrived in Taiwan for two months of meeting for Christians. What a welcome."[16] The Chinese Christians had asked her to come for a ninetieth birthday celebration. When she deplaned, she was handed a full speaking schedule.

From Taipei Bertha wrote to her secretary Mrs. McCarley, "I meant to send back a note from Los Angeles, but was too tired to write when I boarded the plane."[17] So she took a few days to rest before beginning her vigorous schedule. She had a small apartment at the seminary with Dr. and Mrs. Charles Culpepper Jr., and the president of the seminary. She took her dinners with the Culpeppers. As she moved from church to church, she met former primary Sunday school pupils who were now pastors, doctors, professors in schools, and in various other callings—all living for the Lord. "What joy!" she exclaimed.

Bertha was grieved over the difference that industry and commerce had made in Taiwan in the outreach opportunities since she left. Hundreds of thousands of young people were living in industrial dormitories where they worked, entertaining themselves with television. No one was permitted to enter the dorms to witness or invite them to church. It made the work difficult.

Still, it all brought back many happy memories, not only of Taiwan days but also of China as well. Bertha was very critical of the American government for officially recognizing the mainland Chinese government—especially critical of Presidents Nixon and Carter. She actually sent a very caustic telegram to President Carter, questioning how our government could recognize a regime that enslaved millions. She especially felt the sting of how the Communists treated the pastors. They had to submit their sermons to the proper governmental office each week; then they would "edit them" to make them politically correct, Communist style. If the pastor made any changes from the Communist version when he actually preached the message, he would be immediately arrested and was either put in prison or killed. Bertha grieved over it all. Nonetheless, she had a wonderful time among her old friends and churches and God blessed her ministry.

In a letter of thanksgiving to her friends in Taiwan upon her return to America, she wrote, "I was filled with the joyous hope of seeing you. It had not occurred to me that you would be so happy to see me. All of your loving kindness and precious appreciation expressed in so many ways melted my heart. To quote your own expression, I say 'ten thousand thanks' to you and just as many praises to the Lord for all that you mean to me. I doubt if anyone else ever ate as much delicious Chinese food in two months as I did while with you."[18]

Ninety Years Young

An article appeared in the *Spartanburg Herald* on November 16, 1978, in honor of Bertha's ninetieth birthday. In the article the writer quoted C. C. Colton: "Men will wrangle for religion; write for it; fight for it; die for it; anything but live for it." The writer went on, "Colton couldn't have known Bertha Smith, when he wrote those words more than a century ago. The native of Cowpens, Baptist missionary to China, founder of a prayer center, leader of retreats for pastors, church leaders and others, has been living for it a very long time."[19] It was a real encouragement as were letters from friends.

"How much you mean to me at Christmas!" Bertha wrote to friends. "Since my dear sister Jennie went to heaven, friends who express themselves at Christmas time mean more to me than ever before. This year your cards with their enclosures were more welcome than ever. Why? I am out of my home living at Peniel a few weeks while our home—house— is being rolled back and renovated in other ways." [20]

The Old House

In a letter written to Jennie in 1957, Bertha commented on her wish for different shrubs when the town widened the street. She said, "If they take off too much looks like our house might have to be rolled back. Wouldn't that be a calamity!"[21] And they literally did; they rolled the house back some two hundred feet and put it into a more beautiful spot surrounded by trees. It was not a calamity after all. But it was quite an old home now and needed considerable repair. The house had been listed on the National Registry of Historic Places, so Bertha appealed to South Carolina senator Throm Thurmond for governmental assistance for restoration. It is uncertain she received any governmental help, but it all turned out well nonetheless. Later Bertha could say, "I'm sitting in a most delightful sun parlor, the plate glass windows having been given by a family in Tennessee. The opposite side of the home provides the same pleasure. Other additions are a utility room and extra bath, with most of the material being used donated by a friend. Because I have a friend in Kentucky who loves his wife and his wife loves me, our family home since 1895, which had several times surrendered a portion of its front yard to street widening, has now been moved. This was done by one of the best known house moving men in the U.S. for only what it cost him. The home is willed to Peniel at my crossing over."[22]

Peniel Blessings

"Every year gets busier and more interesting," Bertha wrote near the close of 1978. Besides meetings in churches and associations and her trip to Taiwan, she held nine retreats at Peniel. The conferences were rich. Bertha wrote, "The Lord must have chosen those who came and prepared their hearts for either a 'crystal clear' assurance of their salvation, or a deeper longing for a daily life of glorious victory. One precious friend with us for the fifth retreat became so convicted of his old sinful nature that he laid hold on what he had often heard here. . . . When we were all on our knees, having all sins forgiven up-to-date and old self so assigned to the cross that we were on praying ground when that dear Brother was given such a sense of the holiness of God that, like Job of old, he exclaimed, 'I'm vile! I abhor myself and repent in dust and ashes!'"[23]

A little later a deacon with a radiance on his face entered the chapel and exclaimed, "Miss Bertha, I am saved!" When she asked when, he replied, "Just five minutes ago." Another deacon had a similar experience. In another conference, she said, "five good church members in one evening [who] gave similar testimonies. That was the night I got to bed at one o'clock in the morning." Peniel became for many akin to a mini Shantung Revival.

One of the reasons for such dynamic happenings at the retreats at Peniel centered on prayer and fasting. In 1978 fourteen days were set aside for prayer and fasting, one day a month with two in September and October. These were not just days of personal prayer and fasting for Miss Bertha, but for the entire Peniel staff.

God met every need at Peniel as a result of the prayer of faith. On one occasion, a certain sum of money was needed and Friday had been set as the deadline to meet the obligation. At eleven o'clock that morning a check was received for the amount that was needed. Bob Dollar, then chairman of the Peniel trustees, said, "God is never late is He?" Miss Bertha replied, "No, He's never too early either." She would always be "earthy Bertha."

December 1978 marked the twentieth year since Miss Bertha's retirement from the Foreign Mission Board, yet her American ministry went on unabated. She was rather reminiscent at times about the great things she had seen transpire in earlier days in her beloved denomination, the Southern Baptist Convention. Some might say she had been around too long because at times she was critical of some things she saw in the SBC at the moment. Others cheered her on because she had the courage to express what they themselves felt, but perhaps lacked the courage to say or to act upon. In a letter to a Baptist State Director of Evangelism, she wrote what she felt about modern trends in worship, especially singing:

> Now, if we could only have for music the grand "preacher singing" that we had fifteen and twenty years ago with these speakers, the Holy Spirit could come down.

> Our big general meetings have become a pattern for our churches, and congregational singing at our Baptist churches is sickening. Only a little handful in the congregation sings. When I ask them why, they say that they do not know the hymns.

> It is not any group or any individual that I do not appreciate. It is just that it is robbing the congregation of the time they ought to have of

singing together instead of listening to artists. Our special meetings are not times to be entertained.[24]

Early in January 1979 Bertha wrote to the director of the Baptist Book Store in Taipei, Mr. Joseph Chang, apologizing for not writing to all of the people who had been kind to her on her visit to Taiwan the previous year. She confessed, "I lost the notebook in which I had all the names and addresses and have had letters written, waiting to find it, and have not." In the same letter to Mr. Chang she expressed her heartbreak over President Carter's recognition of Red China, as mentioned earlier. On December 15, 1978, President Jimmy Carter announced that the United States would establish normal diplomatic relations with mainland China on January 1, 1979. This would end the diplomatic recognition of Taiwan. She related to Mr. Chang that President Carter had received over six thousand telegrams, 77percent of which opposed what he did. Bertha also sent him a caustic telegram of two hundred words. The fact that President Carter was a Southern Baptist did not deter her from fully expressing herself. The telegram read:

You are hastening the downfall of America! By making friends with God's enemy God has become your enemy. You can never pray again while making an ally of murderers and thieves who confiscated private property and murdered Christians by the thousands.

Are you ignorant of what has happened in China? As a Baptist Missionary in China for 31 years I saw one third of the human family pass from freedom to slavery under the Communist regime.

Fortunately I got out to Taiwan with a million Chinese refugees who lost everything. For 31 years those left behind could never receive a letter from or send one to Taiwan without being shot.

Sarah Perkins, that charming Baptist young woman who went to China from the Governor's Mansion in Georgia will rise in the judgment and condemn you for making an ally of a wicked nation in league with the Devil, who kept her and many other Christians in solitary confinement, many for life. She, for three years and never the same again. Those Christians, dragged out of their homes and imprisoned for having family worship and singing after churches were closed, had no one to plead for their release.

You have betrayed the nation. You are a Balam serving your country to please money-makers. You are a traitor to every person who has ever fought or died for liberty and freedom. From George Washington's day to Vietnam Americans will rise up in the day of judgment and condemn you.

How will you face the Christians in America who elected you? How can you expect the Lord to have mercy on your soul when you have placed the nation under God's holy wrath?[25]

Miss Bertha was not reluctant to express herself in most vehement terms. But she felt that China and its people demanded it.

Turbulent times for Miss Bertha's Southern Baptist Convention were beginning in 1979. For some years there had been a measure of unrest among the more conservative Southern Baptists. They charged that some Convention seminaries and agencies had permitted the infiltration of more liberal views than the traditional evangelicalism of Southern Baptists would allow. A concerted effort emerged to bring about change. It started what has been called the "Conservative Resurgence" that raged on through the remaining years of Miss Bertha's life.

Bertha, clearly conservative in her theological views, in many respects supported the movement. However, she would not have affirmed some of the methodologies that were used on both sides of the spectrum of the theological battle that racked Southern Baptists the rest of her days. She recognized that correct doctrine must always emanate in holy living, and that meant acting in love and graciousness towards one's fellow believers. As John Wesley said concerning the controversies that raged in his day, "They killed love by the truth." So often that becomes the fallout of theological battles. Truth is vital and must be maintained, but so must love. And there is no dichotomy between the two; actually, one supports and is vital to the other. It is regrettable that Miss Bertha did not see the resolution of the conflict that ran through her Convention. But now the last eight years of Miss Bertha's life began to unfold.

21

Upheld by His Omnipotent Hand

The Prayer Garden at Peniel Prayer Center, Cowpens, South Carolina. *Credit: Melten*

When 1980 dawned, Americans were distressed over the hostage situation in Iran. It had been two months since the American Embassy had been taken over and all Americans present taken into custody by the Iranians. It was election year. Who would be elected president the following November? Would Jimmy Carter remain in office? Moreover, secularism deepened. Cults were rising in number in America and morals continued to erode. Violence escalated. Crime and drugs ran rampant. Random shootings began to grip sections of large cities. Many churches were apathetic and in decline. The nation was beginning to move into what has been termed the "post-modern era." And most churches were oblivious of it. Miss Bertha was more keenly aware than ever of the need for revival. She scheduled thirty different conferences and engagements for the new year. She was still emphasizing the same revival truths.

A New Thrust for Revival

On the schedule that Bertha sent to friends and admirers, she laid out the basic purpose of being in Christ. Her sketchy outline declares:

God's Purpose accomplished in Christ.... "in"

The results of Christ's Work

Ephesians 2:1–22 .... (2:1–10, 13–18).

CENTRAL TRUTH: Paul emphasized how responding to the salvation God provided in Christ resulted in Changed life-styles and unity between Jews and Gentiles....

This epistle opened in praising God for his blessings in choosing believers in Christ. Paul prayed for insight on their behalf that they might recognize the fullness of God's power and grace.

In Chapter 2 he proceeded to establish the hopeless condition of unsaved persons.

UNBELIEVERS DESCRIBED AS:

Being in a state of spiritual death.

Lives are ruled by Satan, "prince of the power of the air"

Being selfish and indulgent both lost in sin without Christ 2:13

Christ raised both Jews and Gentiles through the same power with which He raised Christ from the dead, raised all believers from spiritual death in Christ, that He might show His grace in coming ages . . . 4–7

The source and means of salvation . . . 8–10

By grace through faith . . .

The place of works in a Christian life is after salvation . . .

A natural expression of the believer's walk with the Lord . . .

Trespasses . . . wandering from the right path

Sins . . . missing the mark of God's calling . . .

Verse 3. . . . Conversion . . . Manner of Life .... Sins of the "mind": pride, ambition, envy, covetousness, and the like . . .

Verse 4. "But God" introduce attributes of God which bring hope to those without hope . . .

"Rich in mercy . . . Overflowing. . . Abundant . . . Wealth of God . . ."

The source of His mercy is His great love . . . His care, concern, tenderness, and warm, personal sharing of the lives of His saints is beyond human comprehension . . . can't define it but you can experience His love.

Heavenly places "made alive . . ." God's action in each believer's life is a parallel of His action in Christ's life . . .

"His riches of His grace" His redemption will stand throughout time and eternity . . .[1]

A Mishap and a Blessing

Bertha described an incident that took place a few days before her ninety-second birthday while she was off speaking. The date of the occurrence was November 16, 1980: "While rushing around the motel room at my accustomed rapid pace packing to come home from a meeting, my foot slipped from under me. As I fell, my left arm struck a bedside table and broke some bones near the wrist." She had to spend time in the hospital. Upon her discharge, she was invited to stay in the home of a doctor whose wife and sister were nurses. She remained in the doctor's home for three days while awaiting a second x-ray before leaving for her own home in Cowpens. Shepard Averitt had come to work with her earlier in the year, and Bertha felt it necessary to call him to cancel all of her engagements for the remainder of the year. The doctor had overheard her talk with Brother Shepard. As soon as she hung up the telephone he said, "Miss Bertha, you have been such a blessing to us we cannot bear the thought of you canceling any of your speaking engagements. My wife and I want her sister to see you home, travel with you to all your engagements, assist you with all your visual aids in speaking, and just look after you in general for the next eight weeks. I will pay her plane fare and motel expenses." Miss Bertha said, "Now what about that! Praise the Lord evermore!" So the itinerary was kept intact, but it was not all over yet.

Many Christians have difficulty receiving from others; they find it easier to give. But without receivers, there can be no givers. Miss Bertha knew how to do both. It was easier for her to receive the news of assistance with travel, however, than the medical news the doctor gave. Her arm had to be broken again and reset. Wearing a cast for an additional period of time did not come as welcome news. But by February, when she wrote to her praying friends, she said, "Praise the Lord evermore! The broken arm is healed! It is now being exercised and hot water soaked back into usefulness. A special thanks to all who had a part in the volume of prayer that ascended to the Lord for me."[2]

Bertha announced in her December newsletter that fourteen of her most-used messages had been recorded on videotape and were available for rental in groups of seven. She also announced that her latest book, *Our Lost World*, would be released by Broadman Press in January. One wonders when she had time to write. *Our Lost World* is a survey of the various mission areas and the tremendous need on each field. It proved helpful to seminaries, individual Christians, and church study groups.

Spiritual Warfare

Miss Bertha had no qualm about dealing with the devil. Strange as it may appear to some, She would often rebuke him right in the middle of a message or teaching. So it was no surprise to Bertha when the demons in a woman attending a retreat at Peniel caused the woman much discomfort during the teaching sessions. When truth is being taught, demons cannot hide. The woman's story was like lifting a page out of one of the four Gospels. All the characteristics of genuine demon possession were there. The person recording the account penned these words:

> [The victim said], "I hear voices. They say to me there is no God. Jesus is not Deity. Hurt someone. Go into anger rages. I'm afraid I'll lose all control and hurt my children. I have heard these voices since I was five years old. I joined the church when I was ten. I've never been saved. I believe I have demons."

> Miss Bertha, Shep Averitt, and Jim joined hands in a circle around her. She was on her knees in the center. As we prayed to the Father and then in the name of the Lord Jesus Christ, we commanded the Devil to leave her, come out of her and all imps and demons to leave and go back to hell, have no power over her anymore.

> Suddenly she fell over and with extreme strength, grabbed Miss Bertha around the legs almost causing her to fall, then she kicked and jerked, her body trembling, hands drawing, and shaking vehemently. As we continued to demand all demons to leave in the name of the Lord Jesus Christ, she fell over limp on Miss Bertha's lap and just wept.

> Then she asked the Lord Jesus to come in and save her and thanked Him. She would not raise up her face. When asked why she said, "I am embarrassed." She sat through the remainder of the retreat hungry-hearted. Amazed.[3]

Those in partnership with Miss Bertha enabled her to deal with such tough situations by their constant prayer support. A friend from Florence, Alabama, wrote a brief note to say, "We remember you in prayer every day." No doubt, much of the success of Miss Bertha's ministry was due to the many people who prayed for her regularly.

Birthday Blessings

Bertha's birthdays often became a source of support. A friend from Lightfoot, Virginia, sent a check for fifty dollars "in memory of your birthday." Such a continual flow of gifts not only sustained Bertha, but furthered the work of Peniel. Gifts of money would also come in at Christmas for Peniel in honor of the birth of our Lord. Needs were regularly met. She received one birthday greeting that included a request for prayer: "The enemy has tried to rob me of the knowledge I have of 'Christ in me.' Oh, Miss Bertha, please pray for strength for me to be steadfast, unmovable and clothed at all times with the whole armor of God—and having done all to stand! I need to sit at your feet and hear your wise words of spiritual wisdom, endowed from above." At times like these Miss Bertha no doubt reflected on the days when she sat at the feet of R. A. Torrey and Ruth Paxon.

A friend once wrote to Bertha, "There is something amiss in my Christian life. I love the Lord, but my commitments are of the mind. I find myself intellectualizing Christian precepts rather than accepting them through childlike faith."[4] Miss Bertha had a ready answer for that. Bertha would never bypass the mind. She believed in education and a good firm intellectual grasp of the Christian faith. But she insisted that the truths of Christ are designed to be experienced as well. The spiritual as well as the intellectual must be kept in proper perspective and balance.

On the last day of the year, the chairman of the board of a bank in Texas wrote, "It was so good to receive your newsletter. I can hardly believe how the Lord continues to bless you spiritually and physically these days! To think, at your age, you are still as active as someone 23 instead of 93, just blows my mind!" He went on to say, "I appreciate so much the influence you have had on my life these many years. Only in Eternity will you be able to see the fruits of your labor." A check for the ministry was enclosed. It seemed a token of God's grace to close out the year.

Zeal for the Lost

Miss Bertha never lost her zeal for leading lost people to Christ or to inspire witnessing for the Lord among Christians. Right up to the end of her life, she kept evangelism on her priority list. In 1982 she received a letter from a friend in Juneau, Alaska, who shared, "Our major contribution this year is an intense dedication to soul-winning. Those of us who look for our Lord's soon return . . . view each new year as the possible year of this longed for event. Yet, there are so many still unsaved it gives one mixed emotions." As seen so often, Bertha had a real gift, not only for inspiring people to a deeper Spirit-filled life, but also for laying the burden of evangelism and witnessing on their hearts. Consequently, Miss Bertha was in constant demand for evangelism conferences. In that setting she became a tremendous challenge to preachers and pastors. Real revival always results in real evangelism.

In her Christmas letter to friends Miss Bertha said, "Another year passing on means that I am writing again to report on Peniel Prayer Center and on other ways that I have used the Lord's time." In her report she included personal testimonies. One had written, "Happy birthday! I'm not sure of the date of your birthday, but I will never forget the day you led me, a dead church member, to my spiritual birthday—September 17, 1979. How thankful I am for you! You will be happy to know that I am now teaching a weekly Bible class on Philippians in a doctor's home, with a nursery. Twenty-eight women come."[5]

Bertha thanked her friends for upholding her in prayer as she led twelve Christian Life Conferences, helped in two Spiritual Awakening Conferences for the Home Mission Board, led gospel meetings for three weeks in Belize, and for the eighteenth year had a delightful week with the Missions Department at Southwestern Seminary. Some report for a ninety-four-year-old woman!

Another Year: And God's Provision

"The One who owns the cattle on a thousand hills must have sold a few more cows." That's how Miss Bertha liked to express God's provision.

In August Bertha had another fall and broke her right shoulder. Though she was quite agile for her age, at times it caught up with her. Bertha gave her account of the event: "Having always done anything I needed to do, I went after a howling stray dog with a broom one evening, and stumbled over the lid of a buried gas tank. I arose from my fall with two splits in my shoulder bone and one split in the ball of my arm bone. The result was my having to cancel six Christian life conferences and the September Peniel Prayer Retreat. One of my gentlemen friends called the next day to say, 'Miss Bertha, do you not know that dogs chase cats?! Cats do not chase dogs!' Alas, I am too old to practice what I know in emergencies."[6]

More Mundane Matters

There were still mundane things to take care of at Peniel Center. Bertha inquired about some unfinished furniture from the Harris Pine Mills in Valdosta, Georgia. She was always on the lookout for good quality, reasonably priced, furnishings for Peniel. Being very frugal, she managed the business affairs well. She also knew well how to use what was at hand. Instead of paper clips she often used straight pins to hold two pieces of paper together. When she filled up a loose leaf notebook, rather than buy a new binder, she would remove the papers, tie them together with

string, store them, then fill the binder with new paper. Once, while in Formosa, she wanted choir robes for the children, little capes that would
come a little below the waist. She purchased cheap white cloth for two
U.S. dollars, enough to make seven robes, and as she described it, "cut up
an old black taffeta skirt that belonged to my bathrobe and made great big
bows."[7] She did all of the sewing herself.

Bertha and Southern Baptists

Miss Bertha was always faithful to attend scheduled meetings and conferences led by the Southern Baptist Convention. If at all possible she
would attend Woman's Missionary Union and Foreign Mission Weeks at
Ridgecrest, the WMU Annual Meeting, and the Southern Baptist Convention Annual Session. In 1984 a friend wrote, "Miss Bertha, we trust the
Southern Baptist Convention annual meeting was all you prayed for it to
be." Bertha prayed earnestly for the Convention, especially in light of its
conflicts and difficulties previously discussed. She was good leaven in the
lump, with her insistence upon genuine biblical spirituality in all things.

She sent her annual letter out on November 23, 1984, saying, "It seems
such a short time since our letter of last year. In all of the 25 years of my
retirement this has been one of the fullest and richest. Since my field of
labor changed, every year I declare that my schedule will be lighter than
the previous year. For some reason this never has been the outcome. For
1985, you will see that I have finally cut down my schedule."[8]

The years were beginning to take a measure of their toll. Bertha related
to her friends that "for the first time in fifty years, apart from a few acci-
dents, I lost a week of work because of sickness." While in Shreveport at
the end of October, she had to go to the hospital because of a blood clot at
the base of her brain. The doctors thought surgery might be necessary,
but "due to the many people that were praying for me," she said, "that was
not the case." The doctor told her it was a miracle that she completely
recovered and suffered no permanent damage. She graciously thanked
those who had prayed and asked them to continue praying and to "tell the
Lord that I am not nearly ready to stop the life I am living to go to heaven
or to sit in a rocker on the porch and watch the cars pass by. With all my
heart I prefer to be the one rushing somewhere to tell people something
of what He has taught me!" She closed her letter by asking them to pray
"that each time I speak 'Rivers of living water' will flow."

During the year Bertha lost her secretary, but while speaking in
Detroit, God provided her with another—Michael J. Thompson. He had
majored in computer science and had a good job. But, as Bertha related,

"gave it up to come and work with me." After serving a period with Miss Bertha, the Lord called him to preach. That almost had become a pattern.

In the News Again

The Pathway News reprinted a story covering the life, activities, and ministries of Miss Bertha that had previously been printed in *The Daily News Journal* of Murfreesboro, Tennessee. It appeared in March 1985, the year she turned ninety-seven. After covering her life pilgrimage, it ended with, "She is in such demand as a speaker that bookings as far ahead as 1988 have been made. That year will be her 100th birthday, and also the 100th anniversary of Woman's Missionary Union of the Southern Baptist Convention." A fine tribute!

Even though Bertha kept busy with her work, she never lost her vision for a real revival to sweep all of America. She said on one occasion, "I cannot imagine any sin committed before Noah's flood that is any worse than what we are having today."[9] How her beloved country and its churches needed a fresh awakening! She had a marvelous gift to instill this vision for an awakening in others. In 1985 a friend wrote, "We are praying the Lord for a real revival amongst our people." Miss Bertha did not live to see a national revival, but if one comes to America, she will certainly have made major contributions toward it.

Continuing Concern

Bertha's eyesight was impaired now, and she could see very little because of a blinding membrane behind the lens of her one good eye. She quoted all Scripture or had her secretary read lengthy passages. One Sunday morning her teaching centered on Psalm 103. She stood there, straight, and as tall as Miss Bertha could stand, with Bible in hand as though she was going to read the passage. Then she placed it on the podium and said, "I don't know why I'm holding this. I can't see a word." She then began quoting the first few verses of the psalm, stopping after each verse to make comments. It was awesome to realize how God used this "straight-backed lady." He did uphold her by His omnipotent hand.

Deteriorating Health

Miss Bertha always made a few special requests of the church when they invited her to lead a conference. She liked to stay in a motel in order that she might have time to rest, pray, and study. She ate breakfast in the motel room—oatmeal, fruit, or something simple. She had her main meal at noon. It would usually consist of white meat or fish. "I eat no red meat," she said. Perhaps this helps account for her longevity. But the old lady was beginning to give out.

One Sunday evening, after the service in a local church conference, several gathered round and laid hands on Miss Bertha, asking God to give her healing of her lower vertebrae, to enable her to be able to keep her train of thought, and to be with the doctors as they did surgery on her one good eye; she was to have surgery on December 17. The promises in Psalm 92:12–15 were claimed: "The righteous shall flourish like the palm tree: he shall grow like a cedar in Lebanon. Those that be planted in the house of the LORD shall flourish in the courts of our God. They shall still bring forth fruit in old age; they shall be fat and flourishing; To show that the LORD is upright: he is my rock, and there is no unrighteousness in him." And God heard; the pastor of the church received a call on December 20 from her secretary. He said, "Before laser surgery she could read nothing. Afterwards she could read everything on the chart. The doctors were amazed at such fast recovery." Miss Bertha said, "When you've got your sins forgiven up-to-date, you can expect great things from God."

Two years before, in December 1983, it had been necessary to correct her vision with an implant. Later she had similar surgery on the other eye; it hemorrhaged and was lost. She said, "I've been able to see with one or two eyes longer than most people ever see. So, I'm most thankful for any vision the Lord permits me to keep." After the last surgery she said, "The Lord allowed me to experience blindness for a short while in order to teach me to appreciate the sight of one eye. Praise the Lord with me for all He has taught me!"

Many friends prayed and wrote letters of comfort. In spite of deteriorating health, she kept going strong and kept her schedule. A friend wrote, "I was so pleased to get your 1986 [projected] program and to know how God is still truly helping you to give His love to so many people."[10]

In her newsletter covering 1985 Bertha said, "I believe I speak truly when I say I've seen more lives transformed during 1985 than any of the 26 years since my retirement. While I traveled from New Jersey to Arizona, from Michigan to Florida and many places between, blessings came back to me as I saw the Lord work in hearts."[11] Ed Kvietkus, Jr., was added to the staff to serve as her aide and secretary. Ed was from Columbus, Georgia, and had been licensed to preach. Her previous secretary, who had felt the call to preach, had left to prepare for his ministry. Miss Bertha's schedule for 1986 held fewer engagements. To her friends she wrote, "Personally, I'm doing quite well. I'm learning to cope with a tinge of arthritis. I'm glad it has been so long in getting here. I still feel richly blessed to have the good health that I enjoy!"[12]

In December 1986, she received a gift of $450 for Peniel Center from a Sunday school class. The class members had collected the money to purchase a new dishwasher for the Center, but gave her permission to use it as she saw fit. These gifts were evidence of the continuing love and esteem by which people held her in her old age. Christian evangelical leaders across the country had profound respect for her. On December 18 Reverend Stephen Olford wrote, "Just a wee note to let you know you are in our thoughts, love, and prayers. Thanks be unto God for His unspeakable gift. We love you."[13] The year ended on a very happy, comforting note for Miss Bertha. But time was ticking on.

Bertha's Last Year

Miss Bertha's last full year among us was to be 1987. Miraculously, it proved to be a full and eventful year. Her close friends had an inkling she would not live to her hundredth birthday, her fond wish. But she never failed to submit everything to the providence of God; she knew whatever He wills is best. The friends decided to have a large celebration for her 99th year. Early in the year, Jack Taylor sent a letter to everyone on Miss Bertha's mailing list. He wrote, "We are in the midst of Miss Bertha's 99th year! Praise the Lord that He has anointed her life and ministry for this span of time!" The trustees voted to launch Project 99/99. Their dream was to present her with a check for $99,000 for the continued ministry of Peniel on her 99th birthday. One trustee had already given $1,188.

The celebration was held at First Baptist Church, Cowpens. She received words of congratulations and commendations from many Southern Baptist leaders such as the president of the Southern Baptist Convention, pastors of leading churches, not to mention many others whom she had touched. A wonderful program unfolded on Friday evening, November 13, and then another Saturday morning. Some of her very dear friends and men of God took part. Reverend Manley Beasley spoke on Friday and Reverend Bobby Dollar, who served as a trustee of Peniel Center from its inception, brought the Saturday morning message. It was a gracious time. One of the most wonderful tributes was given by Dr. Cal Guy, Professor of Missions at Southwestern Baptist Theological Seminary. He wrote, "Thank you for those twenty years and for the total ministry that you shared with all of us each time you were at Southwestern Seminary. The class sessions were rewarding and blessed the lives of students. The prayer schedule with the students that you maintained at such great length rendered a very special, unique, and extremely helpful service to the individuals and to the kingdom. . . . It has been a privilege to call you friend during all this time of search in so many hearts for the honest presence and power of God's Holy Spirit."

Deaver and Dorothy Lawton, fellow missionaries in China, wrote, "Our memories of you go way back to Shantung days when you held meetings in the Laichow area. We were blessed and grew spiritually through your messages as you spoke of and in the power and fullness of the Holy Spirit." The same thing could be said of the Lawtons that was said of Miss Bertha, "You greeted us with the love of Jesus glowing from your being. God shined through you." This glow was evident on all the faces of the China missionaries who had experienced revival in Shantung.

Most significantly, during the 99 celebration, Hannibal-LaGrange College in Missouri presented Miss Bertha with a plaque establishing a Chair for Spiritual Development. As part of this professorship, the college offered the following courses: Biblical Interpretation, Foundation of Faith, Dimensions of Prayer, Masterlife, The Spiritual Home, The Person and Work of the Holy Spirit, and a new minor in Spiritual Development. At a celebration at the college held after her death, Jack Taylor said, "Probably as no person in America, Miss Bertha Smith has been used in the spiritual development of members of the Body of Christ. Ending her fruitful missionary career at the appointed time she was called to the Church in America, particularly the flock that is Southern Baptist. She has been faithful to the Holy Spirit who told her to 'Go Home And Tell.' I was one of those whom she told and God used her ministry to transform my life and that of my church. The revival that soon ensued could not have occurred without the influence God exerted through her. I believe that God's hand and heart are in this project."[14] In the newsletter written by Mrs. McCarley on November 16 she stated, "Miss Bertha Smith is surpassed by none for her tenacity of purpose and singleness of aim, a true soldier of Jesus Christ, never wavering and never deviating from her high calling." That statement summed up the spirit of this "Woman of Revival."

In December 1987 Miss Bertha enjoyed the visit of two special people. Ivan Larson, Jr., the son of the missionary couple she had served with in China, and his wife dropped by the house for an overnight visit. Ivan was a little boy growing up in Laichowfu in 1930 and 1931. He was almost startled at Bertha's stamina at ninety-nine. He said, "She was still energetic, gave us a grand tour of her home, even climbing to the third floor without the usual difficulties of age. She guided us through her beautiful Prayer Center, and to the prayer garden. We were royally entertained, spending the night in her home." He continued, "She was always 'Aunt Bertha' to us MKs. All the missionaries spent time together in each other's homes, celebrating birthdays, as well as Thanksgiving and Christmas. On my sixth birthday, in October 1931, she had a gala birthday for me, inviting several other missionary kids. I will never forget her sweetness and love expressed to us kids." She never changed.

The issue would come up from time to time as to the fate of Peniel Prayer Center when God took Miss Bertha home. When asked if she wished it closed, she would exclaim, "No, no, no . . . ! Bertha Smith did not start Peniel Prayer Center; God did, and He intends for it to continue until Jesus comes."[15] That settled the issue.

A Baptist Legend

On January 2, 1988, the Spartanburg *Herald Journal* ran a large feature article written by Allison Buice under the title, "Cowpens Woman Acclaimed Baptist Legend." It reads:

> "To be in her presence is to be in the presence of history," Bridges, news staff member of the Southern Baptist Convention Foreign Mission Board, said.
>
> During an interview at her childhood home in Cowpens this week, the spry, white haired Miss Bertha puttered up and down the narrow staircase in her rambling white framed house, answered phone calls, shuffled through mail and tended to lost souls.
>
> Visiting with a guest from Virginia in the parlor, she matter of factly asked when he was going to give up the fight and surrender his life to Christ. Only then would he find peace, she said.
>
> The exchange may have seemed a bit abrupt to many, but for Miss Bertha, it was merely a continuation of her lifelong dedication to Christian service.
>
> "She says what she thinks—lets the chips fall where they may," explained Martha Franks, 86, of Laurens. Miss Franks, also a missionary for more than 40 years, worked with Miss Bertha in China and Taiwan. "She's very direct and emphatic and with her there is no gray. It's either black or white. She is the most remarkable woman."
>
> Hundreds of books including works by theologian C. S. Lewis to a modern day murder mystery line bookshelves throughout Miss Bertha's house. Family photographs fill the walls, accompanied by plaques with inspirational verses in the sunny kitchen, one plaque reads: "He Is Altogether Lovely." In an upstairs bedroom that boasts an antique family bed and chest, another plaque reassures guests: "Jesus Never Fails."

Outside, behind the house, a prayer garden stands. Idle benches sit throughout. Three crosses stand in the center, with a makeshift tomb nearby. The crosses and the tomb are there to remind visitors of Christ's crucifixion and resurrection. The garden has often been used for sunrise Easter services. Photographs of past services show an array of bright colored flowers and visitors. Giving a tour of her home, Miss Bertha stopped in her bedroom to pose for a photograph. In hand was her favorite Bible, a King James version with well worn pages. A favorite verse, Proverbs 3:5: "Trust in the Lord with all thine heart and lean not unto thine own understanding"—has given her great strength through the years, she said.

The Last Days

The Woman's Missionary Union of the Southern Baptist Convention held its centennial celebration in Richmond, Virginia, in May 1988. Thousands planned to attend; it promised to be a grand event: celebrating 100 years of missionary promotion and education. Miss Bertha longed to be there and to take part in this celebration since they were both soon to be one hundred. She was slated to be an honored personality. However, her health was deteriorating rapidly and the doctor absolutely forbade her to go. She was bitterly disappointed. It was evident that the time of her homegoing drew near. Yet, just one month before her death, she led a Chinese businessman in Spartanburg to Christ.

Home Going

Miss Bertha was admitted to Mary Black Memorial Hospital on May 18, 1988. The end was clearly in sight. Her reward was prepared by her Lord, and it was time for her to claim it. After lingering for twenty-five days, she was promoted into the presence of the Lord Jesus Christ. Like a true pilgrim, she stepped into the river as the trumpet sounded on the other shore. Grace had led her all the way, and now grace threw heaven's gate open wide. What a reception that must have been when our dear Miss Bertha entered in. The multitudes she had touched were almost incalculable, and each one surely embraced her and welcomed her home. Above all, she saw her Lord whom she loved and served so faithfully. How thrilled she must have been to realize fully how much God had used her faithful service. In 1950 there were only five million believers in China. At Miss Bertha's final homegoing, just thirty-eight years later, the number of Christians in the great nation numbered fifty to seventy million; and the Shantung Revival played no small part in that harvest.

So we grieve not, though we feel the deep loss. For our Lord said, "Blessed are those who die in the Lord, and their works to follow them." If anyone had "works to follow," it was Miss Bertha. Her works followed her to heaven's shore and great is her reward. But her works continue to follow her here below. We still experience the blessing of her dedicated life. Peniel Prayer Center carries on, but more significantly, the fragrance of her anointed life lingers in so many. Those of us whom she touched can never be the same. And that is the final tribute to this little giant, this "Woman of Revival."

Epilogue

Bertha Smith *Credit: Melten*

Miss Bertha had wished to be 100 before God called her to His higher service. It looked like she might just attain that goal, but on June 12, 1988, during the annual meeting of the Southern Baptist Convention, just five months before her 100th birthday, she heard the trumpet and crossed over. She missed her goal by just five months. Yet, perhaps she didn't. The Chinese age a person not by the birth date but by the year of birth. So Chinese style, Miss Bertha was one hundred years old when God called her to His side. And that would have pleased her well.

A spiritual saga has ended: Therefore, final tribute is in order:

Prayer Warrior Emeritus

It is inconceivable to think of her doing anything other than what she knew was the highest good to mankind—that of praying for others. Lifting others to the throne of grace and asking our blessed Lord to turn them His way so that the prayed-for-one would recognize his need and come to Jesus for that need to be met. Hers was a high calling—that of talking to

God about men and then talking to men about God. To those who knew her, she was exemplary with a zest for life and particularly a love for God's people. A staunch, stalwart soldier of the Cross of Calvary was she!

America might rightfully sing, Oh, to Miss Bertha, how great a debt of gratitude we owe for the many, many prayers she offered to God on our behalf. The Lord Jesus Christ was her Supreme Commander and she fearlessly fought the enemy by faith and faithfulness in praying. We who remain could do no better than to follow her pattern of useful service unto the Master. . .

Like many other "graduated" saints she being dead yet speaketh through her books, tapes, memorable teachings, and through lives that were changed as a result of her intervening and interceding. May God raise up a mighty band of prayer warriors like unto Miss Bertha Smith for His Name's honor and glory.[1]

—Carlene P. Dodson

The Chinese never say "goodbye." Their word for farewell is Zi-gen, which means "I'll see you again." So we can say to Miss Bertha, Woman of Revival, Zi-gen: we will see you again.

Endnotes

Chapter 1

1. Bertha Smith, *Go Home and Tell* (Nashville: Broadman Press, 1965), 10.

Chapter 2

1. Bertha Smith, *The Life and Times of the Cowpens Battleground Community*, 17.
2. Ibid., 17.
3. Ibid., 18.
4. Bertha Smith, *How the Spirit Filled My Life* (Nashville: Broadman Press, 1973), 14–19.
5. Ibid., 12.
6. Ibid., 13.
7. Ibid., 20.
8. Ibid., 22–23.

Chapter 3

1. J. Donald McManus, *Martha Franks: One Link in God's Chain* (Wake Forest: Stevens Book Press, 1990), 28–29.
2. Audiotape, Archives, Peniel Prayer Center, Cowpens, South Carolina.
3. From audiotape in Archives at Peniel Prayer Center.
4. Bertha Smith, *How the Spirit Filled My Life* (Nashville: Broadman Press, 1973), 25.
5. Ibid., 26.
6. Ibid.
7. Catherine Allen, *A Century to Celebrate: History of the Woman's Missionary Union* (WMU: Birmingham, Ala., 1987), 264.

Chapter 4

1. Bertha Smith, *Go Home and Tell* (Nashville: Broadman Press, 1965), 2.
2. Ibid., 5.
3. Ibid., 6.
4. Ibid., 6.

5. Ibid., 7–8.
6. Ibid., 8.
7. From teaching tape in Archives, Peniel Prayer Center.
8. Bertha Smith, *How the Spirit Filled My Life*, 27.
9. Bertha Smith, *Go Home and Tell*, 6.
10. Bertha Smith, *How the Spirit Filled My Life*, 31.
11. Archives, Peniel Prayer Center.
12. Bertha Smith, *How the Spirit Filled My Life*, 33.

Chapter 5

1. J. I. Packer, *Keep In Step with the Spirit* (Old Tappan, New Jersey: Fleming H. Revell, 1984), 25–28.
2. Bertha Smith, *Go Home and Tell*, 12.
3. Ibid., 13.
4. Charles L. Culpepper, *The Shantung Revival* (Dallas, Crescendo Publications, 1971), 13–14.
5. Bertha Smith, *Go Home and Tell*, 15–17.

Chapter 6

1. Marie Monsen, *The Awakening: Revival in China* (China Inland Mission: 1986 in USA), 22.
2. Ibid., 28.
3. Ibid., 30.
4. Marie Monsen, *A Present Help* (China Inland Mission, 1959), 70.
5. Ibid., 71.
6. Bertha Smith, *Go Home and Tell*, 21.
7. Ibid., 22–23.
8. Ibid., 26–27.

Chapter 7

1. Bertha Smith, *Go Home and Tell* (Nashville: Broadman Press, 1965), 41.
2. J. Donald McManus, *Martha Franks: One Link in God's Chain* (Lancaster, South Carolina: Taxahaw Publications, 1990), 43.

Endnotes

3. Ibid., 43.
4. Ibid., 90.
5. Bertha Smith, *Go Home and Tell*,48.
6. Ibid., 44.
7. Ibid., 45–46.
8. Ibid.
9. Bertha Smith, *Go Home and Tell*, 49.
10. Ibid., 49.
11. Ibid., 50.
12. Archives, Peniel Prayer Center

Chapter 8

1. Bertha Smith, *Go Home and Tell* (Nashville: Broadman Press, 1965), 29.
2. Ibid., 32.
3. Ibid., 33–34.
4. Ibid., 37.
5. Ibid., 37–38.
6. Charles Culpepper, *The Shantung Revival*, 15.
7. Ibid., 19.
8. Ibid., 23.
9. Ibid., 25.
10. Ibid., 26.
11. Ibid., 35–36.
12. Ibid., 37–38.
13. Ibid., 38–39.
14. Ibid., 41–42.
15. Ibid., 43–45.
16. Ibid., 50.
17. Ibid., 51.
18. Ibid., 52.
19. Ibid., 52.

Chapter 9

1. Charles L. Culpepper, *The Shantung Revival*, 27.
2. Ibid., 28.
3. Ibid., 33–34.
4. Bertha Smith, *Go Home and Tell*, 51.
5. Ibid., 54.
6. Ibid.
7. Ibid., 54–55.
8. Ibid., 57.
9. Ibid., 58.
10. Ibid., 64.
11. Ibid., 65.
12. Ibid., 65–66.
13. Ibid., 67.
14. Ibid.
15. Ibid., 68.
16. Ibid., 69.
17. Ibid., 70.

Chapter 10

1. Bertha Smith, Personal Letter, January 1935, Archives, Peniel Prayer Center.
2. Ibid.
3. Bertha Smith, *Go Home and Tell*, 60.
4. Ibid., 61.
5. Ibid., 64.
6. Archives, Peniel Prayer Center.
7. Bertha Smith, Personal Letter, November 1934, Archives, Peniel Prayer Center.
8. Ibid.
9. Ibid.
10. Bertha Smith, *Go Home and Tell*, 53.
11. Bertha Smith, Personal Letter, November 1934, Archives, Peniel Prayer Center.
12. Ibid.
13. Ibid.
14. Ibid.
15. Ibid.

16. Ibid.
17. Ibid.
18. Ibid.

Chapter 11

1. Personal letter, April 1937, Archives, Peniel Prayer Center.
2. Ibid.
3. Ibid.
4. Ibid.
5. Ibid.
6. Ibid.
7. Bertha Smith, *Go Home and Tell*, 74.
8. Ibid., 74.
9. Ibid., 75.
10. Ibid., 76.
11. Ibid., 76.
12. Ibid., 81.
13. Ibid.
14. Ibid., 82.
15. Ibid., 83.
16. Ibid., 85.
17. Ibid., 88.
18. Ibid., 95.
19. Ibid., 91.
20. Ibid., 90.
21. Ibid., 97.
22. Ibid., 97–98.
23. Ibid., 98.
24. Ibid., 102.
25. Ibid.
26. Ibid., 105.
27. Ibid., 105–106.
28. Ibid., 107.

Chapter 12

1. Letter, Archives, Peniel Prayer Center.
2. Bertha Smith, *Go Home and Tell*, 109.
3. Ibid., 111.
4. Source unknown.

Chapter 13

1. Video of 60th Anniversary of Miss Bertha's Sailing to China, Archives, Peniel Prayer Center.
2. Fern Harrington, Personal Letter, May, 1948, Archives, Peniel Prayer Center.
3. Video of 60th Anniversary of Miss Bertha's Sailing to China.
4. Bertha Smith, *Go Home and Tell*, 113.
5. Fern Harrington, *The Communist Siege of Yenchow*, *June–July 1948*, Archives, Peniel Prayer Center.
6. Fern Harrington, Personal Letter, June 6, 1948, Archives, Peniel Prayer Center.
7. Bertha Smith, *Go Home and Tell*, 115.
8. Ibid.
9. Fern Harrington, Personal Letter, June 14, 1948, Archives, Peniel Prayer Center.
10. Bertha Smith, *Go Home and Tell*, 116.
11. Ibid., 118.
12. Ibid.
13. Ibid., 119–120.
14. Video of 60th Anniversary of Miss Bertha's Sailing to China, Archives, Peniel Prayer Center.
15. Ibid.
16. Ibid.
17. Bertha Smith, *Go Home and Tell*, 126.
18. Bertha Smith, Personal Letter, Summer 1948, Archives, Peniel Prayer Center.
19. Ibid.

Endnotes

Chapter 14

1. Bertha Smith, *Go Home and Tell*, 130.
2. Ibid., 131.
3. Bertha Smith, 1950 Annual Report, Archives, Peniel Prayer Center.
4. Bertha Smith, *Go Home and Tell*, 132.
5. Ibid., 132.
6. Ibid.
7. Ibid., 133.
8. Bertha Smith, Report from Personal Files, Archives, Peniel Prayer Center.
9. Ibid.
10. Ibid.
11. Juliette Mather, *Taiwan As I Saw It* (Nashville: Broadman Press, 1965), 22.
12. Bertha Smith, Personal Writings, Archives, Peniel Prayer Center.
13. Bertha Smith, *Go Home and Tell*, 135.
14. Ibid., 135.
15. Bertha Smith, Personal Letter, January 1949, Archives, Peniel Prayer Center.
16. Bertha Smith, *Go Home and Tell*, 136.
17. Ibid., 136.
18. Bertha Smith, Personal Writings, Archives, Peniel Prayer Center.
19. Bertha Smith, Personal Letter to Friends, September 21, 1949, Archives, Peniel Prayer Center.
20. Ibid.
21. Bertha Smith, *Go Home and Tell*, 138–139.

Chapter 15

1. Bertha Smith, Personal Letter to Friends, 139.
2. Ibid., 140.
3. Bertha Smith, Personal Report, 1949, Archives, Peniel Prayer Center.
4. Bertha Smith, *Go Home and Tell*, 141.
5. Bertha Smith, Personal Letter, April 27, 1949, Archives, Peniel Prayer Center.
6. Ibid.
7. Ibid.
8. Ibid.
9. Ibid.
10. Ibid.
11. Ibid.
12. Ibid.
13. Bertha Smith, *Go Home and Tell*, 145–146.
14. Ibid., 148.

Chapter 16

1. Bertha Smith, Personal Letter, November 18, 1952, Archives, Peniel Prayer Center.
2. Ibid.
3. Archives, Peniel Prayer Center.
4. Bertha Smith, Personal Letter, January 14, 1953, Archives, Peniel Prayer Center.
5. Bertha Smith, Personal Letter, March 11, 1953, Archives, Peniel Prayer Center.
6. Bertha Smith, Personal Letter, June 18, 1955, Archives, Peniel Prayer Center.
7. Bertha Smith, Personal Letter, April 15, 1955, Archives, Peniel Prayer Center.
8. Bertha Smith, General Letter, October 8, 1954, Archives, Peniel Prayer Center.
9. Ibid.
10. Ibid.
11. Bertha Smith, Personal Letter, April 20, 1955, Archives, Peniel Prayer Center.
12. Bertha Smith, Personal Letter, June 3, 1955, Archives, Peniel Prayer Center.
13. Bertha Smith, General Letter, April 20, 1955.

14. Bertha Smith, Personal Letter, July 18, 1955, Archives, Peniel Prayer Center.
15. Bertha Smith, Personal Letter, December 10, 1955, Archives, Peniel Prayer Center.
16. Ibid.
17. Ibid.
18. Harry Raley, Personal Letter, January 7, 1957, Archives, Peniel Prayer Center.
19. Bertha Smith, Personal Letter, March 23, 1956, Archives, Peniel Prayer Center.
20. Bertha Smith, Personal Letter, April 5, 1956, Archives, Peniel Prayer Center.
21. Bertha Smith, Personal Letter, May 7, 1956, Archives, Peniel Prayer Center.
22. Ibid.
23. Bertha Smith, Personal Letter, November 5, 1956, Archives, Peniel Prayer Center.
24. Bertha Smith, Personal Letter, November 26, 1956, Archives, Peniel Prayer Center.
25. Bertha Smith, Personal Letter, January 7, 1957, Archives, Peniel Prayer Center.
26. Bertha Smith, Letter to Friends, June 13, 1957, Archives, Peniel Prayer Center.
27. Bertha Smith, Personal Letter, February 27, 1957.
28. Bertha Smith, Personal Letter, March 5, 1957.
29. Bertha Smith, Personal Letter, May 26, 1957, Archives, Peniel Prayer Center.
30. Bertha Smith, Personal Letter, July 22, 1957, Archives, Peniel Prayer Center.
31. Bertha Smith, *Go Home and Tell*, 150.
32. Bertha Smith, Personal Letter, January 4, 1958, Archives, Peniel Prayer Center.
33. Bertha Smith, Personal Letter, March 11, 1958, Archives, Peniel Prayer Center.
34. Ibid.
35. Bertha Smith, Newsletter, May 26, 1958, Archives, Peniel Prayer Center.
36. Bertha Smith, Personal Letter, July 21, 1958, Archives, Peniel Prayer Center.
37. Bertha Smith, *Go Home and Tell*, 153.
38. Ibid., 153–54.
39. Tape, Archives, Peniel Prayer Center.
40. Ibid.

Chapter 17

1. Archives, Peniel Prayer Center.
2. Bertha Smith, Personal Letter, February 26, 1959, Archives, Peniel Prayer Center.
3. Ibid.
4. Bertha Smith, Personal Letter, January 28, 1959, Archives, Peniel Prayer Center.
5. Bertha Smith, Personal Letter, April 2, 1959, Archives, Peniel Prayer Center.
6. Bertha Smith, Personal Letter, April 5, 1959, Archives, Peniel Prayer Center.
7. Bertha Smith, Personal Letter, May 4, 1959, Archives, Peniel Prayer Center.
8. Edwina Robinson, Letter, May 11, 1959, Archives, Peniel Prayer Center.
9. Bertha Smith, Personal Letter, June 19, 1959.
10. Bertha Smith, Personal Letter, June 14, 1959, Archives, Peniel Prayer Center.
11. Bertha Smith, Personal Letter, August 16, 1959, Archives, Peniel Prayer Center.
12. Bertha Smith, Personal Letter, August 22, 1959, Archives, Peniel Prayer Center.
13. Bertha Smith, Personal Letter, September 9, 1959, Archives, Peniel Prayer Center.

Endnotes

Chapter 18

1. Bertha Smith, Personal Letter, January 10, 1959, Archives, Peniel Prayer Center.
2. Bertha Smith, Personal Letter, November 12, 1955, Archives, Peniel Prayer Center.
3. Ibid.
4. Archives, Peniel Prayer Center.
5. Ibid.
6. Archives, Peniel Prayer Center.
7. Ibid.
8. Ibid.
9. Ibid.
10. Ibid.
11. Ibid.
12. Ibid.
13. Ibid.
14. Letter, October 1963, Archives, Peniel Prayer Center.
15. Letter penned in Ft. Worth, April 13, 1964, Archives, Peniel Prayer Center.
16. Archives, Peniel Prayer Center.
17. Bob Beaty, Personal Correspondence.
18. Archives, Peniel Prayer Center.
19. Ibid.
20. Ibid.
21. Ibid.
22. Ibid.
23. Ibid.
24. Ibid.
25. Ibid.
26. Ibid.
27. Ibid.

Chapter 19

1. Archives, Peniel Prayer Center.
2. Archives, Peniel Prayer Center.
3. Ibid.
4. Ibid.
5. Author's personal correspondence from Robert Dollar.
6. Ibid.
7. Archives, Penial Prayer Center.
8. Ibid.
9. Author's correspondence.
10. Archives, Peniel Prayer Center.
11. Ibid.
12. Betty Russell, Letter, January 20, 1994, Archives, Peniel Prayer Center.
13. Archives, Peniel Prayer Center.
14. Ibid.
15. Bertha Smith, Personal Letter, June 24, 1974, Archives, Peniel Prayer Center.
16. Archives, Peniel Prayer Center.
17. Bennet and Spencer, Letter, December 23, 1974, Archives, Peniel Prayer Center.
18. Archives, Peniel Prayer Center.

19. Ibid.
20. Ibid.

Chapter 20

1. Archives, Peniel Prayer Center.
2. Ibid.
3. Ibid.
4. Ibid.
5. Ibid.
6. Ibid.
7. Bertha Smith, Personal Letter, February 26, 1955, Archives, Peniel Prayer Center.
8. Archives, Peniel Prayer Center.
9. Ibid.
10. Ibid.
11. Tape, Archives, Peniel Prayer Center.
12. All quotes on the celebration are on videotape, Archives, Peniel Prayer Center.
13. Archives, Peniel Prayer Center.
14. Ibid.
15. Ibid.
16. Ibid.
17. Ibid.
18. Ibid.
19. Ibid.
20. Ibid.
21. Bertha Smith, Personal Letter, June 27, 1957, Archives, Peniel Prayer Center.
22. Archives, Peniel Prayer Center.
23. Ibid.
24. Ibid.
25. Ibid.

Chapter 21

1. Archives, Peniel Prayer Center.
2. Ibid.
3. Ibid.
4. Ibid.
5. Ibid.
6. Ibid.
7. Bertha Smith, Personal Letter, November 22, 1955, Archives, Peniel Prayer Center.
8. Ibid.
9. Tape, Archives, Peniel Prayer Center.
10. Archives, Peniel Prayer Center.
11. Ibid.
12. Ibid.
13. Ibid.
14. Ibid.
15. Archives, Peniel Prayer Center.

Epilogue

1. Archives, Peniel Prayer Center.